Bloom's Modern Critical Views

African American Poets: Wheatley-Tolson
Edward Albee
American and Canadian Women Poets, 1930–present
American Women Poets, 1650–1950
Maya Angelou
Asian-American Writers
Margaret Atwood
Jane Austen
James Baldwin
Honoré de Balzac
Samuel Beckett
Saul Bellow
The Bible
William Blake
Jorge Luis Borges
Ray Bradbury
The Brontës
Gwendolyn Brooks
Elizabeth Barrett Browning
Robert Browning
Italo Calvino
Albert Camus
Lewis Carroll
Willa Cather
Cervantes
Geoffrey Chaucer
Anton Chekhov
Kate Chopin
Agatha Christie
Samuel Taylor Coleridge
Joseph Conrad
Contemporary Poets
Stephen Crane
Dante
Daniel Defoe
Don DeLillo
Charles Dickens
Emily Dickinson
John Donne and the 17th-Century Poets
Fyodor Dostoevsky
W.E.B. DuBois
George Eliot
T. S. Eliot
Ralph Ellison
Ralph Waldo Emerson
William Faulkner
F. Scott Fitzgerald
Sigmund Freud
Robert Frost
Johann Wolfgang von Goethe
George Gordon, Lord Byron
Graham Greene
Thomas Hardy
Nathaniel Hawthorne
Ernest Hemingway
Hispanic-American Writers
Homer
Langston Hughes
Zora Neale Hurston
Aldous Huxley
Henrik Ibsen
John Irving
Henry James
James Joyce
Franz Kafka
John Keats
Jamaica Kincaid
Stephen King
Rudyard Kipling
Milan Kundera
D. H. Lawrence
Ursula K. Le Guin
Sinclair Lewis
Bernard Malamud
Christopher Marlowe
Gabriel García Márquez
Cormac McCarthy
Carson McCullers
Herman Melville
Arthur Miller
John Milton
Molière
Toni Morrison
Native-American Writers
Joyce Carol Oates
Flannery O'Connor
Eugene O'Neill
George Orwell
Octavio Paz
Sylvia Plath
Edgar Allan Poe
Katherine Anne Porter
J. D. Salinger
Jean-Paul Sartre
William Shakespeare: Histories and Poems
William Shakespeare: Romances
William Shakespeare: The Comedies
William Shakespeare: The Tragedies
George Bernard Shaw
Mary Wollstonecraft Shelley
Percy Bysshe Shelley
Alexander Solzhenitsyn
Sophocles
John Steinbeck
Tom Stoppard
Jonathan Swift
Amy Tan

Bloom's Modern Critical Views

Alfred, Lord Tennyson
Henry David Thoreau
J. R. R. Tolkien
Leo Tolstoy
Mark Twain
John Updike
Kurt Vonnegut
Alice Walker
Robert Penn Warren
Eudora Welty
Edith Wharton
Walt Whitman
Oscar Wilde
Tennessee Williams
Thomas Wolfe
Tom Wolfe
Virginia Woolf
William Wordsworth
Richard Wright
William Butler Yeats

Modern Critical Views

SAMUEL TAYLOR COLERIDGE

Edited and with an introduction by

Harold Bloom

Sterling Professor of the Humanities

Yale University

CHELSEA HOUSE PUBLISHERS

New York ◇ Philadelphia

Printed and bound in the United States of America

10 9 8 7

∞ The paper used in this publication meets the minimum requirements of the American National Standard for Permanence of Paper for Printed Library Materials, Z39.48-1984.

Library of Congress Cataloging-in-Publication Data
Main entry under title:
Samuel Taylor Coleridge.
(Modern critical views)
Bibliography: p.
Includes index.
1. Coleridge, Samuel Taylor, 1772–1834—Criticism and interpretation—Addresses, essays, lectures.
I. Bloom, Harold. II. Series.
PR4484.S26 1986 821′.7 85-46059
ISBN 0-87754-684-3

Contents

Editor's Note

This book brings together a comprehensive selection of the most distinguished criticism devoted to Coleridge's writings during the past quarter century, arranged in the order of its publication. I am grateful to Cathy Caruth for her erudition and insight in helping me choose these critical essays.

The introduction surveys Coleridge's poetic career as a powerful instance of the anxiety of influence. With my earlier readings of "Dejection: An Ode," "To William Wordsworth," "Limbo," and "Ne Plus Ultra," the chronological sequence of this volume begins, to be followed directly by Kenneth Burke's exuberant response to "Kubla Khan."

Owen Barfield, who among all living critics is closest in spirit to Coleridge, integrates some critical aspects of Coleridge's quest for "Method." Related inquiries are carried out by M. H. Abrams, dean of Romantic scholars, in his account of Coleridge's grand conceptual image, "A Light in Sound," and by a great allegorical critic, Angus Fletcher, in his analysis of Coleridgean threshold personifications. E. S. Shaffer's profoundly learned excavation of the origins of "Kubla Khan" in Coleridge's abandoned vision of a projected epic on the fall of Jerusalem is joined here by Kathleen Coburn's unique insight into the cognitive art of Coleridge's extraordinary Notebooks. Two great generations of Coleridge scholars culminate in Thomas McFarland's discovery of the origin of the poet-critic's theory of Secondary Imagination in the philosophy of the German metaphysician, Tetens.

A younger generation of scholars is represented by the seven remaining essays in this volume, starting with Jerome Christensen's examination of the mode of marginalia in the *Biographia Literaria*. Leslie Brisman's dialectical account of Coleridge's Christian supernaturalism partly turns upon Coleridge's own antithesis that is also at the center of Timothy Corrigan's investigation of the language of science in the *Biographia Literaria.*

Four readings of Coleridge's most famous poems conclude this volume, with each reading exemplifying a distinguished instance of contemporary modes of advanced literary criticism. Arden Reed on "Frost at Midnight" and Susan J. Wolfson on "The Ancient Mariner" both show a deconstructive awareness in analyzing problematical elements in Coleridge's rhetoric. Ken Frieden's exegesis of "Kubla Khan" and Camille Paglia's overview of "Christabel" combine psychoanalytical and rhetorical perspectives so as to achieve startling yet central insights into Coleridge at his most magical, and at his most disturbing.

Introduction

I

Coleridge, the youngest of fourteen children of a country clergyman, was a precocious and lonely child, a kind of changeling in his own family. Early a dreamer and (as he said) a "character," he suffered the loss of his father (who had loved him best of all the children) when he was only nine. At Christ's Hospital in London, soon after his father's death, he found an excellent school that gave him the intellectual nurture he needed, as well as a lifelong friend in the future essayist Charles Lamb. Early a poet, he fell deeply in love with Mary Evans, a schoolfellow's sister, but sorrowfully nothing came of it.

At Jesus College, Cambridge, Coleridge started well, but temperamentally he was not suited to academic discipline and failed of distinction. Fleeing Cambridge, and much in debt, he enlisted in the cavalry under the immortal name of Silas Tomkyn Comberback but kept falling off his horse. Though he proved useful to his fellow dragoons at writing love letters, he was good for little else but stable-cleaning, and the cavalry allowed his brothers to buy him out. He returned to Cambridge, but his characteristic guilt impeded academic labor and when he abandoned Cambridge in 1794 he had no degree.

A penniless young poet, radical in politics, original in religion, he fell in with the then equally radical bard Robert Southey, remembered today as the Conservative Laureate constantly savaged in Byron's satirical verse. Like our contemporary communards, the two poetical youths projected what they named a "pantisocracy." With the right young ladies and, hopefully, other choice spirits, they would found a communistic agrarian-literary settlement on the banks of the Susquehanna in exotic Pennsylvania. At Southey's urging, Coleridge made a pantisocratic engagement to the not very brilliant Miss Sara Fricker, whose sister Southey was to marry. Pantisocracy died aborning, and Coleridge in time woke up miserably to find himself unsuitably married, the greatest misfortune of his life.

He turned to Wordsworth, whom he had met early in 1795. His poetry influenced Wordsworth's and helped the latter attain his characteristic mode. It is not too much to say that Coleridge's poetry disappeared into Wordsworth's. We remember *Lyrical Ballads* (1798) as Wordsworth's book, yet about a third of it (in length) was Coleridge's, and "Tintern Abbey," the crown of the volume except for "The Rime of the Ancient Mariner," is immensely indebted to Coleridge's "Frost at Midnight." Nor is there much evidence of Wordsworth admiring or encouraging his friend's poetry; toward "The Ancient Mariner" he was always very grudging, and he was discomfited (but inevitably so) by both "Dejection: An Ode" and "To William Wordsworth." Selfless where Wordsworth's poetry was concerned, Coleridge had to suffer his closest friend's neglect of his own poetic ambitions.

This is not an easy matter to be fair about, since literature necessarily is as much a matter of personality as it is of character. Coleridge, like Keats (and to certain readers, Shelley), is lovable. Byron is at least always fascinating, and Blake in his lonely magnificence is a hero of the imagination. But Wordsworth's personality, like Milton's or Dante's, does not stimulate affection for the poet in the common reader. Coleridge has, as Walter Pater observed, a "peculiar charm"; he seems to lend himself to myths of failure, which is astonishing when the totality of his work is contemplated.

Yet it is his life, and his self-abandonment of his poetic ambitions, that continue to convince us that we ought to find in him parables of the failure of genius. His best poetry was all written in the year and half in which he saw Wordsworth daily (1797–8), yet even his best poetry, with the single exception of "The Ancient Mariner," is fragmentary. The pattern of his life is fragmentary also. When he received an annuity from the Wedgwoods, he left Wordsworth and Dorothy to study language and philosophy in Germany (1798–9). Soon after returning, his miserable middle years began, though he was only twenty-seven. He moved near the Wordsworths again and fell in love, permanently and unhappily, with Sara Hutchinson, whose sister Mary was to become Wordsworth's wife in 1802. His own marriage was hopeless, and his health rapidly deteriorated, perhaps for psychological reasons. To help endure the pain he began to drink laudanum, liquid opium, and thus contracted an addiction he never entirely cast off. In 1804, seeking better health, he went to Malta but returned two years later in the worst condition of his life. Separating from Mrs. Coleridge, he moved to London and began another career as lecturer, general man-of-letters, and periodical editor, while his miseries augmented. The inevitable quarrel with Wordsworth in 1810 was ostensibly reconciled in 1812, but real friendship was not reestablished until 1828.

From 1816 on, Coleridge lived in the household of a physician, James

Gillman, so as to be able to keep working and thus avoid total breakdown. Prematurely aged, his poetry period over, Coleridge entered into a major last phase as critic and philosopher, upon which his historical importance depends; but this, like his earlier prose achievements, is beyond the scope of an introduction to his poetry. It remains to ask, What was his achievement as a poet, and extraordinary as that was, why did his poetry effectively cease after about 1807? Wordsworth went on with poetry after 1807 but mostly very badly. The few poems Coleridge wrote, from the age of thirty-five on, are powerful but occasional. Did the poetic will not fail in him, since his imaginative powers did not?

Coleridge's large poetic ambitions included the writing of a philosophic epic on the origin of evil and a sequence of hymns to the sun, moon, and elements. These high plans died, slowly but definitively, and were replaced by the dream of a philosophic *Opus Maximum*, a huge work of synthesis that would reconcile German idealist philosophy with the orthodox truths of Christianity. Though only fragments of this work were ever written, much was done in its place—speculations on theology, political theory, and criticism that were to influence profoundly conservative British thought in the Victorian period and, in quite another way, the American transcendentalism led by Emerson and Theodore Parker.

Coleridge's actual achievement as poet divides into two remarkably diverse groupings—remarkable because they are almost simultaneous. The daemonic group, necessarily more famous, is the triad of "The Ancient Mariner," "Christabel," and "Kubla Khan." The "conversational" group includes the conversation-poem proper, of which "The Eolian Harp" and "Frost at Midnight" are the most important, as well as the irregular ode, such as "Dejection" and "To William Wordsworth." The late fragments, "Limbo" and "Ne Plus Ultra," are a kind of return to the daemonic mode. For a poet of Coleridge's gifts, to have written only nine poems that really matter is a sorrow, but the uniqueness of the two groups partly compensates for the slenderness of the canon.

The daemonic poems break through the orthodox censor set up by Coleridge's moral fears of his own imaginative impulses. Unifying the group is a magical quest-pattern which intends as its goal a reconciliation between the poet's self-consciousness and a higher order of being, associated with Divine forgiveness; but this reconciliation fortunately lies beyond the border of all these poems. The Mariner attains a state of purgation but cannot get beyond that process. Christabel is violated by Geraldine, but this too is a purgation rather than a damnation, as her utter innocence is her only flaw. Coleridge himself, in the most piercing moment in his poetry, is tempted to assume the state of an Apollo-rebirth—the youth with flashing eyes and floating hair—but he withdraws from his vision of a poet's paradise, judging it to be only another purgatory.

The conversational group, though so immensely different in mode, speaks more directly of an allied theme: the desire to go home, not to the past but to what Hart Crane beautifully called "an improved infancy." Each of these poems, like the daemonic group, verges upon a kind of vicarious and purgatorial atonement in which Coleridge must fail or suffer so that someone he loves may succeed or experience joy. There is a subdued implication that somehow the poet will yet be accepted into a true home this side of the grave if he can achieve an atonement.

Where Wordsworth, in his primordial power, masters the subjective world and aids his readers in the difficult art of feeling, Coleridge deliberately courts defeat by subjectivity and is content to be confessional. But though he cannot help us to feel, as Wordsworth does, he gives us to understand how deeply felt his own sense of reality is. Though in a way his poetry is a testament of defeat, a yielding to the anxiety of influence and to the fear of self-glorification, it is one of the most enduringly poignant of such testaments that literature affords us.

II

"Psychologically," Coleridge observed, "consciousness is the problem"; and he added somberly: "Almost all is yet to be achieved." How much he achieved Kathleen Coburn and others are showing us. My concern here is the sadder one of speculating yet again about why he did not achieve more as a poet. Walter Jackson Bate has meditated, persuasively and recently, upon Coleridge's human and literary anxieties, particularly in regard to the burden of the past and its inhibiting poetic splendors. I swerve away from Bate to center the critical meditation upon what might be called the poetics of anxiety, the process of misprision by which any latecomer strong poet attempts to clear an imaginative space for himself.

Coleridge could have been a strong poet, as strong as Blake or Wordsworth. He could have been another mighty antagonist for the Great Spectre Milton to engage and, yes, to overcome, but not without contests as titanic as those provided by Blake's *The Four Zoas* and Wordsworth's *The Excursion*, and parental victories as equivocal as those achieved with Blake's *Jerusalem* and Wordsworth's *The Prelude*. But we have no such poems by Coleridge. When my path winds home at the end of this Introduction, I will speculate as to what these poems should have been. As critical fathers for my quest I invoke first Oscar Wilde, with his glorious principle that the highest criticism sees the object as in itself it really is not, and second, Wilde's critical father, Walter Pater, whose essay of 1866 on "Coleridge's Writings" seems to me still the best short treatment of Coleridge, and this after a century of commentary. Pater, who knew his debt to Coleridge, knew also the anxiety Coleridge caused him, and Pater therefore came to a further and subtler knowing. In the Organic analogue, against which the entire soul of the great Epicurean critic rebelled, Pater recognized the product of Coleridge's profound anxieties as a creator. I begin therefore with Pater on Coleridge, and then will move immediately deep into the Coleridgean interior, to look upon Coleridge's fierce refusal to take on the ferocity of the strong poet.

This ferocity, as both Coleridge and Pater well knew, expresses itself as a near-solipsism, and Egotistical Sublime, or Miltonic godlike stance. From 1795 on, Coleridge knew, loved, envied, was both cheered and darkened by the largest instance of that Sublime since Milton himself. He studied constantly, almost involuntarily, the glories of the truly modern strong poet, Wordsworth. Whether he gave Wordsworth rather more than he received, we cannot be certain; we know only that he wanted more from Wordsworth than he received, but then it was his endearing though exasperating weakness that he always needed more love than he could get, no matter how much he got: "To be beloved is all I need,/And whom I love, I love indeed."

Pater understood what he called Coleridge's "peculiar charm," but he resisted it in the sacred name of what he called the "relative" spirit against Coleridge's archaizing "absolute" spirit. In gracious but equivocal tribute to Coleridge he observed:

> The literary life of Coleridge was a disinterested struggle against the application of the relative spirit to moral and religious questions. Everywhere he is restlessly scheming to apprehend the absolute; to affirm it effectively; to get it acknowledged. Coleridge failed in that attempt, happily even for him, for it was a struggle against the increasing life of the mind itself. . . . How did his choice of a controversial interest, his determination to affirm the absolute, weaken or modify his poetic gift?

To affirm the absolute, Pater says—or, as we might say, to reject all dualisms except those sanctioned by orthodox Christian thought—is not *materia poetica* for the start of the nineteenth century, and if we think of a poem like the "Hymn before Sun-Rise, in the Vale of Chamouni," we are likely to agree with Pater. We will agree also when he contrasts Wordsworth favorably with Coleridge, and even with Goethe, commending Wordsworth for "that flawless temperament . . . which keeps his conviction of a latent intelligence in nature within the limits of sentiment or instinct, and confines it to those delicate and subdued shades of expression which perfect art allows." Pater goes on to say that Coleridge's version of Wordsworth's instinct is a philosophical idea, which means that Coleridge's poetry had to be "more dramatic, more self-conscious" than Wordsworth's. But this in turn, Pater insists, means that for aesthetic success ideas must be held loosely, in the relative spirit. One idea that Coleridge did not hold loosely was the Organic analogue, and it becomes clearer as we proceed in Pater's essay that the aesthetic critic is building toward a passionate assault upon the Organic principle. He quotes Coleridge's description of Shakespeare as "a nature humanized, a genial understanding, directing self-consciously a power and an implicit wisdom deeper even than our consciousness." "There," Pater comments, with bitter eloquence, "'the absolute' has been affirmed in the sphere of art; and thought begins to congeal." With great dignity Pater adds that Coleridge has "obscured the true interest of art." By likening the work of art to a living organism, Coleridge does justice to the impression the work may give us, but he "does not express the process by which that work was produced."

M. H. Abrams, in his *The Mirror and the Lamp*, defends Coleridge against Pater by insisting that Coleridge knew his central problem "was to use analogy with organic growth to account for the spontaneous, the inspired, and the self-evolving in the psychology of invention, yet not to commit himself as far to the elected figure as to minimize the supervention of the antithetic qualities of foresight and choice." Though Abrams calls Pater "short-sighted," I am afraid the critical palms remain with the relative spirit, for Pater's point was not that Coleridge had no awareness of the dangers of using the Organic analogue but rather that awareness, here as elsewhere, was no salvation for Coleridge. The issue is whether Coleridge, not Shakespeare, was able to direct "self-consciously a power and an implicit wisdom deeper than consciousness." Pater's complaint is valid because Coleridge, in describing Shakespeare, Dante, Milton, keeps repeating his absolute formula that poems grow from within themselves, that their "wholeness is not in vision or conception, but in an inner feeling of totality and absolute being." As Pater says, "that exaggerated inwardness is barren" because it "withdraws us too far from what we can see, hear, and feel," because it cheats the senses and emotions of their triumph. I urge Pater's wisdom here not only against Coleridge, though I share Pater's love for Coleridge, but against the formalist criticism that continued in Coleridge's absolute spirit.

What is the imaginative source of Coleridge's disabling hunger for the Absolute? On August 9, 1831, about three years before he died, he wrote in his Notebook: "From my earliest recollection I have had a consciousness of Power without Strength—a perception, an experience, of more than ordinary power with an inward sense of Weakness. . . . More than ever do I feel this now, when all my fancies still in their integrity are, as it were, drawn *inward* and by their suppression and compression rendered a mock substitute for Strength—" Here again is Pater's barren and exaggerated inwardness, but in a darker context than the Organic principle provided.

This context is Milton's "universe of death," where Coleridge apprehended death-in-life as being "the wretchedness of *division*." If we stand in that universe, then "we think of ourselves as separated beings, and place nature in antithesis to the mind, as object to subject, thing to thought, death to life." To be so separated is to become, Coleridge says, "a soul-less fixed star, receiving no rays nor influences into my Being, *a Solitude which I so tremble at, that I cannot attribute it even to the Divine Nature.*" This, we can say, is Coleridge's Counter-Sublime, his answer to the anxiety of influence, in strong poets. The fear of solipsism is greater in him than the fear of not individuating his own imagination.

As with every other major Romantic, the prime precursor poet for Coleridge was Milton. There is a proviso to be entered here; for all these poets—Blake, Wordsworth, Shelley, Coleridge (only Keats is an exception)—there is a greater Sublime poetry behind Milton, but as its author is a people and not a single poet, and as it is far removed in time, its greatness does not inhibit a new imagination—not unless it is taken as the work of the Prime Precursor Himself, to whom all creation belongs. Only Coleridge, among these poets, acquired a double Sublime anxiety of influence. Beyond the beauty that has terror in it of Milton, was beauty more terrible. In a letter to Thelwall, December 17, 1796, Coleridge wrote: "Is not Milton a *sublimer* poet than Homer or Virgil? Are not his Personages more sublimely cloathed? And do you not know, that there is not perhaps *one* page in Milton's *Paradise Lost*, in which he has not borrowed his imagery from the *Scriptures*?—I allow, and rejoice that *Christ* appealed only to the understanding & the affections; but I affirm that, after reading Isaiah, or St. Paul's Epistle to the Hebrews, Homer & Virgil are disgustingly *tame* to me, & Milton himself barely tolerable." Yet these statements are rare in Coleridge. Frequently, Milton seems to blend with the ultimate influence, which I think is a normal enough procedure. In 1796, Coleridge also says, in his review of Burke's *Letter to a Noble Lord*: "It is lucky for poetry, that Milton did not live in our days. . . . " Here Coleridge moves toward the center of his concern, and we should remember his formula: "Shakespeare was all men, potentially, except Milton." This leads to a more ambiguous formula, reported to us of a lecture that Coleridge gave on November 28, 1811: "Shakespeare became all things well into which he infused himself, while all forms, all things became Milton—the poet ever present to our minds and more than gratifying us for the loss of the distinct individuality of what he represents." Though Coleridge truly professes himself more than gratified, he admits loss. Milton's greatness is purchased at the cost of something dear to Coleridge, a principle of difference he knows may be flooded out by his monistic yearnings. For Milton, to Coleridge, is a mythic monad in himself. Commenting upon the apostrophe to light at the commencement of the third book of *Paradise Lost*, Coleridge notes: "In all modern poetry in Christendom there is an under consciousness of a sinful nature, a fleeting away of external things, the mind or subject greater than the object, the reflective character predominant. In the *Paradise Lost* the sublimest parts are the revelations of Milton's own mind, producing itself and evolving its own greatness; and this is truly so, that when that which is merely entertaining for its objective beauty is introduced, it at first seems a discord." This might be summarized as: where Milton is not, nature is barren, and its significance is that Milton is permitted just such a solitude as Coleridge trembles to imagine for the Divine Being.

Humphry House observed that "Coleridge was quite unbelievably modest about his own poems; and the modesty was of a curious kind, sometimes rather humble and over-elaborate." As House adds, Coleridge "dreaded publication" of his poetry, and until 1828, when he was fifty-six, there was nothing like an adequate gathering of his verse. Wordsworth's attitude was no help, of course, and the Hutchinson girls and Dorothy no doubt followed Wordsworth in his judgments. There was Wordsworth, and before him there had been Milton. Coleridge presumably knew what "Tintern Abbey" owed to "Frost at Midnight," but this knowledge nowhere found expression. Must we resort to psychological speculation in order to see what inhibited Coleridge, or are there more reliable aids available?

In the *Biographia Literaria* Coleridge is not very kind to his pre-Wordsworthian poetry, particularly to the "Religious Musings." Yet this is where we must seek what went wrong with Coleridge's ambitions—here, and if there were space, in "The Destiny of Nations" fragments (not its arbitrarily yoked-together form of 1817), and in the "Ode to the Departing Year," and in the "Monody on the Death of Chatterton" in its earlier versions. After Wordsworth had descended upon Coleridge, supposedly as a "know-thyself" admonition from heaven but really rather more like a new form of the Miltonic blight, then Coleridge's poetic ambitions sustained another kind of inhibition. The Miltonic shadow on early Coleridge needs to be studied first, before a view can be obtained of his maturer struggles with influence.

With characteristic self-destructiveness, Coleridge gave "Religious Musings" the definitive subtitle: "A Desultory Poem, Written on the Christmas Eve of 1794." The root-meaning of "desultory" is "vaulting," and though Coleridge consciously meant that his poem skipped about and wavered, his imagination meant "vaulting," for "Religious Musings" is a wildly ambitious poem. "This is the time. . ." it begins, in direct recall of Milton's "Nativity" Hymn, yet it follows not the Hymn but the most sublime moments of *Paradise Lost*, particularly the invocation to Book III. As with the 1802 "Hymn before Sun-Rise," its great fault as a poem is that it never stops whooping; in its final version I count well over one hundred exclamation points in just over four hundred lines. Whether one finds this habit in Coleridge distressing or endearing hardly matters; he just never could stop doing it. He whoops because he vaults; he is a high jumper of the Sublime, and psychologically he could not avoid this. I quote the poem's final passage with relish and with puzzlement, for I am uncertain as to how good it may be, though it seems awful. Yet its awfulness is at least Sublime; it is not the drab, flat awfulness of Wordsworth at *his* common worst in *The Excursion* or even (heresy to admit this!) in so many passages of *The Prelude*—passages that we hastily skip by, feeling zeal and relief in getting at the great moments. Having just shouted out his odd version of Berkeley—that "life is a vision shadowy of truth"—Coleridge sees "the veiling clouds retire" and God appears in a blaze upon His Throne. Raised to a pitch of delirium by this vision, Coleridge soars aloft to join it:

> Contemplant Spirits! ye that hover o'er
> With untired gaze the immeasurable fount
> Ebullient with Creative Deity!
> And ye of plastic power, that interfused
> Roll through the grosser and material mass
> In organizing surge! Holies of God!
> (And what if Monads of the infinite mind?)
> I haply journeying my immortal course
> Shall sometime join your mystic choir! Till then
> I discipline my young and novice thought
> In ministeries of heart-stirring song,
> And aye on Meditation's heaven-ward wing
> Soaring aloft I breathe the empyreal air
> Of Love, omnific, omnipresent Love,
> Whose day-spring rises glorious in my soul
> As the great Sun, when he his influence
> Sheds on the frost-bound waters—The glad stream
> Flows to the ray and warbles as it flows.

Scholars agree that this not terribly pellucid passage somehow combines an early Unitarianism with a later orthodox overlay, as well as quantities of

Berkeley, Hartley, Newton, Neoplatonism, and possibly more esoteric matter. A mere reader will primarily be reminded of Milton and will be in the right, for Milton counts here and the rest do not. The Spirits Coleridge invokes are Miltonic angels, though their functions seem to be more complicated. Coleridge confidently assures himself and us that his course is immortal, that he may end up as a Miltonic angel and so perhaps also as a monad of the infinite mind. In the meantime, he will study Milton's "heart-stirring song." Otherwise, all he needs is love, which is literally the air he breathes, the sunrise radiating out of his soul in a stream of song, and the natural sun toward which he flows, a sun that is not distinct from God. If we reflect on how palpably sincere this is, how wholehearted, and consider what was to be Coleridge's actual poetic course, we will be moved. Moved to what? Well, perhaps to remember a remark of Coleridge's: "There are many men, especially at the outset of life, who, in their too eager desire for the end, overlook the difficulties in the way; there is another class, who see nothing else. The first class *may* sometimes fail; the latter rarely succeed." Whatever the truth of this for other men, no poet becomes a strong poet unless he starts out with a certain obliviousness of the difficulties in the way. He will soon enough meet those difficulties, however, and one of them will be that his precursor and inspirer threatens to subsume him, as Coleridge is subsumed by Milton in "Religious Musings" and in his other pre-Wordsworthian poems. And here I shall digress massively before returning to Coleridge's poetry, for my discourse enters now upon the enchanted and baleful ground of poetic influence, through which I am learning to find my way by a singular light—one that will bear a little explanation.

I do not believe that poetic influence is simply something that happens, that it is just the process by which ideas and images are transmitted from earlier to later poets. In that view, whether or not influence causes anxiety in the later poet is a matter of temperament and circumstance. Poetic influence thus reduces to source-study, of the kind performed upon Coleridge by Lowes and later scholars. Coleridge was properly scornful of such study, and I think most critics learn how barren an enterprise it turns out to be. I myself have no use for it as such, and what I mean by the study of poetic influence turns source-study inside out. The first principle of the proper study of poetic influence, as I conceive it, is that no strong poem has sources and no strong poem merely alludes to another poem. The meaning of a strong poem *is* another strong poem, a precursor's poem which is being misinterpreted, revised, corrected, evaded, twisted askew, made to suffer an inclination or bias which is the property of the later and not the earlier poet. Poetic influence, in this sense, is actually misprision, a poet's taking or doing amiss of a parent-poem that keeps *finding* him, to use a Coleridgean turn of phrase. Yet even this misprision is only the first step that a new poet takes when he advances from the early phase where his precursor floods him to a more Promethean phase where he quests for his own fire—which must nevertheless be stolen from his precursor.

I count some half-dozen steps in the life cycle of the strong poet as he attempts to convert his inheritance into what will aid him without inhibiting him by the anxiety of a failure in priority, a failure to have begotten himself. These steps are revisionary ratios, and for the convenience of a shorthand, I find myself giving them arbitrary names that are proving useful to me and perhaps can be of use to others. I list them herewith, with descriptions but not examples, as this can only be a brief sketch; I must get back to Coleridge's poetry, with this list helpfully in hand, to find my examples in Coleridge.

1. *Clinamen*, which is poetic misprision proper, I take the word from Lucretius, where it means a "swerve" of the atoms so as to make change possible in the universe. The later poet swerves away from the precursor by so reading the parent-poem as to execute a *clinamen* in relation to it. This appears as the corrective movement of his own poem, which implies that the precursor poem went accurately up to a certain point but then should have swerved, precisely in the direction that the new poem moves.
2. *Tessera*, which is completion and antithesis; I take the word not from mosaic-making, where it is still used, but from the ancient Mystery cults, where it meant a token of recognition—the fragment, say, of a small pot which with the other fragments would reconstitute the vessel. The later poet antithetically "completes" the precursor by so reading the parent-poem as to retain its terms but to mean them in an opposite sense, as though the precursor had failed to go far enough.
3. *Kenosis*, which is a breaking device similar to the defense mechanisms our psyches employ against repetition-compulsions; *kenosis* then is a movement toward discontinuity with the precursor. I take the word from St. Paul, where it means the humbling or emptying-out of Jesus by himself when he accepts reduction from Divine to human status. The later poet, apparently emptying himself of his own afflatus, his imaginative godhood, seems to humble himself as though he ceased to be a poet, but this ebbing is so performed

in relation to a precursor's poem-of-ebbing that the precursor is emptied out also, and so the later poem of deflation is not as absolute as it seems.

4. *Daemonization*, or a movement toward a personalized Counter-Sublime in reaction to the precursor's Sublime; I take the term from general Neoplatonic usage, where an intermediary being, neither Divine nor human, enters into the adept to aid him. The later poet opens himself to what he believes to be a power in the parent-poem that does not belong to the parent proper but to a range of being just beyond that precursor. He does this, in his poem, by so stationing its relation to the parent-poem as to generalize away the uniqueness of the earlier work.
5. *Askesis*, or a movement of self-purgation which intends the attainment of a state of solitude; I take the term, general as it is, particularly from the practice of pre-Socratic shamans like Empedocles. The later poet does not, as in *kenosis*, undergo a revisionary movement of emptying but of curtailing: he yields up part of his own human and imaginative endowment so as to separate himself from others, including the precursor, and he does this in his poem by so stationing it in regard to the parent-poem as to make that poem undergo an *askesis* also; the precursor's endowment is also truncated.
6. *Apophrades*, or the return of the dead; I take the word from the Athenian dismal or unlucky days upon which the dead returned to reinhabit the houses in which they had lived. The later poet, in his own final phase, already burdened by an imaginative solitude that is almost a solipsism, holds his own poem so open again to the precursor's work that at first we might believe the wheel has come full circle and we are back in the later poet's flooded apprenticeship, before his strength began to assert itself in the revisionary ratios of *clinamen* and the others. But the poem is now *held* open to the precursor, where once it *was* open, and the uncanny effect is that the new poem's achievement makes it seem to us not as though the precursor were writing it, but as though the later poet himself had written the precursor's characteristic work.

These then are six revisionary ratios, and I think they can be observed, usually in cyclic appearance, in the life's work of every post-Enlightenment strong poet—which in English means, for practical purposes, every post-Miltonic strong poet. Coleridge, to return now to where I began, had the potential of the strong poet but—unlike Blake, Wordsworth, and the major poets after them down to Yeats and Stevens in our time—declined the full process of developing into one. Yet his work, even in its fragmentary state, demonstrates this revisionary cycle in spite of himself. My ulterior purpose in this discussion is to use Coleridge as an instance because he is apparently so poor an example of the cycle I have sketched. But that makes him a sterner test for my theory of influence than any other poet I could have chosen.

I return to Coleridge's first mature poetry and to its *clinamen* away from Milton, the Cowperizing turn that gave Coleridge the Conversation Poems, particularly "Frost at Midnight." Hazlitt quotes Coleridge as having said to him in the spring of 1798 that Cowper was the best modern poet, meaning the best since Milton, which was also Blake's judgment. Humphry House demonstrated the relation between "Frost at Midnight" and *The Task*—a happy one, causing no anxieties, where a stronger poet appropriates from a weaker one. Coleridge used Cowper as he used Bowles, Akenside, and Collins, finding in all of them hints that could help him escape the Miltonic influx that had drowned out "Religious Musings." "Frost at Midnight," like *The Task*, swerves away from Milton by softening him, by domesticating his style in a context that excludes all Sublime terrors. When Coleridge rises to his blessing of his infant son at the poem's conclusion he is in some sense poetically "misinterpreting" the beautiful declaration of Adam to Eve: "With thee conversing I forget all time," gentling the darker overtones of the infatuated Adam's declaration of love. Or, more simply, like Cowper he is not so much humanizing Milton—that will take the strenuous, head-on struggles of Blake, Wordsworth, Shelley, Keats—as he is making Milton more childlike, or perhaps better, reading Milton as though Milton loved in a more childlike way.

The revisionary step beyond this, an antithetical completion or *tessera*, is ventured by Coleridge only in a few pantheistic passages that sneaked past his orthodox censor, like the later additions to "The Eolian Harp" or the veiled vision at the end of the second verse paragraph of "This Lime-Tree Bower My Prison." With his horror of division, his endless quest for unity, Coleridge could not sustain any revisionary impulse which involved his reversing Milton or daring to complete that sacred father.

But the next revisionary ratio, the *kenosis* or self-emptying, seems to me almost obsessive in Coleridge's poetry, for what is the total situation of the Ancient Mariner but a repetition-compulsion, which his poet breaks for himself only by the writing of the poem and then only momentarily? Coleridge had contemplated an Epic on the Origin of Evil, but we may ask, Where would Coleridge, if pressed, have located the origin of evil in himself? His Mariner is neither depraved in will nor even disobedient, but merely ignorant, and the spiritual machinery his crime sets into motion is so ambiguously presented as to be finally beyond analysis. I would ask the question, What was Coleridge trying (not necessarily consciously) to do for himself by writing the poem? And by this question I do not mean Kenneth Burke's notion of trying to do something for oneself as a person. Rather, what was Coleridge the poet trying to do for himself as poet? To which I would answer: trying to free himself from the inhibitions of Miltonic influence by humbling his poetic self and so humbling the Miltonic in the process. The Mariner does not empty himself out; he starts empty and acquires a Primary Imagination through his suffering. But for Coleridge the poem is a *kenosis*, and what is being humbled is the Miltonic Sublime's account of the origin of evil. There is a reduction from disobedience to ignorance, from the self-aggrandizing consciousness of Eve to the painful awakening of a minimal consciousness in the Mariner.

The next revisionary step in clearing an imaginative space for a maturing strong poet is the Counter-Sublime, the attaining of which I have termed *daemonization*, and this I take to be the relation of "Kubla Khan" and "Christabel" to *Paradise Lost*. Far more than "The Rime of the Ancient Mariner," these poems demonstrate a trafficking by Coleridge with powers that are *daemonic*, even though the "Rime" explicitly invokes Neoplatonic daemons in its marginal glosses. Opium was the avenging *daemon* or *alastor* of Coleridge's life, his Dark or Fallen Angel, his experiential acquaintance with Milton's Satan. Opium was for him what wandering and moral tale-telling became for the Mariner—the personal shape of repetition-compulsion. The lust for paradise in "Kubla Khan," Geraldine's lust for Christabel—these are manifestations of Coleridge's revisionary daemonization of Milton, these are Coleridge's Counter-Sublime. Poetic Genius, the genial spirit itself, Coleridge must see as daemonic when it is his own rather than when it is Milton's.

It is at this point in the revisionary cycle that Coleridge begins to back away decisively from the ferocity necessary for the strong poet. He does not sustain his *daemonization*; he closes his eyes in holy dread, stands outside the circumference of the *daemonic* agent, and is startled by his own sexual daring out of finishing "Christabel." He moved on to the revisionary ratio I have called *askesis*, or the purgation into solitude, the curtailing of some imaginative powers in the name of others. In doing so, he prophesied the pattern for Keats in "The Fall of Hyperion," since in his *askesis* he struggles against the influence of a composite poetic father, Milton-Wordsworth. The great poems of this *askesis* are "Dejection: An Ode" and "To William Wordsworth," where criticism has demonstrated to us how acute the revision of Wordsworth's stance is, and how much of himself Coleridge purges away to make this revision justified. I would add only that both poems misread Milton as sensitively and desperately as they do Wordsworth; the meaning of "Dejection" is in its relation to "Lycidas" as much as in its relation to the "Intimations" ode, even as the poem "To William Wordsworth" assimilates *The Prelude* to *Paradise Lost*. Trapped in his own involuntary dualisms, longing for a monistic wholeness such as he believes is found in Milton and Wordsworth, Coleridge in his *askesis* declines to see how much of his composite parent-poet he has purged away also.

After that, sadly enough, we have only a very few occasional poems of any quality by Coleridge, and they are mostly not the poems of a strong poet—that is, of a man vaulting into the Sublime. Having refused the full exercise of a strong poet's misprisions, Coleridge ceased to have poetic ambitions. But there are significant exceptions—the late manuscript fragment "Limbo" and the evidently still-later fragment "Ne Plus Ultra." Here, and I think here only, Coleridge experiences the particular reward of the strong poet in his last phase—what I have called the *apophrades* or return of the dead: not a Counter-Sublime but a negative Sublime, like the *Last Poems* of Yeats or *The Rock* of Stevens. Indeed negative sublimity is the mode of these Coleridgean fragments and indicates to us what Coleridge might have become had he permitted himself enough of the perverse zeal that the great poet must exhibit in malforming his great precursor. "Limbo" and "Ne Plus Ultra" show that Coleridge could have become, at last, the poet of the Miltonic abyss, the bard of Demogorgon. Even as they stand, these fragments make us read Book II of *Paradise Lost* a little differently; they enable Coleridge to claim a corner of Milton's Chaos as his own.

Pater thought that Coleridge had succumbed to the Organic analogue because he hungered too intensively for eternity, as Lamb had said of his old school-friend. Pater also quoted De Quincey's summary of Coleridge: "He wanted better bread than can be made with wheat." I would add that Coleridge hungered also for an eternity of generosity between poets, as between people—a generosity that is not allowed in a world where each poet must struggle to individuate his own breath and this at the expense of his forebears as much as of his contemporaries. Perhaps also, to modify De Quincey, Coleridge wanted better poems than can be made without misprision.

I suggest then that the Organic analogue, with all its pragmatic neglect of the processes by which poems have to be produced, appealed so overwhelmingly to Coleridge because it seemed to preclude the anxiety of influence and to obviate the poet's necessity not just to unfold like a natural growth but to develop at the expense of others. Whatever the values of the Organic analogue for literary criticism—and I believe, with Pater, that it does more harm than good—it provided Coleridge with a rationale for a dangerous evasion of the inner steps he had to take for his own poetic development. As Blake might have said, Coleridge's imagination insisted upon slaying itself on the stems of generation—or, to invoke another Blakean image, Coleridge lay down to sleep upon the Organic analogue as though it were a Beulah-couch of soft, moony repose.

What was our loss in this? What poems might a stronger Coleridge have composed? The *Notebooks* list *The Origin of Evil, an Epic Poem; Hymns to the Sun, the Moon, and the Elements—six hymns*; and, more fascinating even than these, a scheme for an epic on "the destruction of Jerusalem" by the Romans. Still more compelling is a March 1802 entry in the *Notebooks*: "Milton, a Monody in the metres of Samson's Choruses—only with more rhymes/—poetical influences—political-moral-Dr. Johnson/." Consider the date of this entry—only a month before the first draft of "Dejection"—and some sense of what *Milton, a Monody* might have been begins to be generated. In March 1802, William Blake, in the midst of his sojourn at Hayley's Felpham, was deep in the composition of *Milton: a Poem in 2 Books, To Justify the Ways of God to Men.* In the brief, enigmatic notes for *Milton, a Monody* Coleridge sets down "—poetical influences—political-moral-Dr. Johnson," the last being, we can assume, a refutation of Johnson's vision of Milton in *The Lives of the Poets*, a refutation that Cowper and Blake would have endorsed. "Poetical influences," Coleridge says, and we may recall that this is one of the themes of Blake's *Milton*, where the Shadow of the Poet Milton is one with the Covering Cherub, the great blocking-agent who inhibits fresh human creativity by embodying in himself all the sinister beauty of tradition. Blake's *Milton* is a kind of monody in places, not as a mourning for Milton, but as Milton's own, solitary utterance as he goes down from a premature Eternity (where he is unhappy) to struggle again in fallen time and space. I take it though that *Milton, a Monody* would have been modeled upon Coleridge's early "Monody on the Death of Chatterton" and so would have been Coleridge's lamentation for his Great Original. Whether, as Blake was doing at precisely the same time, Coleridge would have dared to identify Milton as the Covering Cherub, as the angel or *daemon* blocking Coleridge himself out from the poet's paradise, I cannot surmise. I wish deeply that Coleridge had written the poem.

It is ungrateful, I suppose, as the best of Coleridge's recent scholars keep telling us, to feel that Coleridge did not give us the poems he had it in him to write. Yet we have, all apology aside, only a double handful of marvelous poems by him. I close therefore by attempting a description of the kind of poem I believe Coleridge's genius owed us and which we badly need, and always will need. I would maintain that the finest achievement of the High Romantic poets of England was their humanization of the Miltonic Sublime. But when we attend deeply to the works where this humanization is most strenuously accomplished—Blake's *Milton* and *Jerusalem*, Wordsworth's *Prelude*, Shelley's *Prometheus Unbound*, Keats's two *Hyperions*, even in a way Byron's *Don Juan*—we sense at last a quality lacking, a quality in which Milton abounds for all his severity. This quality, though not in itself a tenderness, made Milton's Eve possible, and we miss such a figure in all her Romanic descendants. More than the other five great Romantic poets, Coleridge was able, by temperament and by subtly shaded intellect, to have given us a High Romantic Eve, a total humanization of the tenderest and most appealing element in the Miltonic Sublime. Many anxieties blocked Coleridge from that rare accomplishment, and of these the anxiety of influence was not the least.

HAROLD BLOOM

Wisdom and Dejection: Four Poems

"DEJECTION: AN ODE"

There is only one voice in "Dejection: An Ode." In this poem Coleridge does not argue with himself, though he has need to do so. But the voice is turned against itself with an intensity that only the greatest poets have been able to bring over into language. The ode's continuity as argument presents no problems; "Dejection" overtly rejects the dialectic of Wordsworth's memory-as-salvation. The logic of "Dejection" is that human process is irreversible: imaginative loss is permanent, and nature intimates to us our own mortality always.

The puzzle of "Dejection" is why and how it rejects as *imaginative argument* the Wordsworthian myth. The myth was initially a Coleridgean creation, in the "conversation poems" of 1795–98, where it is beautifully stated, though always with misgivings. The "why" of rejection belongs to a study of how Coleridge's poetry itself discourses on poetic limits. The "how" is a lesson in the Romantic uses of self-directed argument.

The epigraph to Wordworth's "Intimations" ode is a motto of natural piety. Against its rainbow Coleridge sets the natural emblem most in opposition: the new Moon, with the old Moon in its arms. In "Dejection" the storm is predicted, comes on, and finally is "but a mountain-birth," sudden and soon over. The poem's new moon is the Wordsworth surrogate, "Dear Lady! friend devoutest of my choice"; its old moon, Coleridge himself. The principal difference, then, between the two odes is that Wordsworth uses one protagonist passing through

---

From *The Visionary Company: A Reading of English Romantic Poetry.* © 1961 by Harold Bloom. Cornell University Press, 1961. Originally entitled "Samuel Taylor Coleridge."

several states of being while Coleridge undertakes the lesser imaginative task and risks pathos by doubling the human element yet keeping the voice single. The poem's speaker is doomed to imaginative death; all hope for joy devolves upon the "Lady."

By evading individual progression-through-contraries, Coleridge has no ostensible need for poetic logic. But this evasion could not in itself make a poem of any value; flat personal despair joined to altruism and benevolence is hardly a formula for poetic power. "Dejection" is imaginatively impressive because Coleridge does not succeed in altogether distinguishing himself from the Lady whose joy he celebrates. The curious and yet extraordinarily successful effect is like that of a saint seeking to disavow Christian doctrine by avowing its efficacy for others, less sinful than himself.

Study of "Dejection: An Ode" can well begin backwards, with a consideration of the lines that enable the poem to end on the word "rejoice":

> To her may all things live, from pole to pole,
> Their life the eddying of her living soul!

The image of the eddy is the summary figure of the poem: the flux of nature throughout has prepared for it. Joy, as the effluence of Life, overflows as sound, light, cloud, shower; as a composite luminous and melodic mist of the soul; now solid, now liquid, now vaporous, now pure light or pure sound. This is repetitious summary, but the poem's repetitiveness is meaningful here. The myth of Wordsworth's Child is being rejected; the glory comes and goes, without relation to infancy, childhood, youth, maturity. The progression is simply linear and it is irreversible:

> There was a time when, though my path was rough,
>   This joy within me dallied with distress,
> And all misfortunes were but as the stuff
>   Whence Fancy made me dreams of happiness:
> For hope grew round me, like the twining vine,
> And fruits, and foliage, not my own, seemed mine.
> But now afflictions bow me down to earth

The eddy has stopped its pole-to-pole movement; the cycle of joy is over. Taken literally, Coleridge's myth of dejection is a bizarre reinforcement of a single stage in the poetic argument of "Resolution and Independence":

> We poets in our youth begin in gladness,
> But thereof comes in the end despondency and madness.

If "Dejection" had only its stanzas I to VI and its climactic in stanza VIII, it could not be defended from the charge of pathos. The usually evaded stanza

VII, which is generally considered a transitional mood piece, controls the poem's logic and equips it to avoid self-indulgence. The structure of the poem is in two units: stanzas I, VII, VIII, and stanzas II–VI. The first group are respectively devoted to the pre-storm calm, the storm itself, and the subsequent calm, which is analogous to the peace at the end of a formalized tragedy. The middle stanzas are argument, between Coleridge-as-Wordsworthian and Coleridge-in-dejection, with the latter dialectically triumphant. The connecting unit between the groups opens stanza VII, in which the "viper thoughts" of II–VI are dismissed as "Reality's dark dream":

I turn from you, and listen to the wind,
Which long has raved unnoticed.

As he listens to the wind, he resolves his poem. The resolution is purely dialectical in that the stanza offers a set of assumptions that *include* the opposing Wordsworthian and Coleridgean views on the relationship between external nature and the poet's creative joy. Certainly the resolution is indirect, and perhaps too ingenious. But the curious seventh stanza cannot be ignored as an embarrassing digression; it is the crisis of the poem, akin to the silence between the eighth and ninth stanzas of the "Intimations" ode. There the dialectic rises to poetic finality because it is a dialectic of discourse itself. The conflict of discourse and silence is resolved in favor of silence, with the result that the discourse, when it begins again, can move in reverse and state the contrary of the preceding stanzas.

Part of the functional obscurity of Coleridge's stanza VII is its reference to the child as Otway might present her, where we would expect one of the solitary creatures of Wordsworth's poetry. The problem here is merely a genetic one, related to the successive "Edmund" and "lady" substitutions for Wordsworth in the "Dejection" ode. Originally Coleridge had written:

As William's self had made the tender Lay—

This vanished together with:

A boat becalm'd! dear William's Sky Canoe

after the present line 36 of the ode, identifying the crescent moon with the visionary sky-boat of *Peter Bell*. So vanished also Coleridge's "I too will crown me with a Coronal" in direct answer to Wordsworth's "My heart hath its coronal," also vanished from the final version. Otway, like Chatterton, was a figure of Romantic myth: the poet as hungry outcast in the storm of organized society. Any poet of the time who cited either Chatterton or Otway can be assumed to be speaking of himself in his exemplary role. The lost child of stanza VII could easily be Wordsworth's Lucy Gray, or Blake's Little Girl

Lost, without the natural piety of the one or the cyclic function of the other.

The tone of stanza VII is complex, for it presents the Wind as a bad actor, overplaying, or a worse poet, raving bombast. The Eolian Harp is not the fit instrument for this Wind, as the harp is needlessly subtle, in itself too bare of easily negative associations. The Wind's song is unnaturally terrible: "worse than wintry." But the analogue to the Wind's song is what has been spoken while the song "long has raved unnoticed," that is, stanzas II–VI of Coleridge's ode, stanzas "perfect in all tragic sounds," written by a poet "e'en to frenzy bold."

The Eolian Harp sends forth a diminishing series of unhappy ravings, toning down from torture to rout to losing one's way, "a Tale of less affright," a "tender lay," and one that is "tempered with delight." But where is the "delight" in Coleridge's citation of the tale?

> 'Tis of a little child
> Upon a lonesome wild,
> Not far from home, but she hath lost her way:
> And now moans low in bitter grief and fear,
> And now screams loud, and hopes to make her mother hear.

The child does not find its way home in Coleridge's poem. And yet this is the agency of resolution in the poem's emergence from conflict. The poet in his last stanza keeps vigil far from sleep, but his vigil is in some way not specified an atonement for his friend, who will awaken from a gentle sleep lifted in spirit and attuned in voice by Joy. The descent of the saving and shaping Spirit in that blessed sleep is announced in the phrase "with wings of healing." Coleridge has rejected the myth of Wordsworth's salvation, and yet he avers that Wordsworth is saved. The puzzle can be summarized in the question: what is involved in the "thus" that opens the poem's last line?

> Thus mayest thou ever, evermore rejoice.

Our only evidence for a reply is either *in* the final stanza, or in that and its relationship to the preceding "lost child" stanza. As in the "Intimations" ode, the dialectic turns over *between* the stanzas; the overt continuity is a puzzle to the Corporeal Understanding but a challenge to the Intellectual Powers, to employ Blake's characterization of the nature of Vision, not Allegory. The Intellectual Powers are the imagination, and the imagination, assuming the perfect unity of "Dejection" as a work of art, goes to work upon the problem of continuity here by pondering the implications of the perfect unity of stanza VIII with the remainder of the poem.

That unity is necessarily imagistic as well as argumentative, but to separate unities so is to create only another cloven fiction. What we have in "Dejection" could be studied as an imagistic dialectic or a dialectical image, the eddy and its widely assorted components. The eddy is, in the poem, inseparably both image and argument. As image it comprehends (as Abrams demonstrates) all of the subordinate imagery of the poem. As argument, it *is* the poem, or more precisely, the poem's partially concealed emblem. The eddying movement of joy in the flux of nature is a cyclic signature of all things, both in "Dejection" and in "Intimations." But in Wordsworth the signature is distorted, with more powerful poetic results than Coleridge obtains by his clean comprehensiveness of imagistic presentation.

In Wordsworth, the eddy is broken twice, once at the pole of Nature, and once at the pole of Man. After the first break, Nature serves as a kindly nurse or foster mother, until the movement of joy can be (partially) restored. The second break, at Man's pole, takes place in the sleep of death that the sensual and proud, that poor, loveless, ever-anxious crowd, enjoy as best they can when the true joy of the creation of self is gone. The composing of the "Intimations" ode is the awakening from this sleep of death, the flowing-on again of the joyous waters of continuity.

Coleridge's imaginative severity, his heightened sense of poetic limits, gives us a stricter argument and a more confined image. The movement breaks at only one pole, man's, because the movement can emanate out only from man. For:

> we receive but what we give,
> And in our life alone does Nature live

Out of the soul alone eddies the mysterious element-of-elements, self-creating joy, to borrow John Clare's phrase. Joy, the Imagination itself, the great I Am, the word of primal creation, issues forth as a light, a glory, a fair, luminous cloud, an ultimate voice which is the strong music of the soul. The light, glory, and luminous cloud are what the child Wordsworth *saw*; the potent music is what he *heard*. The "fountain-light of all our day," a "master-light of all our seeing," is how the "Intimations" ode finally summarizes them.

In his sixth stanza Coleridge says that the visitations of his affliction, his *acedia*, suspend his shaping spirit of Imagination: suspend, not abolish. Suspension is reinforced by "almost" as a qualifier in the stanza's last line. Joy still moves out of Coleridge but fitfully; the eddy is haphazard, has lost its perfection of movement.

In stanza VII, when Coleridge sends these "viper thoughts" from him, he chooses the healing power of Wordsworth's "Lucy Gray" as being appropriate for his state. He accepts it as comfort, where he rejects the consolation of "Intimations." But his Lucy is hardly Wordsworth's. Coleridge's follows the phrasing of one of his letters to Poole; Wordsworth's neither moans low nor screams loud. Before being lost, Lucy is as blithe as the mountain roe. After her absorption into Nature (or, more accurately, her absorption of Nature into her) we have a myth:

> —Yet some maintain that to this day
> She is a living child;
> That you may see sweet Lucy Gray
> Upon the lonesome wild.
>
> O'er rough and smooth she trips along,
> And never looks behind;
> And sings a solitary song
> That whistles in the wind.

The final touch is the poem's initial affirmation; Wordsworth himself has *seen* her. Coleridge's odd tribute is to supply the poem's missing middle, and then to accept the given of it, without incorporating any trace of the *textus receptus* in his final version of "Dejection." But the reference is there, and the reference does its work. Lucy's absorption is a proof of the imaginative finality of the eddy. Joy survives, though some of us do not, not wholly. And yet we all of us survive, some only partially, in it. Which, by a "commodious vicus of recirculation," takes us back to "Dejection"'s final stanza again.

The "Intimations" ode ends by celebrating "the human heart by which we live." The Wordsworth Lady in "Dejection"'s climax is to rise "with light heart," lifted by joy, attuned by it in voice. All things will live "to her"; for their life literally will be the pole-to-pole eddying of her living and creative soul. The unspoken question, or reservation, is in the missing "but to me?" The grief of Lucy Gray is absorbed into the eddy of creativity as thoroughly as if it had never been. But the Coleridgean lost child and the ruined man, blasted at the roots, are not to be subsumed by poetry. Wordsworth is saved, not by his own myth, as he avers, but because he is a "simple spirit, guided from above." Coleridge's passionate undersong, poised dialectically against the serenity of his poem's resolution, evidences that his comparative damnation came because he lacked both Wordsworth's guidance (egotism, as we call it now) and Wordsworth's saving simplicity. Coleridge could not be a fanatic, even of the Imagination.

"TO WILLIAM WORDSWORTH"

The conversation poem "To William Wordsworth" is Coleridge's immediate reply to having heard Wordsworth read the entire *Prelude* aloud to him during January 1807. On the night Wordsworth finished, January 7, Coleridge composed the greater part of his beautiful but ambiguous tribute to:

> what within the mind
> By vital breathings secret as the soul
> Of vernal growth, oft quickens in the heart
> Thoughts all too deep for words

The reference to the final line of the "Intimations" ode attaches this poem to the "Dejection" ode as well. Indeed, the debate of "Dejection" is carried on here again, five years after the earlier poem. Coleridge says that *The Prelude*'s theme is:

> of moments awful,
> Now in thy inner life, and now abroad,
> When power streamed from thee, and thy soul received
> The light reflected, as a light bestowed

We receive but what we give, is the way Coleridge previously had phrased this sad truth. But the tone is different now. Coleridge both praises Wordsworth's power and implies that Wordsworth is deluded in assigning the power to Nature. This curious double emphasis is carried through the poem, but in varying and disguised forms.

Coleridge praises *The Prelude* as being "more than historic," a "prophetic" poem dealing with "the building up of a Human Spirit," a high theme that Wordsworth has the distinction of being the first to sing aright. He emphasizes, rather more than Wordsworth does, the mystery of the subject. Wordsworth sees overt manifestations, both in Nature and in his own inner life. Coleridge speaks of "vital breathings secret as the soul of vernal growth"; Nature and Man are parallel mysteries. The shift from Wordsworth's thoughts too deep for tears to Coleridge's thoughts too deep for words is part of the same pattern. It is as though Coleridge desires to replace the naturalist in Wordsworth by a premature mystic.

When Coleridge turns to Wordsworth and the Revolution, his emphasis again results in a subtle distortion of Wordsworth's doctrine and poem. *The Prelude*'s crisis is slighted in this account of it:

> —Of that dear Hope afflicted and struck down,
> So summoned homeward, thenceforth calm and sure
> From the dread watch-tower of man's absolute self,
> With light unwaning on her eyes, to look
> Far on—herself a glory to behold,
> The Angel of the vision

Poor Hope begins as a revolutionary humanist in this passage but is baptized in the course of it and ends an Angel. Wordsworth's hope is revived by memory, by spots of time and their consequences. Coleridge completes his revision of *The Prelude* by deftly importing the "Ode to Duty" into it:

> Then (last strain)
> Of Duty, chosen Laws controlling choice,
> Action and joy

The true glory of the 1805 *Prelude* is that the soul is still an impulse to herself as the poem closes. It was just afterwards that Wordsworth supplicated for a new control, and composed the palinode of "Peele Castle." The chastened Coleridge, himself somewhat broken, is rather too quick to welcome deviations from the religion of Nature.

More extraordinary is Coleridge's complex emotional reaction to his friend's achievement:

> Ah! as I listened with a heart forlorn,
> The pulses of my being beat anew:
> And even as Life returns upon the drowned,
> Life's joy rekindling roused a throng of pains

The pains, not the joy, dominate the lines that follow. Coleridge feels keen pangs of love for Wordsworth, but they awaken in him with the turbulent outcry of a weeping babe. As Coleridge apprehends his friend's achievement (and his own part in it) he reproaches himself for his own failure:

> Sense of past Youth, and Manhood come in vain,
> And Genius given, and Knowledge won in vain;
> And all which I had culled in wood-walks wild,
> And all which patient toil had reared, and all,
> Commune with thee had opened out—but flowers
> Strewed on my corse, and borne upon my bier
> In the same coffin, for the self-same grave!

The decorum of including this in a poem of ostensible tribute is strange. Sense of past youth, the cullings of "wood-walks wild," the natural gift of genius, the liberation of communion with another: these are all the themes of *The Prelude*. The implication of Coleridge's lines is: where is *my* poem on the growth of my own mind?

Coleridge attempts to check his lament, but again his diction betrays his sense of being overthrown upon his own ground:

> That way no more! and ill beseems it me,
> Who came a welcomer in herald's guise,
> Singing of Glory, and Futurity,
> To wander back on such unhealthful road,
> Plucking the poisons of self-harm! And ill
> Such intertwine beseems triumphal wreaths
> Strew'd before thy advancing!

This must have been a very uncomfortable poem for Wordsworth to read. Coleridge wanders back as Wordsworth advances. The only two activities possible for Coleridge are either to pluck the poisons of self-harm on the now unhealthful road of memory, or else to strew triumphal wreaths before his friend. Another three years were to pass, then the inevitable quarrel came.

The final sections of "To William Wordsworth" are profoundly moving, for in them Coleridge, with immense effort, breaks out of his selfhood communings, and achieves a sense of another. Though he still refers to his past mind as "nobler" than his present, and speaks of himself as listening to Wordsworth's reading "like a devout child" with passive soul, he does begin to manifest a revival of sensibility, and end to torpor and self-pity:

> by they various strain
> Driven as in surges now beneath the stars,
> With momentary stars of my own birth,
> Fair constellated foam, still darting off
> Into the darkness; now a tranquil sea,
> Outspread and bright, yet swelling to the moon.

Coleridge, in this passage, is compared to the sea; Wordsworth's poem to a wind. The poem drives Coleridge along at certain moments as the wind causes the ocean to surge. The aroused Coleridge both moves beneath the stars, symbols here of creativity, and momentarily creates his own stars, which dart off into the oceanic darkness. In a very brilliant phrase, "fair constellated foam," the stars are seen as a direct effluence from Coleridge's own being, the foam on the waves of his surging consciousness. Even when not so active, he is still, under the influence of Wordsworth's oral delivery, a tranquil sea, outspread and bright, receptive to natural influences and swelling to the moon. The sexual element in the passage ought not to be avoided; it is so manifestly there. Coleridge had always insisted that Wordsworth's genius was more masculine than that of any other poet, and Coleridge's own Imagination tends to be feminine, as a close reading of "Christabel" ought to make clear. Wordsworth's account of Nature is that of a lover describing his mistress. Coleridge's

Nature is less of a Muse, and blends at last into the male Godhead of Hebraic and Christian tradition. In this poem, which joins "Dejection" as a prophecy of the crisis between Wordsworth and Coleridge, "Dejection"'s argument with the "Intimations" ode comes to a climax. Wordsworth's is the male dream of a perpetually given grace, a generous presence of love and beauty which cannot cease. Coleridge's is a reduced vision of reality; we get back what we give, and need more love than we can hope to get, for we need more than we can give.

For Coleridge, Wordsworth is still "my comforter and guide," strong in himself, and powerful enough to give his friend strength. When the reading is done, and Coleridge's tributary poem ends also, the dependent poet is lost in imaginative reverie:

> Scarce conscious, and yet conscious of its close
> I sate, my being blended in one thought
> (Thought was it? or aspiration? or resolve?)
> Absorbed, yet hanging still upon the sound—
> And when I rose, I found myself in prayer.

The one thought, probably only an aspiration, but hopefully a resolve, is the thought of emulation, and the prayer is for a release of imaginative power. But the closing line is tribute also; to have participated in *The Prelude* is to have found in poetry a more than superfluous means of grace.

"LIMBO"

The poem responding to *The Prelude* is Coleridge's last meditation in the mode that his "conversation poems" had pioneered. After January 1807 he bade farewell to Nature as a muse. The sonnet "To Nature" may be as late as 1820 in composition, but its tone is altogether defensive and nostalgic:

> It may indeed be phantasy, when I
> Essay to draw from all created things
> Deep, heartfelt, inward joy that closely clings;
> And trace in leaves and flowers that round me lie
> Lessons of love and earnest piety.

This is at a dead end of vision. The poet can be only mildly defiant, and seek to justify Nature by attaching her for sanction to God as a "poor sacrifice" to the higher sacramentalism. Sometime about 1817, Coleridge scribbled a nightmare-like fragment in a notebook, and called it "Limbo." The flight from Nature leads to an Ulro as frightening as Blake's state of negations:

The sole true Something—This! In Limbo's Den
It frightens Ghosts, as here Ghosts frighten men.
Thence cross'd unseiz'd—and shall some fated hour
Be pulveris'd by Demogorgon's power,
And given as poison to annihilate souls

The substance of substances, or "sole true Something" in "Dejection: An Ode" was still "this light, this glory, this fair luminous mist." Now Coleridge is on the other side of dejection, in a den of quietude which knows an essence of annihilation. Ghosts dwell in Limbo, a state whose very name (Latin *limbus*) means border or edge, and where no judgment is possible, and non-being reigns. "The sole true Something," the dread substanceless substance, frightens ghosts in Limbo, as ghosts frighten us here. The "Thence cross'd unseiz'd" refers to the Acheron, the river in Hades over which Charon the boatman ferries the dead. In lines crossed out of the fragment, Coleridge says that the dread thing skimmed in the wake of Charon's boat and mocked his demand for a farthing fare. It can cross the gulf between existence and non-existence, for it has attributes both of what is and of what is not. It is thus the essence or soulless soul of chaos, and shall at a darkly fated time be ground into a poison by Demogorgon, the god of the primordial abyss, and used to annihilate souls. Even now, the fragment goes on to affirm, it shrinks souls who dread "the natural alien of their negative eye," just as moles dread light.

So far these are the metaphysics of nightmare, and the rhetoric of the fragment is oppressive. Coleridge's horror of mere matter, his aversion to metaphysical materialism, so dominates these lines as to give them an undoubted but perhaps illicit power. They play upon our obsessive fear of formlessness, and it needs no Coleridge to do that; any director of a horror film can do more. The fragment becomes poetry when Coleridge recovers himself, and speculates upon Limbo:

—where Time and weary Space
Fettered from flight, with night-mare sense of fleeing,
Strive for their last crepuscular half-being;—
Lank Space, and scytheless Time with branny hands
Barren and soundless as the measuring sands

Limbo cannot let Time and Space go but keeps them in dim and twilight form, else it vanishes into a still farther abyss. But their stay is reluctant; as in a nightmare they strive to flee but stand fast just this side of existent being. They are unmeaning, "as moonlight on the dial of the day." The juxtaposed images of the moon and the sundial suddenly liberate Coleridge's imagination into a lovely vision of "Human Time" as opposed to the horror of Limbo's minimal clock time:

> An Old Man with a steady look sublime,
> That stops his earthly task to watch the skies;
> But he is blind—a Statue hath such eyes;—
> Yet having moonward turn'd his face by chance,
> Gazes the orb with moon-like countenance,
> With scant white hairs, with foretop bald and high,
> He gazes still,—his eyeless face all eye;—
> As 'twere an organ full of silent sight,
> His whole face seemeth to rejoice in light!
> Lip touching lip, all moveless, bust and limb—
> He seems to gaze at that which seems to gaze on him!

This, with its rhapsodic ecstasy, is one of the great and genuinely difficult passages in Coleridge's poetry. Flanked on each side "by the mere horror of blank Naught-at-all," these lines both exemplify and celebrate the revival of poetic joy and creativity within the poet who utters them. They stand with the chant at the close of "Kubla Khan," the beautiful movement that ends "Frost at Midnight," and the vision of the infant gazing at the moon in "The Nightingale." These, with the moonlight episodes in "Christabel" and *The Ancient Mariner*, are Coleridge's moments of pure Imagination. Of all these, the vision by moonlight in "Limbo" is the most desperate and poignant, and is equivalent to Keat's suffering vision of the unveiled face of Moneta in *The Fall of Hyperion*. What Coleridge sees, like Keats, is beyond tragedy, and past all pathos.

Human time is measured here, as in Blake, by the intensity of apprehension and creation which goes into it, not by duration. The Old Man who is Time's Human emblem is very like Rilke's Angel, blind and containing the forms of reality within himself. But Rilke's Angel gazes within. Coleridge's sublime Old Man watches the skies with a steady look. Yet he has a statue's blind eyes; the Byzantine suggestion anticipates Yeats. As he gazes moonward he is one moon reflecting light upon another, Human Time receiving and giving again to a symbolic Eternity. Coleridge finely says that the Old Man's eyeless face is all eye, full of silent sight. The sight of Eternity is presumably a speaking one, as in certain moments of awakened Imagination in Coleridge and Wordsworth. Finally, Human Time is transfigured in the joy of the light coming down upon the Old Man. Lip touches lip in response, but all is moveless, for this is a mouth that has, as Yeats was to say in a similar moonlit context, no moisture and no breath. And yet the statue is all but animate, as

Coleridge breathlessly cries out the last line of his vision; the gaze between Old Man and moon seems mutual. Against the materialist and dim temporal form of Limbo, Coleridge has set an idealistic image of humanized temporality; against the nightmare, a dream of desire. The dream dissolves, and the poem ends, not in the Purgatory curse of growthless, dull Privation, the lurid thought haunting "Dejection: An Ode," but in the Hell of a fear far worse, the future state of positive Negation. The myth of Nature had failed Coleridge, or he it. The philosopher-theologian in him found what seemed a rock to build upon, but the poet found only a fear of blind matter, and the torments of the formless, a poet's true Hell.

"NE PLUS ULTRA"

The nature of that inferno Coleridge explored at least once more, in a fragment probably inscribed in 1826, after the notebook draft of "Limbo." Positive Negation is an oxymoron requiring illustration. The apocalypse of the brief "Ne Plus Ultra" fragment is as vivid an exemplification as nightmare can achieve. I quote it entire, as it is all one indivisible movement:

Sole Positive of Night!
Antipathist of Light!
Fate's only essence! primal scorpion rod—
The one permitted opposite of God!—
Condensed blackness and abysmal storm
Compacted to one sceptre
Arms the Grasp enorm—
The Intercepter—
The Substance that still casts the shadow Death!—
The Dragon foul and fell—
The unrevealable,
And hidden one, whose breath
Gives wind and fuel to the fires of Hell!
Ah! sole despair
Of both th' eternities in Heaven!
Sole interdict of all-bedewing prayer,
The all-compassionate!
Save to the Lampads Seven
Reveal'd to none of all th' Angelic State,
Save to the Lampads Seven,
That watch the throne of Heaven!

The Lampads Seven are seven lamps of fire burning before the Divine Throne in Revelation 4 : 5, where they are called the seven Spirits of God. The two Eternities in Heaven are probably Divine Love and Divine Knowledge. "Ne Plus Ultra" means the acme, usually the highest point of perfection, further than or beyond which one cannot go. Here it means the lowest point of imperfection, the nadir of positive Negation, the Dragon that is Death, Chaos, Satan. The poem is a startled apprehension revealing the names and nature of this great beast, which coils itself formlessly at the outer borders of the ordered world.

This Antagonist is the negation of all values. He is darkness against light, and fate's only reality against the Will of God. Yet he is part of that Will—its one permitted opposite. All of natural blackness and storm are compactly condensed in him. He stands, eternally, between prayer and its compassionate fruition.

Coleridge died on July 25, 1834. Some eight months before, he had composed his own epitaph, pathetic and characteristic:

> Stop, Christian passer-by!—Stop, child of God,
> And read with gentle breast. Beneath this sod
> A poet lies, or that which once seem'd he.
> O, lift one thought in prayer for S. T. C.;
> That he who many a year with toil of breath
> Found death in life, may here find life in death!

For Coleridge, the Intercepter found his chief formless form as death in life. Death in life defeated the poet, but for Coleridge the theory of poetry was at last not the theory of life. The Imagination in Blake and Wordsworth sought life in life, and prevailed in Blake until the end. Coleridge initiated what he himself could not approve, and wrote his own epitaph many times before his death. The poems live; the theology and philosophy have only a life in death.

KENNETH BURKE

"Kubla Khan": Proto-Surrealist Poem

Let's begin at the heart of the matter, and take up the "problems" afterwards. Count me among those who would view this poem both as a marvel, and as "in principle" *finished* (and here is a "problem," inasmuch as Coleridge himself refers to "Kubla Khan" as a "fragment").

Conceivably, details could be added, to amplify one or another of the three movements. And some readers (I am not among them) might especially feel the need of transitional lines to bridge the ellipsis between the middle and final stanzas. But as regards the relationship among the three stages of the poem's development, its unfolding seems to me no less trimly demarcated than the strophes of a Greek chorus, or (more relevantly) the Hegelian pattern of thesis, antithesis, and synthesis. Whatever may have got lost, the three stanzas in their overall progression tick off a perfect form, with beginning, middle, and end respectively. Thus:

Stanza One (Thesis) amplifies the theme of the beatific vision. Stanza Two (Antithesis) introduces and develops the sinister, turbulent countertheme (plus, at the close, a notably modified recall of the contrasting first theme). And the Third Stanza fuses the two motives in terms of a beatific vision (the "damsel with a dulcimer") seen by a poetic "I," the mention of whom, despite the euphoria, leads to the cry, "Beware! Beware!" and to talk of a "dread" that, however "holy," in a sinister fashion is felt to befit the idealistic building of this particular air castle.

In *The Road to Xanadu*, John Livingston Lowes brought an infectious combination of research and spirited delight to the tracking down of possible

---

From *Language as Symbolic Action: Essays on Life, Literature, and Method.* University of California Press, 1966.

literary sources behind Coleridge's great poems of Fascination (an enterprise further justified by the fact that Coleridge was so notoriously omnivorous a reader, and one of his memorandum books listed texts containing many references to caverns, chasms, mazes, sunken rivers, fountains, and the like). By consulting Lowes the reader will discover that nearly every notable term or reference in the poem appeared (often with quite relevant applications and combinations) in other passages that Coleridge is quite likely to have seen. But though greatly enjoying the charm of Lowes's presentation, and having on many occasions consulted his book when working on Coleridge, I should begin by pointing out that our present job involves a quite different trend of investigation (an investigation in which Lowes's book can be of great help, though his interest is directed otherwise).

There is a sense in which poets can be said to have special nomenclatures, just as scientists or philosophers do. But this situation is concealed from us by the fact that, rather than inventing a special word for some particular conceptual purpose, or pausing to define some particular application he is giving to a word in common usage, a poet leaves the process implicit, even though he uses the common idiom in his peculiar way. (For instance, the term "fish" in Theodore Roethke's poems would have little in common with the article of food we might buy in a market or order in a restaurant.) And by collating all the contexts that help define a word as it figures in a given poet's work, we can discern respects in which it is part of a nomenclature essentially as specialized as "entelechy" in the philosophy of Aristotle, or "relativity" with particular reference to the theories of Einstein. So, thinking along those lines, insofar as I'd risk looking up from the immediate text, I'd tend to ask about uses of a given term in other works *by Coleridge* rather than asking (like Lowes) about possible sources in *other* writers. For instance, people have doubtless talked about fountains since they could talk at all. And Coleridge's reference to the sacred river, Alph, does unquestionably suggest the ancient myth of the river Alpheus that sank into the ground and emerged as the fountain Arethusa (a belief which Lowes shows to have merged with notions about the sources of the Nile). I'd tend to start matters from a concern with the themes of submergence and emergence, with the Alpheus-Arethusa *pattern* as a symbolizing of *rebirth*, regardless of who else happened to speak of it. Or take this comment in Lowes:

> In April, 1798, Coleridge who had been suffering from an infected tooth, wrote as follows, in a letter to his brother George:
>
> > Laudanum gave me repose, not sleep; but you, I believe, know how divine that repose is, *what a spot of enchantment, a green*

> *spot of fountain and flowers and trees in the very heart of a waste of sands!*

Now when Coleridge wrote that, he was recalling and echoing, consciously or unconsciously, something else. For in the Note Book (which, as we know, belongs to this same period) appears this memorandum:

> —*some wilderness-plot, green and fountainous* and unviolated by Man.

Lowes then asks, "Is it possible to discover what lies behind this note?" He proceeds to discover, in Bartram's *Travels*, the expressions "blessed unviolated spot of earth!" and "the enchanting spot." And he notes that two pages earlier Bartram had written: "the dew-drops twinkle and play. . . on the tips of the lucid, green savanna, sparkling" beside a "serpentine rivulet, meandering over the meadows." As approached from Lowes's point of view, the serpentine, meandering rivulet would seem to touch upon the "sacred river,/ Five miles meandering with a mazy motion"; the "dew-drops" might impinge upon "honey-dew"; and so on. But of primary importance for *our present investigations* is not the question of where Coleridge may have read words almost identical with "spot of enchantment," but the fact that he used the expression in this particular context (in association with laudanum). And the reference to "honey-dew" would lead us, not to such a reference as *Bartram's* "dew-drops," but rather to a pair of quite contrasting references in "The Ancient Mariner," the first a dew like the sweat of anguish ("From the sails the dew did drip"), the second the dew of refreshment after release from the dreadful drought ("I dreamt that they were filled with dew;/And when I awoke, it rained"). Or we might recall the voice "As soft as honey-dew" that, though gentle, pronounced a fatal sentence: "The man hath penance done,/And penance more will do." And above all, I should rejoice to encounter in another poem ("Youth and Age") an explicit recognition of this term's convertibility: "Dew-drops are the gems of morning,/But the tears of mournful eve." In a juvenile poem, there is a related expression, "inebriate with dew." And I should never feel wholly content until I could also fit in one of the jottings from *Anima Poetae* that widens the circle of associations by reference to "a voice that suits a dream, a voice in a dream, a voice soundless and yet for the *ear* and not for the *eye* of the soul" (for often eye and ear can represent quite different orders of motivation).

In brief, the student of any one poet's nomenclature has more to learn from a concordance of his work (a purely *internal* inspection of a term's "sources" in its own range of contexts) than from an inspection of possible borrowings (except in the broadest sense, as when a scholar cites usages by an older writer's contemporaries to help establish the likelihood that a given term was being used in a sense local to that period but now obsolete).

In fact, the many interesting documents which Lowes assembles as inductive proof of expressions which Coleridge derived or adapted from his reading, might with much justice be interpreted quite differently, as indication that Coleridge was but responding "naturally" to the implications of such imagery. For instance, one might conceivably not require a prior text to help him discover that the image of a maze can adequately stand for a certain kind of emotional entanglement or "amazement," and that the greenery of an oasis in a desert provides an adequate image for an idea of refuge. And presumably travel books select such things to talk about for the very reason that their sheer "factuality" follows along the grooves of man's spontaneous imagination. Be that as it may, Lowes's study of possible derivation with regard to possible private literary sources contains much material that can be applied to the study of "associations" in two senses that Lowes was not concerned with: (1) their relation to "mythic" or "archetypal" forms of thought that do not rely on historical sources for their derivation; and (2) their relation to a nomenclature that, at notable points, may be uniquely Coleridgean (in that they possess personal connotations not to be found in any dictionary, and not precisely appreciated by us who read them, as it were, without quite the proper accent).

In any case, for the most part, we shall interpret the poem by looking for what now would often be called "archetypal" sources rather than for Lowes's possible derivations from other sources (while occasionally considering the areas at which the two kinds of inquiry seem to overlap).

Even if, as regards its actual origin, we choose to accept without question Coleridge's statement that the poem is the spontaneous product of a dream (and thus arose without artistic purpose), when viewing it as a work of art we must ask what kind of effect it "aims" to produce. I'd propose to answer that question roundabout, thus:

In the *Poetics*, among the resources that Aristotle says contribute to the effectiveness of tragedy as a literary species he lists a sense of the "marvelous" (*to thaumaston*). The overall purpose involved in tragedy is "catharsis," while various other resources serve in one way or another to make the sense of purgation most effective. The Cornelian "theater of admiration" played down the principle of catharsis as exemplified in the Attic plays. And it so altered the proportions of the tragic ingredients that one particular kind of the "marvelous" (the cortège-like neoclassic pomp of such plays' courtly style) rose in the scale from a means to an end. The appeal to our sense of the marvelous takes many other forms, and among the variations I would include Coleridge's great "Mystery" poems (or poems of "Fascination"): "Kubla Khan," "The Ancient

Mariner," and "Christabel." Indeed, they come closer to a sense of the marvelous that Aristotle had in mind, since he was discussing ways whereby the playwright might endow a plot with the aura of supernatural fatality; and in his *Biographia Literaria* Coleridge says of his part in the volume of "Lyrical Ballads" containing work by him and Wordsworth:

> it was agreed, that my endeavours should be directed to persons and characters supernatural, or at least romantic; yet so as to transfer from our inward nature a human interest and a semblance of truth sufficient to procure for these shadows of imagination that willing suspension of disbelief for the moment, which constitutes poetic faith.

And previously in the same text:

> the incidents and agents were to be, in part at least, supernatural; and the excellence aimed at was to consist in the interesting of the affections by the dramatic truth of such emotions, as would naturally accompany such situations, supposing them real. And real in *this* sense they have been to every human being who, from whatever source of delusion, has at any time believed himself under supernatural agency.

Though Coleridge does not mention "Kubla Khan" in this connection (it was not published at that time), when judged as a poem it obviously appeals by producing much the same kind of effect. That is, its *mystery* endows it with a feeling of *fatality*. Presumably "The Ancient Mariner" also had its "archetypal" origins in a dream, told to Coleridge by a friend of his, though greatly modified, as Wordsworth testifies, by Coleridge's own additions. And few works have a more strangely dreamlike quality than "Christabel." The sinister element that lies about the edges of these poems attains its blunt documentary completion in the nightmares of guilt, remorse, or woe he describes in "The Pains of Sleep," with such clinical testimony as the lines:

> The third night, when my own loud scream
> Had waked me from the fiendish dream,
> O'ercome with sufferings strange and wild,
> I wept as I had been a child;
> And having thus by tears subdued
> My anguish to a milder mood,
> My punishments, I said, were due
> To natures deepliest stained with sin,—

For aye entempesting anew
The unfathomable hell within,
The horror of their deeds to view,
To know and loathe, yet wish and do!
Such griefs with such men well agree,
But wherefore, wherefore fall on me?

Before considering "Kubla Khan" in detail, I cite this piece (which Coleridge himself specifically mentions as a "contrast") because of my conviction that it brings out the full implication of the sinister potentialities one finds faint traces of in the predominantly euphoric state symbolized by pleasure dome, Edenic garden, and "a damsel with a dulcimer" (surely one of the most euphonious lines in the language). And now, to the poem in detail:

The first stanza, obviously, is the beatific vision of an Edenic garden, enclosed ("girdled round") in a circle of protection. In the third stanza the idea of encirclement will take on quite different connotations ("Weave a circle round him thrice"). To the generally recognized connotations of "Alph" as both "Alpheus" and "Alpha," I would offer but one addition; yet I submit that it is essential to an understanding of many notable details in the poem. As I have tried to show in my *Grammar of Motives* on "the temporizing of essence") and in my *Rhetoric of Religion* (particularly the section on "The First Three Chapters of *Genesis*"), the proper narrative, poetic, or "mythic" way to deal with fundamental motives is in terms of *temporal* priority. In this mode of expression, things deemed most basic are said to be *first in time*. So a river whose name suggests the first letter of the alphabet in an ancient language (one can as well hear the Hebrew form, "Aleph") is indeed well named. And fittingly, therefore, the forests are called "ancient as the hills." For this stanza is designed to convey in narrative, or "mythic" (or "archetypal") terms the very *essence* of felicity (the creative "joy" that, in his poignant ode "Dejection," written about two years later, Coleridge will bemoan the permanent loss of, since his "genial spirits fail," and he "may not hope from outward forms to win/The passion and the life, whose fountains are within").

True, in the first stanza, there is no specific reference to a fountain. But when we recall the passage already quoted from a letter to his brother (concerning a "divine repose" that is like "a spot of enchantment, a green spot of fountain and flowers and trees in the very heart of a waste of sands"), we can see how, so far as the associations within Coleridge's private nomenclature were concerned, the reference to "sunny spots of greenery" (plus the connotations of Alph) had already set the terministic conditions for the explicit emergence of a fountain. And the thought might also induce us to ask whether, beyond such a "spot of enchantment" there might also be lurking some equivalent to the "waste of sands" for which it is medicinal.

In any case, given what we now know about the imagery of man's ideal beginnings, would we not take it for granted that the "caverns" traversed by the river are leading us "back" to such a "sunless sea" as the womb-heaven of the amniotic fluid by which the fetus was once "girdled round" in Edenic comfort? (In one of his fragments, Coleridge characteristically depicts a "sot" luxuriating on a couch and exclaiming: "Would that this were work—*utinam hoc esset laborare!*") In Lowes you can find literary "sources" for the fact that the caverns are "measureless." It is also a fact that they *should* be measureless for the simple reason that they connote an ideal time wholly alien to the knowledge of numbers. On the other hand, the garden spot is measured ("twice five miles") since such finiteness helps suggest connotations of protective enclosure, as with the medieval ideal of the *hortus conclusus* which Leo Spitzer has discussed in his monograph on "Milieu and Ambiance."

How far should we carry such speculations? We need not insist on it, but inasmuch as forests are of *wood* (thereby bringing us into the fate-laden Greek-Roman line of thought that commingles ideas of wood, matter, and mother: *hyle, dynamis, mater, materia, potentia*) the reference to them reinforces the feminine connotations of such a guarded and guardian garden.

So far as Coleridgean terminology in general is concerned, we might also note that green is not an unambiguous color. Christabel is to Geraldine as a dove is to a green snake coiled about her ("Swelling its neck as she swelled hers"). And when reading that Alph is a "sacred river," we might bear in mind the well-known but sometimes neglected etymological fact that in Latin usage either a priest or a criminal was *sacer*, as with the fluctuancies between French *sacre* and *sacré* (the same ambiguities applying to Greek *hagios* and to the Hebrew concept of the "set apart," *qodesh, qadesh*).

As for "stately": We might recall that Geraldine's bare neck was "stately." And cutting in from another angle, I might cite a prose passage that I consider so basic to Coleridge's thinking, I keep finding all sorts of uses for it. It is from *The Friend*, where the exposition is divided into what he calls "landing-places." He is here discussing the sheer *form* of his presentation (the emphasis is mine):

> Among my *earliest* impressions I still distinctly remember that of my *first* entrance into the *mansion* of a neighboring baronet, *awfully* known to me by the name of the great house, its exterior having been long *connected in my childish imagination* with the *feelings and fancies* stirred up in me by the perusal of the Arabian Nights'

> Entertainments. Beyond all other objects, I was most struck with the magnificent staircase, relieved at well-proportioned intervals by spacious landing-places, this adorned with grand or showy plants, the next looking out on an extensive prospect through the *stately* window. . . while from the last and highest the eye commanded the *whole spiral ascent* with the marble pavement of the great hall; from which it seemed to spring up as if it merely used the ground on which it rested. My readers will find no difficulty in *translating these forms of the outward senses into their intellectual analogies*.

In sum, I'd say that references to the "decreeing" of this "stately pleasure-dome" combine connotations of infantile ("first" or "essential") felicity with concepts of hierarchal wonder. Though on its face the term fits well with the euphoria that so strikingly pervades the whole first stanza, and we shall later see the term applied to a hero, there is also the fact, as regards Coleridge's nomenclature in general, that it also applies to the sinister serpent-woman, Geraldine. Viewed in this light, it might be said to possess latent possibilities of trouble, an ambiguous announcement of a "problematical" theme that would become explicit later.

Similarly, despite my interpretation of "sunless" as uterine, I must concede its deathy connotations, particulary in view of the fact that the "sunless sea" will later be redefined as the "lifeless ocean." At best, we are on the edges of that midway, Life-in-Death stage which played so important a part in the sufferings of the Ancient Mariner. Or, otherwise put, any connotations of *rebirth* also imply connotations of *dying*.

In any case, the overall benignant tenor of the first stanza is so pronounced, the poetic conditions are set for a contrast, if the imaginative logic of the poem makes such a turn desirable. Thus, the second stanza is an amplification of the sinister meanings subsumed in the opening outcry: "But oh! that deep romantic chasm which slanted/Down the green hill athwart a cedarn cover!" On their face, chasms are cataclysmic, ghastly, and chaotic. "Athwart" on its face is troublous, to the extent that it has "thwart" in it. And as regards Coleridge's particular nomenclature, we might well adduce as evidence, from "Fears in Solitude," the lines, "the owlet Atheism,/Sailing on obscene wings athwart the noon," though part of the damage here may be associated also with the time of day, since it was "The bloody Sun, at noon" that visited such torture on the Ancient Mariner. (More on these lines later.)

Though you may have felt that I was straining things as regards the ambiguities of "sacred" in the first stanza, surely you will grant that in this middle stanza such disturbances come to the fore, as regards the synonym "holy" with reference to "A savage place! . . . enchanted" (recall the "spot of enchantment") and "haunted/By woman wailing for her demon-lover!" I take it that the theme of the demon lover will return in a slightly transformed state near the end of the poem. As for the phase of the moon, Lowes notes: It was under the aegis of the "waning moon" that the Mariner's cure began. (It would be more accurate to say his *partial* cure; for we should always remember that that "grey-beard loon" was subject to periodic *relapses*, and then his anguish again drove him to confess his sense of guilt.)

Coleridge has so beautifully interwoven description of *natural motions* with words for *human actions*, one is hardly aware of the shifts between the two kinds of verbs (beginning as early as the pleasure dome, which is described as being *decreed*). Thus one hardly notes the "as if" in his reference to the "fast quick pants" with which the fountain is "breathing." All the descriptions are so saturated with *narrative*, one inevitably senses in them a principle of *personality*. (Ruskin's "pathetic fallacy" is carried to the point where everything is as active as in a picture by Breughel.) Though the observation applies to the poem throughout, we might illustrate the point by listing only the more obvious instances in the middle stanza: slanted, athwart, enchanted, waning, haunted, wailing, seething, breathing, forced, half-intermitted, vaulted, rebounding, flung up, meandering, ran, sank, heard, prophesying.

I would view this general hubbub as something more than a way of making descriptions vivid (though it certainly is at least that). I would take it also to indicate that this indeterminate mixture of motion and action is in effect a poetized *psychology*, detailing not what the reader is to *see* but what *mental states* he is thus empathically and sympathetically *imitating* as he reads.

I stress the notion because of my belief that it provides the answer to the problem of the "sunless sea" synonymized in the second stanza as a "lifeless ocean." Though the reciprocal relation between the destination of the river and the emergence of the fountain justifies one in looking upon them as standing for aspects of a life force that bursts into creativity and sinks into death, I would contend that the central significance of this stream is somewhat more specific. The poem is figuring stages in a *psychology*—and in this sense the river is, first of all, the "stream of consciousness" (which is in turn inextricably interwoven with the river of *time*). That is, the design is not just depicting in general the course of *life and death*, plus connotations of rebirth. Rather, the poem is tracing in terms of imagery the very *form* of thinking (which is necessarily integral with a time process, inasmuch as the form of thinking must unfold through time.) It is as though, like Kantian transcendentalism, Coleridge were speculating epistemologically on the nature of consciousness, *except* that he is in effect talking of intuition in terms that are themselves the embodiment of what he is talking *about*. That's why Coleridge could say in his introduction to the poem:

> The Author. . .could not have composed less than from two to three hundred lines; if that indeed can be called composition in which all the images rose up before him as *things*.

In this respect, I repeat, the poem could be viewed as a highly personal, *poetic* analogue of Kantian transcendentalism, which sought *conceptually* to think about itself until it ended in a schematization of the forms necessarily implicit in its very act of thinking.

I have several reasons for wanting to insist that the image of the sacred river, in its journey to and from an ultimate reservoir of the "sunless" or "lifeless" is to be viewed thus, as more specifically tied to the *psychology of idealism* than just a figuring of life and death in general. For one thing (as per my paper, "Thanatopsis for Critics: a Brief Thesaurus of Deaths and Dyings," *Essays in Criticism*, October 1952) since poets at their best write only what they profoundly know (and beyond all doubt, "Kubla Khan" is one kind of poetry at its best) and inasmuch as no living poet has experienced death, I take it for granted that, when a poet speaks of death, he is necessarily talking about something else, something witnessed *from without*, like a funeral, whereas this poem is wholly *from within*. Similarly, as regards fictions about the "supernatural," we need but consider the conduct of the "dead" sailors in "The Ancient Mariner" to realize that in the realm of the "supernatural" there *is* no death. Even in the "double death" of the orthodox Christian's Hell, the miserable wretches somehow carry on eternally. Or Whitman's paeans to Death indicate how Death becomes rather like the ultimate, maternal repository from which the forms of conscious life emerge (a pattern that also infuses thoughts on the ultimate end and source of things, in the second part of Goethe's *Faust*). Or think of the similar return to the "buttonmoulder," in *Peer Gynt*. And to cap things, recall Coleridge's "Epitaph," asking the reader to pray "That he who many a year with toil of breath/Found death in life, may here find life in death!"

Further, the realm of "essence" can never "die." For instance, what destruction of all existing life in the universe could alter the essential "fact" that, if *a* is greater than *b* and *b* is greater than *c*, then *a* is greater than *c*? And what obliteration can be so total as to alter the fact that Napoleon's character, or "essence," must go on having been exactly what it was?

If, on the other hand, we think of the river as more specifically interweaving the stream of time and the stream of consciousness (what Coleridge called the "streamy nature of association"), all comes clear. For there *is* a sense in which both time and thought continually hurry to their "death," yet are continually "reborn," since the death of one moment is incorporated in the moment that arises out of it, and the early stages of a thought process are embedded in its fulfillment. Nor should we forget Coleridge's original declared intention with regard to the "supernatural, or at least romantic" as a device to transfer from our "inward nature" various "shadows of imagination."

For these reasons, if you choose to see the river and the fountain as figuring ultimately the course of life and death, I'd ask you at least to think of these more specific "transcendental" qualifications as relevant adjectives to your nouns. And certainly a note like this, in the Gutch Memorandum Notebook, is on our side: "There is not a new or strange opinion—Truth returns from banishment—a river run underground—fire beneath embers—." Also, in his Notebooks, when saying that in the best part of one's nature man must be solitary, he adds: "Man exists herein to himself & to God alone—Yea, in how much only to God—how much lies *below* his own Consciousness."

In any case, there is no questioning the fact that the Coleridgean nomenclature elsewhere does clearly give us personal (moral, psychological) equivalents for fountains and streams with mazy motion. The most relevant for our purposes is in "Dejection," a poem specifically concerned with the loss of such impulsive poetic ability as distinguishes "Kubla Khan":

> My genial spirits fail;
> And what can these avail
> To lift the smothering weight from off my breast?
> It were a vain endeavour,
> Though I should gaze for ever
> On that green light that lingers in the west:
> I may not hope from outward forms to win
> The passion and the life, whose fountains are within.

In an expression some years later, he gives the word a decidedly moral twist, in referring to "my conscience, the sole fountain of certainty." In one letter, he refers to "the pure fountain of all my moral religious feelings and comforts,—I mean the absolute Impersonality of the Deity." And in a formal letter of condolence, written before the production of "Kubla Khan," he had given us a related moral significance for "chaff": "The pestilence of our lusts must be scattered, the strong-layed Foundations of our Pride blown up, and the stubble and chaff of our Vanities burnt, ere we can give ear to the inspeaking Voice of Mercy, 'Why *will* ye die?'" True, Lowes finds references to fountains that hurled forth various kinds of fragments, but he also cites a reference to an "inchanting and amazing chrystal fountain"; hence so far as "sources" in his sense are concerned, Coleridge could just as well have given us a fountain *without* "chaff." Thus, from the standpoint of "mythic" or "archetypal" sources, I'd say that Coleridge's creative fountain was a bit "problematical," as with the countertheme of this stanza generally; in effect this spirited (or breathy) upheaval had not yet separated the wheat from the tares, though it was intensely involved in the process of doing so.

"Mazy" is a word that turns up often in Coleridge. It's as characteristically his as "dim." (Though there is no "dim" in the poem itself, the introduction quotes lines that refer to "the fragments dim of lovely forms.") And if you want the range of troublous moral connotations that are packed into that word "mazy," consult a passage in "Religious Musings" (an earlier, somewhat bombastic poem that Charles Lamb greatly admired). Here Enmity, Mistrust, "listening Treachery" and War are said to falsely defend the "Lamb of God" and "Prince of Peace," whom

> (in their songs
> So bards of elder times had haply feigned)
> Some Fury fondled in her hate of man,
> Bidding her serpent hair in mazy surge
> Lick his young face, and at his mouth imbreathe
> Horrible sympathy!

"Religious Musings" is quite a storehouse for expressions that reveal the moral implications in many of the most characteristic images found in the Mystery, or "Fascination," Poems.

Though Lowes cites a text that refers to the prophecy of war (and in connection with *Abyssinia* even, an associate preparation, if you will, of the corresponding adjective in the final stanza), I'd view the line, "Ancestral voices prophesying war," as a narrative way of saying in effect: "This tumultuous scene is *essentially* interwoven with such motives as we connote by the term "war." Or, otherwise put: The war that is to break out *subsequently* is *already implicit* in the nature of things *now*. That is, I would interpret it as a typical stylistic device for the "temporizing of essence." Such is always the significance of "portents," that detect the *presence* of the future.

The stanza does not conclude by a simple return to the pleasure dome of the opening; for three notable details are added: We now learn of the dome's "shadow"; it is said to have "floated midway" on the waves; and the caves are said to be "of ice." Let us consider these additions.

In "The Ancient Mariner" we read that "where the ship's huge shadow lay,/The charmèd water burnt alway/A still and awful red." In a letter to

Southey, written about three years after the probable production of "Kubla Khan," Coleridge says regarding troubles with his wife that his sleep "became the valley of the shadows of Death." (The same letter refers to "her inveterate habits of puny thwarting," a phrase which please bear in mind for later reference, "and unintermitting dyspathy," where the reader must decide for himself whether the participle throws connotative light upon the poem's reference to the fountain's "half-intermitted burst.") In the explicitly moralistic use of imagery in "Religious Musings," we are told that "Life is a vision shadowy of Truth;/And vice, and anguish, and the wormy grave,/Shapes of a dream!"

At this point it's almost imperative that we introduce an aside. For the pejorative reference to "shapes" all but *demands* our attention. "Shape" is characteristically a troublous word in Coleridgese. Thus, in "Religious Musings," see "pale Fear/Haunted by ghastlier shapings than surround/Moon-blasted Madness when he yells at midnight." Likewise, the ominous supernatural specter-bark of "The Ancient Mariner" was "A speck, a mist, a shape." In "The Pains of Sleep" he refers to "the fiendish crowd/Of shapes and thoughts" that "tortured" him. Many other usages could be adduced here. And though, in "Dejection," Coleridge explicitly regrets that he has lost his "shaping Spirit of Imagination," in one of his letters written during the same *annus mirabilis* when the first version of "The Ancient Mariner" and the first part of "Christabel" came into being, he speaks of his body as "diseased and fevered" by his imagination. Nor should we forget the essentially ironic situation underlying "The Eolian Harp," a poem that begins as an address to his wife, but develops into a vision of beatific universal oneness; whereupon he forgets all about his "pensive Sara," until he sees her "mild reproof"—and four lines after the appearance of his characteristic word "dim," he apologizes for "These shapings of the unregenerate mind."

So much for "shadow," and its membership in a cluster of terms that include pejorative or problematical connotations of "shape." "Float" is much less strongly weighted on the "bad" side than "shadow" and "shape." Things can float either malignly or benignly, as with the Mariner's boat at different stages in its journey. In Coleridge's play *Remorse* there is a passage that suggests Shelley's typical kind of idealistically easygoing boat:

> It were a lot divine in some small skiff
> Along some ocean's boundless solitude
> To float forever with a careless course
> And think myself the only being alive!

Thus in "Religious Musings," we read of Edenic delights that "float to earth." But in the same text there are "floating mists of dark idolatry" that "Broke and misshaped the omnipresent Sire." The poem itself has an interesting ambiguous usage, where talk of "Moulding Confusion" with "plastic might" (the Greek derivative "plastic" being his consistently "good" word for "shaping") leads into talk of "bright visions" that "float." And somewhere in between, there is a letter: "My thoughts are floating about in an almost chaotic state." So, when in the next stanza you come to the "floating hair," you are presumably on a ridge that slopes both ways. And the only fairly sure grounds for deciding which way it slopes is given to us on the surface: the accompanying cry, "Beware! Beware!"

We shall consider later the strategic term "midway." But before leaving it for the present, I'd like to suggest that, as regards Coleridge's poem "Love" (which transforms his troubled courtship of Sara Hutchinson into an allegory of knighthood), I doubt whether, under the modern dispensation, he'd have included the line, "When midway on the mount I lay."

We now have only the ice to deal with, and we shall have finished our consideration of the ways in which the closing lines of Stanza Two are not just a return to the theme of Stanza One, but a return *with a difference*. And that difference resides *precisely* in the addition of details more in keeping with the countertheme, though ambiguously so (yet not quite so ambiguously, if we read the poem not just as English but as one particular poetic dialect of English, one vatic nomenclature subtly or implicitly different from all others).

Lowes (as might be expected!) turns up some caverns of ice in another text that Coleridge presumably read (even a quite rare kind of ice that waxes and wanes with the phases of the moon). But we still contend that a "source" in that sense is not relevant to our present problem. For we need but assume that the source chose to talk about ice for the same reason that Coleridge incorporated what had been said in the source; namely: because "ice" has a set of "mythic" or "archetypal" connotations which recommend it to a poet's attention. And we are concerned with "derivation" in that "nonhistoric" but poetically "principled" sense.

It is obvious enough what kind of attitude is linked with the iciness of ice in "The Ancient Mariner." There, ice is purely and simply a horror. And ice is unambiguously unpleasant, insofar as it stands for coldness in the sense that Coleridge had in mind when, in the letter to Southey about his wife's "puny thwarting," he characterized her as "cold in sympathy." And we are still to discuss Coleridge's play, *Remorse*, where "fingers of ice" are located in a "chasm" within a "cavern." (Here the sound of water dropping in the darkness is likened to "puny thwartings.") But regardless of what ominous implications may lurk in the ice, on its face the reference is euphoric.

We are now ready for the windup. In terms of the Hegelian pattern, we should expect the final stanza (a kind of poem-within-a-poem) to "synthesize" the two movements that have gone before. It does so. For the vision of the "Abyssinian maid" is clearly *beatific*, yet the beholder of the vision (as presented in terms of the poem) is also to be identified with *sinister* connotations (as with those that explicity emerge just after a recurrent reference to the "caves of ice"). I refer to the cry, "Beware! Beware!"—and to the development that transforms malignly the principle of encirclement (introduced benignly in Stanza One).

As for the fact that the maid in the vision is said to be "Abyssinian": Derive her as you will along the lines of sources in other books, there's still a tonal likelihood that the lady is "Abyssinian" because, among other things, as so designated she contains within this name for her essence the syllables that spell "abyss." And there, roundabout, would be the "chasm," euphorically transmuted for the last phase.

As for "Mount Abora": Regardless of its possible derivation from other texts (as Lowes suggests), in accordance with theories of "musicality in verse" that I have discussed elsewhere (in connection with Coleridge, an essay reprinted in my book, *The Philosophy of Literary Form*), I would lay great stress upon the fact that *m* and *b* are close tonal cognates, hence these vocables come very close to "Singing of Mount Amora," which is understandable enough.

As for the lines, "Could I revive within me/Her symphony and song": I see in them the euphorically tinged adumbration of the outcry that was to turn up, in "Dejection," only a few years later.

For some reason that it's hard to be clear about, though in a letter Coleridge admonished his son Hartley "not to speak so loud," again and again he applies this epithet to music (even to the bassoon, in "The Ancient Mariner," though that instrument cannot be loud, so far as sheer decibels go). All I can offer, along these lines, is the possibility of a submerged pun, as indicated by an early poem in which Coleridge speaks of "loud, lewd Mirth." Might "loud" *deflectively* connote "lewd," in the depths of the Coleridgean nomenclature? I won't assert so, but there does seem to be the possibility (though it would be a tough one to prove, even if it were absolutely true). In the meantime, we must simply await further advices.

The cavern scenes in Act IV of *Remorse* might well be mentioned in greater detail, since they help so greatly to reveal the sinister possibilities lurking beneath the surface of the terms in "Kubla Khan." Seen in a dream, the cave is "haunted," the villain appearing to his victim in "a thousand fearful shapes." There is a morbid dalliance with "shadows." The threat implicit in the very idea of a chasm is brought out explicitly by the nature of the plot, as the villain hurls his victim "down the chasm." (Chasms, that is, are implicitly a kind of gerundive, a to-be-bewared-of, a to-be-hurled-into). And whereas we are told that the "romantic chasm" of the euphoric poem "slanted/ Down," these apparently innocuous words are seen to have contained, about their edges, malign connotations; for in the victim's premonitory dream of his destruction in *Remorse*, we learn that his foot hung "aslant adown" the edge. At the end of the act, the woman who is to be the *avenger* announces, "The moon hath moved in Heaven, and I am here," (a remarkable transformation of the prime motivating line in "The Ancient Mariner": "The moving Moon went up the sky"). At the start of the last act, the circle appears at its worst: "Circled with evil." (A previous reference to a threatening circle of people surrounding the villain had appeared in the stage directions.) A reference to the "fascination" in the eye of the hero (whom the loving heroine calls "stately") marks the spot from which I would derive the term, "Fascination Poems" as an alternative to "Mystery Poems."

In the light of our analysis, it should be easy to understand why, in the closing poem-within-a-poem, the references to the poet (who is ambiguously one with both the dream and the dreamer) should be so surrounded with connotations of admonition. Yet the poem is essentially euphoric. Hence, even though we are told to *beware*, and to view with *holy dread* (or rather, to deflect-our-eyes-from) the poet who both is this marvel and has conceived it, we end on *Paradise*.

Returning now to a point we postponed when considering "midway on the waves," should we not take into consideration the fact that in the *middle stanza* the notion appears not once but four times: The other explicit places are: "Amid whose swift half-intermitted burst"; "And 'mid these dancing rocks"; "And 'mid this tumult"—while a strong trace of the pattern is also observable in "half-intermitted" and "the mingled measure/From the fountain and the caves." (I take it that "measure," in contrast with "measureless," includes connotations of poetic measure.)

At the risk of being charged with oversubtlety, I'd propose to view that design (a kind of *spatial fixity* in these many motions and actions and action-like motion) as a matter of basic significance. As regards the underlying principle of the poem (its essence or character as a *unity*) these conflicting elements (the beatific and the sinister) are but what we might Spinozistically call two attributes of a common substance. Thus, in the last analysis, the stages of its unfolding melt into a simultaneity, a nodus of motivation that stands "midway" between the extremes. (A stanza of "Religious Musings" where Saints "sweep athwart" the poet's "gaze," develops into agitation thus: "For who of woman born may paint the hour,/When seized in his mid course, the Sun shall wane/Making noon ghastly!" I'd hardly dare press the point; but we might at least recall that the midday sun transfixed the Mariner's boat, and Christabel's troubles took place at midnight. And anyone who is concerned with the strange magic of reversal, as in formulas like "Ave Eva," might also pause to note however uneasily that, quite as Cummings in "God" saw "dog spelled backwards," so "mid" is but a chiastic form of Coleridge's ubiquitous "dim.")

However, even if there is a sense in which the generating principle represented by this poem's action is itself as much an unmoved mover as Aristotle's God (with even an analogue of "negative theology" in "sunless," "lifeless," "measureless," and "ceaseless"), there is also the fact that, as "broken down" into a quasi-temporal sequence, the translation of this essential unity into a series of successive revelations (or tiny "apocalypses") can *begin* with a reference to an Edenic garden, and *end* on the word "Paradise." In this sense, despite the intrinsic immobility of the poem's organizing principle (a "midway" situation that found more explicit dissociative expression in "The Ancient Mariner," both in the figure of the motionless boat, and in the specter, "The Night-mare Life-in-Death"); despite the fact that while the narrative relation between rising fountain and sinking river goes on "turning," the *principle* behind the unfolding is "forever still"; despite these ups and downs en route, the poem as a whole can be called "euphoric."

We are now ready to take up the problem that arises from our insistence upon calling the poem *finished* whereas the author himself called it a "fragment." Here I can best make my point by quoting a passage from my *Philosophy of Literary Form*:

> Imagine an author who had laid out a five-act drama of the rational, intricate, intrigue sort—a situation that was wound up at the start, and was to be unwound, step by step, though the five successive acts. Imagine that this plot was scheduled, in Act V, to culminate in a scene of battle. Dramatic consistency would require the playwright to "foreshadow" this battle. Hence, in Act III, he might give us the battle incipiently, or implicitly, in a vigorous battle of words between the antagonists. But since there was much business still to be transacted, in unwinding the plot to its conclusion he would treat Act III as a mere foreshadowing of Act V, and would proceed with his composition until the promises emergent in Act III had been fulfilled in Act V.
>
> On the other hand, imagine a "lyric" plot that had reduced the intrigue business to a minimum. When the poet had completed Act III, his job would be ended, and despite his intention to write a work in five acts, he might very well feel a loss of inclination to continue into Acts IV and V. For the act of foreshadowing, in

> Act III, would already *implicitly contain* the culmination of the promises. The battle of words would itself by the *symbolic equivalent* of the mortal combat scheduled for Act V. Hence, it would *serve as surrogate* for the *quality* with which he had intended to end Act V, whereat the poet would have no good reason to continue further. He would "lose interest"—and precisely because the quality of Act V had been "telescoped" into the quality of Act III that foreshadowed it (and in foreshadowing it, was of the same substance or essence). Act III would be a kind of ejaculation too soon, with the purpose of the composition forthwith dwindling.

Does not this possibility solve our problem? I believe that, in principle at least, Coleridge actually did dream all those lines, and transcribed them somewhat as an amanuensis might have done. For nearly every writer has jotted down a few bits that he woke up with, and there's no reason why someone couldn't wake up with more. And Mozart apparently could conceive of a work all finished before he wrote it down, so that in effect the act of composition was but the translating of a timeless unity (like a painting or piece of sculpture) into a temporal progression (quite as the observer "reads histories" into a static form when he lets his eye wander from place to place across it, thereby "improvising" developments within its parts). And even a long and complex structure which one works out painfully step by step may involve but the progressive "discovery" of implications already present in the "germ" that set him off in the first place. Why had it even struck him as worth working on, if it had not been for him like a knotted bundle of possibilities which he would untie one by one, as the loosening of each knot set the conditions for the loosening of the next (like a psychoanalyst's patient discovering by free association things that he somehow already knew but didn't know he knew)?

But "Kubla Khan" was the kind of poem that Coleridge's own aesthetic theories were not abreast of. His very attempts to distinguish between "Imagination" and "Fancy" at the expense of the latter serve to indicate my point. "Fancy" wouldn't come into its own until the time of Rimbaud, when it would take on dimensions that Coleridge never explicitly attributed to it. For his concept of Fancy got mixed up with purely mechanical doctrines of associationism which he strongly rejected (a kind of resistance that was probably also tied up with his moralistic attempts to resist the compulsive aspects of his addiction to opium, when it became integrated with the fountain of his creativity). In any case, at the very start of his collaboration with Wordsworth in plans for the *Lyrical Ballads*, the kind of job he set himself really involved an ideal of "Fancy" (but not in the partly pejorative sense that the term took on, in the dialectic of his *Biographia Literaria*). And as an integral aspect of such possibilities there would be the kind of imagistic short-circuiting to which I have referred in my quotation from *Philosophy of Literary Form*.

Thus, when one contemporary critic finds that the expression, "ancestral voices prophesying war" is "too pointless," since "no further use is made of it," the objection would be like contending that, in Eliot's "Gerontion," a line such as "By Hakagawa, bowing among the Titians" is "pointless" because we learn nothing more about Hakagawa. On the contrary, as I have tried to show, the line does to perfection exactly what it is there for, as a narrative way of stating a motivational essence. Yvor Winters' label, "Reference to a non-existent plot," to characterize such usages as Eliot's, helps us see that Coleridge's poem was already moving towards a later elliptical manner, at a time when Southey could have turned "Kubla Khan" into a work as long as *The Ring and the Book*. In this sense, the poem was a "fragment." But it is complete insofar as no further movements are needed (or even possible, without the poem's becoming something else, as when one dream fades into another). The most one can imagine is the addition of a few details that amplify what is already sufficiently there.

All told, the more closely we study the poem in the light of Coleridge's particular nomenclature, the more fully we realize how many of the terms have sinister connotations, as regards their notable use in other contexts. Imagery lends itself well to such shiftiness, and readily transcends the law of excluded middle. In fact, such susceptibility doubtless accounts for much of its appeal, since it can so spontaneously bridge the gulfs of dispute, and can simultaneously confess and be reticent. In line with contemporary interests, one might note that Coleridge explicitly equates the image of the fountain with the principle of what would not be called "creativity." On this point, in addition to references already cited, we might recall in his preface to "Christabel," his objections to "a set of critics . . . who have no notion that there are such things as fountains in the world, small as well as great." At another place he distinguishes between "Springs" and "tanks" ("two Kinds of Heads in the world of literature"). Elsewhere, when on the subject of "knowing" and "being," he sums up by thoughts on "the common fountain-head of both, the mysterious source whose being is knowledge, whose knowledge is being—the adorable I AM IN THAT I AM." In *Anima Poetae* he writes: "Nota bene to make a detailed comparison, in the manner of Jeremy Taylor, between the searching for the first cause of a thing and the seeking the fountains of the Nile—so many streams, each with its particular fountains—and, at last, it all comes to a name." Another note beautifully illustrates how the image takes on other connotations of delight: "Some wilderness-plot—green & fountainous & unviolated by Man." But "creativity" also has its *risks*. And whether or not you would agree that the "problematic" element was heightened in Coleridge's case by the interweaving of the Mystery Poems with the early stages of opium addiction, it still remains a fact that in "Kubla Khan" as enacted in detail, the principle of inspiration is simultaneously welcomed and feared (a secular attitude properly analogous to the theologians' doubts whether a vision of the divine is truly from God or from the Devil in disguise).

OWEN BARFIELD

Ideas, Method, Laws

At one point in Coleridge's remarkable Address to the Royal Society of Literature on the *Prometheus of Aeschylus*, from which we quoted at the con clusion of the preceding chapter, he sums up his interpretation of the myth as follows: "the groundwork of the Aeschylean *mythus* is laid in the definition of idea and law, as correlatives that mutually interpret each the other." This principle is one that is nearly central to Coleridge's cosmology, and an expansion of it may prove the best approach to the meaning of the word *idea*, as he habitually employs it.

It was further observed [elsewhere] that the only plural of reason is ideas of reason. To this it may now be added that *all* ideas are "ideas of reason" in Coleridge's terminology. For the other senses in which the word is most commonly used he himself employs the terms *notion*, *conception* and occasionally *maxim*. It needs also saying that the ideas of reason are not the plural of reason in the ordinary sense, whereby the particular components of a collective noun might be thought of as its plural reference; in the sense, that is, that the plurality of "crowd" is the persons who compose the crowd. An idea is not a component part of reason, because reason, the whole, is present and effective in each idea. Alternatively, we may speak of ideas as "parts" of reason, only if we are prepared to let the term connote *that* relation between a whole and its parts, whereby the particular and the universal are one—*totus in omni parte*. Coleridge himself sometimes uses the term *constituent*.

> as constituents of reason we necessarily contemplate unity and distinctity. Now the latter as the polar opposite to the former

From *What Coleridge Thought.*

> implies plurality: therefore I used the plural, distinctities, and say, that the distinctities considered apart from the unity are the ideas, and reason is the ground and source of ideas.

We need, once again, to be able to distinguish without dividing; and that very ability is itself reason.

It follows that much, if not most, of what has already been said of reason will also apply to the ideas of reason, or any one of them. In neither case is it possible to "account for," or even fruitfully to discuss, the paradox of singular plurality or of identity in difference. It must be accepted because, on examination, we find that it is itself the experiential ground on which all intellectual acceptance and rejection are based. Reason "affirms itself." It is understanding that thinks "of" or "about" things. Reason is the thinking. Itself the creative polarity that engenders many from one, it "comes forth out of the moulds of the understanding" only as the invincible contradiction, the insoluble "problem," of the one and the many.

By the same token the understanding as such can have nothing to say about the relation between reason and the ideas of reason. All it can do is to take note of the fact that to be at once universal and particular is the very nature of the act of thinking, the act of consciousness itself; and this has already been dealt with at some length [elsewhere].

The like consideration applies to the relation between the ideas of reason and the phenomenal world. Seeking an explanation of the "multeity" of nature, we are driven, first, to eliminate our inveterate fancy of a fixed and anterior "outness" of phenomena; secondly, to the discovery that understanding points us back behind itself to reason, to reason as at once the source of living opposites and the lightning flash that arrests them at the entrance to the understanding and reveals them as a stony landscape of logical contradictions bounded by its horizon; thirdly, and consequently, to the presence of reason as the *ground* of the understanding. It would be absurd, or more strictly speaking preposterous, to look "behind" reason for some fancied source, either ("as monkeys put their hands behind a looking-glass") in the phenomenal world, which is itself the product of reason, or in the understanding, of which reason is the ground. A thing cannot be the product of that which it has itself produced; "that the *very* ground, saith Aristotle, is groundless or self-grounded, is an identical proposition."

And so with imagination: having been told that it is characteristic of imagination to apprehend unity in multeity, or the all in each, we can ask why this should be so; and we can be answered: Because that is the nature of reason, and imagination is the mind's approach towards self-knowledge, and thus towards a fuller awareness of the presence of reason within us. But there we must stop. It is meaningless for the understanding to go on and ask: why should, or how can, that be the nature of reason? All the understanding can hope to do is to remove the obstacles which its own confused conceptions have interposed; and that is just the task that Coleridge set himself. When they *are* removed, we may participate in reason; but not by understanding it, only by awakening it within us as we contemplate its effects; or if it is preferred, by meditating it. *Meditation* is a word Coleridge introduced more than once when he was emphasising the "all in each," the universal human nevertheless particularised, which we find in Shakespeare's presentation of his dramatic characters.

It follows then from the nature of reason, and of its relation to the ideas of reason, that nearly everything we can say about an idea is also being said about reason; and vice versa. To ask: how do we apprehend an idea? is to ask: how do we participate in reason? And there is the same difficulty about answering the one question as about answering the other; a difficulty not really met by using carefully chosen words like *participate* (which already transcends the conceptions of the understanding). Nor is it met (though all this may contribute something to the "pointing back") by going farther and attempting to define participation as, let us say, "a felt union with the inner origin of outward forms." Moreover, assuming that it has been apprehended, any attempt to *express* it will involve those "blank misgivings of a creature| Moving about in worlds not realised" of which Wordsworth wrote. It follows in fact from the whole nature of the relation between reason and understanding that "an idea, in the *highest* sense of that word, cannot be conveyed but by a *symbol*"; that is to say, so far as language is concerned, in figurative language.

Here again a modern reader of Coleridge may find that he derives some assistance from the now familiar, though dim, mental image of an unconscious, or subconscious, mind—an image, which itself, of course, flouts the conceptions of the mere understanding, since it amounts to saying "unconscious consciousness." It is significant that Freud, who was avowedly determined to limit himself to a body-bound notion of the unconscious, was nevertheless obliged to rely, via the dream, almost wholly on symbolism. It may also be useful at this point to look at one of Coleridge's own attempts to convey, in figurative language, something of what is involved in the apprehension of an idea. He compares it with the experience of listening to music:

> Music seems to have an *immediate* communion with my Life;. . .
> It converses with the *life* of my mind, as if it were itself the Mind
> of my Life. Yet I sometimes think that a great Composer, a Mozart,
> a Beethoven must have been in a state of Spirit much more akin,

> more analogous to, mine own when I am at once waiting for, watching, and organically constructing and inwardly constructed by, the *Ideas*, the living Truths, that may be re-excited but cannot be expressed by Words, the Transcendents that give the Objectivity to all Objects, the Form to all Images, yet are themselves untranslatable into any Image, unrepresentable by any particular Object, than I can imagine myself to be a Titian or a Sir C. Wren.

To apprehend an idea is to be aware of at once constructing and being constructed by it; it is to be aware, in the same act and moment, of myself and the source of my selfhood; for it is to participate in reason, to become one again with the living opposites that created me and, as growth forces, sustain my own creative being.

It is perhaps, then, by equating reason with "the unconscious," though in a non-Freudian sense, that we can approach most sympathetically Coleridge's numerous references to the "dimness" of ideas, at least on their first appearance in the mind. Clearness is founded on shallowness. It is for the conceptions or notions of the understanding to be clear, and it is when they lack that saving virtue that they become dangerous; for then they filch some of the strength of growth, and of feeling, which belongs by right to ideas, since it is ideas that actually "constitute" our humanity. And that is why deep thinking necessarily entails strong feeling. It will be best to return to this later in the chapter. But we may note here its bearing on the station occupied by imagination between reason and understanding. Whether we think of the mind as in the first place understanding, but ascending towards reason; or of ideas as in the first place "the permanence and self-circling energies of the reason," but descending towards the understanding, we shall not be surprised to find them often enough "in that shadowy half-being, that state of nascent Existence in the Twilight of Imagination, and just on the vestibule of Consciousness . . ." where feeling also has its roots.

In apparent contrast with these references to the dimness of ideas lies the fact that it is precisely on the apprehension of ideas, as distinct from mere conceptions or maxims, that Coleridge bases his important concept of "method." In this volume we are attempting to outline what Coleridge thought, in accordance with a particular selected plan. It would have been possible to choose a different plan altogether and to work outwards, so to speak, from the little group of Essays in the *Friend* in which he himself outlines what he understands by method. Because ideas are the permanence and self-circling energies of reason, they are also in an almost literal sense "the prophetic soul|of the wide world dreaming on things to come" and it is therefore only *their* presence in the mind that can give rise to a knowledge effective for the future as well as analytical of the past; and (which is much the same thing) only that which can produce any radically *new* knowledge. The conceptions of the understanding, "like lights in the stern of a vessel, illumine only the path that has already been past over." Coleridge himself once adduced the literary example of Polonius; but perhaps the best analogy to mere understanding is the idea of the perfect computer. Raise the computer to absolute perfection: reduce the understanding to absolute "mereness": and there need be no significant difference between the two instruments.

Coleridge develops his own idea of method by contrasting it with *classification*—which is arrangement for the convenience of memory or communication. In the sphere of natural science he takes as an outstanding example of classification the system of Linnaeus in botany. After praising the illustrious Swede warmly for his services to the study, he points out that the system amounts nevertheless to "little more than an enormous nomenclature; a huge catalogue, *bien arrangé*, yearly and monthly augmented in various editions, each with its own scheme of technical memory and its own conveniences of reference!" Linnaeus "invented an universal character for the Language of Botany chargeable with no greater imperfections than are to be found in the alphabets of every particular Language"; and alphabetical arrangement is the *terminus ad quem* of nonmethodical (in Coleridge's sense) arrangement. It was in fact as the introduction to an Encyclopedia, the topics in which were to be ordered otherwise than alphabetically, that he evolved his "Treatise on Method."

A *methodical* order must be based, he held, not on notions but on ideas. Above all it requires, in any particular field, the "initiative idea," which Linnaeus lacked. For the plurality of ideas is not a merely numerical one; "there is a gradation of Ideas, as of ranks in a well-ordered State, or of commands in a well-regulated army." And in the case of natural science it is on *this* order that any ultimately fruitful method will need to be based, since this is the actual order of *natura naturans*, and thus the natural order in the mind. Yet the received scientific method—with a few important exceptions—was ignoring it altogether. Coleridge held that the latter was in fact no method at all, but a typically Linnaean, or encyclopedic, classification of disjointed fragments of *natura naturata*. The result was, not the reality of nature, but an arrangement projected upon the phenomena by memory and fancy. Whereas a genuine method must stem from the participating apprehension of related ideas, and thus of that timeless articulation of ultimate reality, out of which *natura naturans* emerges to become ("quenched" now "in the product") the static multeity of *natura naturata*. It is at this stage that method reveals itself as resulting from "the due mean or balance between our passive impressions and the mind's own reaction on the same." And we may think of that mean indifferently as "organisation" in nature or as "imagination" in man.

For there is no getting away from the fact that in Coleridge's system we cannot, in the long view, divide the one from the other, though we can distinguish them sharply enough. Nature is all that is objective, but the relation between mind and nature remains an inseverable polarity. Thus the emergence of ideas from the dimness of instinct, which we have already considered; the fact that the idea then "commences the process of its own transmutation. . . and. . . finishes the process as the understanding"; the fact that "organisation ceasing, mechanism commences"; the fact that "an idea conceived as subsisting in an object becomes a law"—none of these are to be taken as exclusively psychological events or processes.

The most carefully considered formulation of the relations between *idea* and *law* is probably the one that will be found near the beginning of *Church and State*:

> That which, contemplated objectively (that is, as existing externally to the mind), we call a law; the same contemplated subjectively (that is, as existing in a subject or mind), is an idea. Hence Plato often names ideas laws; and Lord Bacon, the British Plato, describes the laws of the material universe as the ideas in nature. *Quod in natura naturata lex, in natura naturante idea dicitur.*

True, there are other ideas besides those that coincide with the laws of nature. In the "Treatise on Method" Coleridge distinguishes Metaphysical Ideas, which "relate to the essence of things as possible," and which "continue always to exist in and for the Mind alone," from Physical Ideas, or "those which we mean to express, when we speak of the *nature* of a thing actually existing and cognizable by our faculties, whether the thing be material or immaterial, bodily or mental." The Essays are closely reasoned and require to be studied at first hand. Here it may suffice to say that, for the relation between ideas and laws, it is physical ideas that are significant. From that point of view metaphysical ideas are mainly of importance because reflection on them—for example on the idea of a perfect circle in geometry—or upon a law of thought, such as the principle of contradiction—may develop our capacity for that "inward beholding" which is our only access to the ideas of reason, whether metaphysical or physical. They can help us to overcome

> the difficulty of combining the notion of an organ of sense, or a new sense, with the notion of the appropriate and peculiar objects

> of that sense . . . the organs of spiritual apprehension having objects consubstantial with Themselves (ὁμοουσία), or being themselves their own objects, that is, self contemplative

and thus to preserve the all-important distinction between a genuine law of nature and a mere hypothesis evolved by fancy for the purpose of saving the appearances.

We may now conveniently complete the quotation from the address on the "Prometheus of Aeschylus," with which this chapter opened:

> the groundwork of the Aeschylean *mythus* is laid in the definition of idea and law, as correlatives that mutually interpret each the other,—an idea, with the adequate power of realizing itself being a law, and a law considered abstractedly from, or in the absence of, the power of manifesting itself in its appropriate product being an idea.

Fortunately however we are not limited to pondering definitions; for in Essays VIII and IX of *The Friend*, Section 2, Coleridge has taken up an expanded these definitions in a careful study of the relation between Plato and Bacon. And these two Essays are important for two more reasons: because they survey the relation between law and idea in the light, as Coleridge observes, of the General History of the Human Mind, and because, in doing so, they solve, or should solve, the difficulty which many have found in perceiving the actual relation—the difference as well as the resemblance—between Plato's doctrine of ideas and Coleridge's.

There is yet a fourth reason why these two Essays should be studied. They suggest that a substantial revision, or at all events readjustment, is called for of the popular image of Bacon's place in the history of science. His view of what constitutes induction is indeed adversely criticised (on the basis, incidentally, of a misunderstanding of which Coleridge makes short work); but he is still, for most, an admired leader of a merciful escape from the leading-strings of Plato, Aristotle and the Middle Ages. To describe him as "the British Plato" is in fact pretty startling in view of his own loudly proclaimed contempt for all three. Coleridge was well aware of this, and the Essays are a carefully documented response to the obvious challenge his judgment invokes. In the first of them (VIII) he briefly reviews the current misunderstanding of what Bacon in fact endeavoured to assert concerning the relation between nature and mind and considers the extent to which Bacon himself was responsible for it, stressing heavily in this regard the latter's brutal rejection of his predecessors. It is this unthinking, and unjustified, rejection, he says, which has been hailed with joy as a great step forward in the growth of science, not the actual teaching, which is in fact very closely allied to Plato's. There *was*, at this point, a step forward in "the education of the mind of the *race*," as he will show in Essay IX, but it was a different and far subtler one than is commonly assumed. But there is also another, a semantic, reason why Bacon is misunderstood; and Coleridge concedes, towards the end of Essay VIII, that

> it will be no easy task to reconcile many passages in the *De Augmentis* and the *Redargutio Philosophiarum* with the author's own fundamental principles, as established in his *Novum Organum*; if we attach to the words the meaning which they *may* bear, or even, in some instances, the meaning which might appear to us, in the present age, more obvious.

We shall not reproduce the arguments and supporting quotations from the *Novum Organum*, of which Essay IX consists. Its two principal contentions are, firstly, that the "lux intellectus" or "lumen siccum," on which Bacon lays repeated emphasis, is not, as had been generally supposed, the shallow clarity of understanding, but is identical with Plato's *nous* or Coleridge's reason; while the famous "idols," on whose correction he was so insistent, are precisely "the limits, the passions, the prejudices, the peculiar habits of the human understanding, natural or acquired. . . the arrogance, which leads man to take the forms and mechanism of his own mere reflective faculty, as the measure and nature of Deity." Bacon's real point is that

> our understanding not only reflects the objects *subjectively*, that is, substitutes for the inherent laws and properties of the objects the relations which the objects bear to its own particular constitution; but that in all its conscious presentations and reflexes, *it is itself only a phaenomenon of the inner sense* [reason], and requires the same corrections as the appearances transmitted by the outward senses [italics not in original].

The second, and more particular, contention he summarises in the following passages:

> Thus the difference, or rather distinction between Plato and Lord Bacon is simply this; that philosophy being necessarily bi-polar, Plato treats principally of the truth, as it manifests itself at the *ideal* pole, as the science of intellect (i.e. *de mundo intelligibili*), while Bacon confines himself, for the most part, to the same truth, as it is manifested at the other, or material pole, as the science of nature (i.e. *de mundo sensibili*).

Plato's *main* concern therefore was with metaphysical ideas—"those objective truths that exist in and for the intellect alone," whereas Bacon's was with those which

> have their signatures in nature, and which (as he himself plainly and often asserts) may indeed be revealed to us *through* and *with*, but never *by* the senses or the faculty of sense.

And hence, Coleridge concludes,

> it will not surprise us, that Plato often calls ideas LIVING LAWS, in which the mind has its own true being and permanence; or that Bacon, vice versa, names the laws of nature *ideas*; and represents . . .*facts of science* and *central phaenomena*, as signatures, impressions and symbols of ideas.

Plato's gaze was turned in one direction, Bacon's in the other; but both were agreed, and it is "often expressed, and everywhere supposed" by Bacon not only

> that there is potentially, if not actually, in every rational being, a somewhat, call it what you will, the pure reason, the spirit, lumen siccum, intellectual intuition etc. etc.

but also

> that in this are to be found the indispensable conditions of all science, and scientific research, whether meditative, contemplative, or experimental.

It was the shift of emphasis, the change of direction of the gaze, that constituted an actual "step" in the general history of the mind, not (as has been very widely assumed) the adoption of a new scientific *method*; most certainly not so, if that method is taken to be a wilful limitation of science to the mere understanding and the senses.

It is, then, in connection with these two Essays on Method, and his remarks on method elsewhere, that the difference between Coleridge's doctrine of ideas and Plato's can be best discerned. Here, too, it is a difference of emphasis or direction rather than of substance. Plato's *nous*, we may say, is Coleridge's reason; for both of them, the hierarchy of ideas which constitutes that *nous* or reason is the articulation of ultimate reality and for both of them these ideas are also the powers that produce and sustain the natural world. But Plato never spoke of an "initiative idea"; he never equated an idea with the *act* of reason individualised, and thus with an individual human thinker. All that Coleridge has to say of the relation between reason and *will* is foreign to him. There is really no word in Greek that corresponds to what we mean by will, and none to what we mean by "subject." That polarity between subject and object, which is at the base of Coleridge's system, is nowhere to be found in Plato. It is only in Coleridge therefore that we find such a concept as that of an "initiative idea," on which method depends. Plato's method was his dialectic. It is only for Coleridge that the articulation of ideas can be itself at the same time method; that it is indeed the only reliable method, since we cannot in the last resort divide the objective ordering of nature from its ordering in and by human reason; since "the mind of man in its own primary and constituent forms represents the law of nature."

That which functions in nature as the principle of "productive unity," is necessarily at the same time functioning in nature's ideal pole, spirit, as that principle of "unity with progression," which is the principle of method. It is always so functioning potentially and is felt, when it first begins to be felt, as instinct. What we call "discovery" is the raising of it from potential to actual by becoming fully conscious of it; and that is the proper, the *methodical*, function of the understanding. ". . . every idea is living, productive, partaketh of infinity, and (as Bacon has sublimely observed) containeth an endless power of semination." "From the first, or initiative Idea, as from a seed, successive Ideas germinate." We are entitled to designate Coleridge's system "organicism" only if, in doing so, we are aware that "semination" and "germinate" here are not mere *metaphors*—unless, of course, by the word *metaphor* we merely allude loosely to the fact that all words referring to the ideal pole of reality have, or at one time had, reference also to the phenomenal pole. Coleridge's organicism is definitely not "a metaphor of mind" in the ordinary sense of the word; it is not "an implicit assertion that all the universe is like some one element in that universe."

"Hypothese non fingo." Newton refused to seek "behind" the law of gravitation for causes or explanations acceptable to a human understanding boggling at the impossible contradiction of "action at a distance." He left that to inferior scientists; and the law of gravitation is one of Coleridge's favourite illustrations of a "law of nature," as distinct from theory or hypothesis. Law differs from hypothesis, as idea differs from abstraction; just as an idea is not a notion "of" or "about" something other than itself, so a true law of nature is not a rule generalized from particular observations of natural behaviour; it is nature behaving. An idea is neither an abstraction nor a thing, but a physical idea *is* at the same time a law of nature. We must still therefore distinguish the idea or law itself from any uncontemplative notion of it. It is the *notion* of a law of gravity which degenerates into fancied invisible string. The very law itself is also the power. Science went astray in its dealings with both matter and space when, instead of accepting gravitation as at once a law of nature and an idea of reason, it began to devise hypotheses which would render it acceptable to the understanding. Where Newton was content to think of, and to quantify, the link that holds the earth to the sun as a vector, the lesser fry in an age of the understanding and the senses must fancy their piece of invisible string or something like it. They could never accept, because they could never understand, that the ultimate explanation of phenomena cannot itself be phenomenal. In the "Treatise on Method" Coleridge put is as follows:

> Every Physical Theory is in some measure imperfect, because it is of necessity progressive; and because we can never be sure that we have exhausted the terms or that some new discovery may not affect the whole scheme of its relations . . . the doctrines of vortices, of an universal ether, of a two-fold magnetic fluid, etc., are *Theories* of Gravitation: but the Science of Astronomy is founded on the *Law* of Gravitation, and remains unaffected by the rise and fall of the Theories.

The true object of science is "that knowledge in which truth and reality are one and the same, that which in the ideas that are present to the mind recognises the laws that govern in Nature if we may not say the laws that are Nature."

Of course the mental activity of forming theories and hypotheses may lead the mind to the apprehension of laws. In fact a sound theory will prove to have been an anticipation of one; it "becomes an IDEA in the moment of its coincidence with an objective law." And here lies the clue to the true function, and the value, of *experiment*. There is naturally much on this subject in the Essays on Method and the "Treatise," but it is not there alone that Coleridge has dealt with it, and in particular one of the Notebooks contains a fairly extensive treatment of the whole relation between idea, law and theory. There are a good many minor difficulties, and it might be worth someone's while to investigate as fully as the records permit such topics as Coleridge's later substitution of *theorems* for metaphysical ideas, his occasional, but only occasional, distinction between *theory* and *hypothesis*, and his more frequent, but not invariable, distinction between *laws* and *rules*. Instead of attempting anything of the sort we shall simply try to outline in our own way, and on our own responsibility, the general scheme of the relation between ideas, theories and laws which appears to result from a general survey of the many and scattered observations of Coleridge relevant thereto. It was on that relation that his methodology was founded.

For this purpose it will be necessary to begin by reverting once more to that "order of the Mental Powers," to which we have already alluded [previously]:

Reason
Imagination
Understanding

Understanding
Fancy
Sense

It will be recalled that the scale is meaningful only if it is conceived in the mode of polarity. So conceived, it may be used, before we proceed farther, to illuminate a little the difficult issue of the peculiar relation between ideas and mind. We have used such terms as *apprehend, contemplate, participate, meditate*. Coleridge himself on one occasion, and in one particular context, went so far as to say that idea *is* mind. But more often he makes the relation equivalent to a perceptual one. This is in accord with the scale, since the mode of polarity involves a relation between the two extremities that is closer to identity, though it is greater in distance, than that between any two other points in the scale or process. Thus, the closer one is to reason, the closer also has one come to its octave, sense, "Reason indeed is much nearer to Sense than to Understanding; for Reason (says our great Hooker) is a direct aspect, an inward beholding, having a similar relation to the intelligible or spiritual, as Sense has to the material or phenomenal." The distinction is that, in the case of reason, we are in a realm where an act may be "one with the product of the act"; we are dealing with "a subject which becomes its own object." And it is for that reason that, as previously mentioned, reflection on metaphysical ideas is a valuable aid. For there we are *obliged* to combine "the notion of an organ of sense. . . with the notion of the appropriate and peculiar objects of that sense." Contemplating *any* idea, the mind contemplates its own energies; contemplating a metaphysical idea, "the mind *exclusively* contemplates its own energies." Reason is "an organ of sense, or a new sense," but it is an organ of *inward* sense and moreover "an organ identical with its appropriate objects." Human reason, as organ, perceives or contemplates the ideas of reason which constitute it, but are nevertheless its own act. Perception of an idea is therefore self-apprehension or self-contemplation; but then so would physical sense-perception be, given full self-consciousness.

Just as the understanding *without* the light of reason, or without the use of reason as an organ turned inward, is a very different matter from the understanding when properly related to reason (a difference Coleridge expressed by the line drawn between understanding and understanding), so is what is ordinarily meant by a law of nature very different from the true law, which is at the same time an idea. We may venture accordingly to parallel Coleridge's gamut with another of our own construction:

Reason (as "the source and birthplace of ideas")
Idea
Law
______
Law
Theory
Sense

We believe that, seen within such a framework, many of Coleridge's observations become more meaningful or at all events less mystifying; such observations, for example, as that "in the infancy of the human mind all our ideas are instincts"; or that the scientist, in forming a theory, is instinctively labouring to extract a law, and further, that "This instinct [note: *not* the theory] is itself but the form, in which the idea, the mental correlative of the law, first announces its incipient germination in his own mind." It would be well to consider also, in this framework, his many allusions to the necessary relation between deep thinking and strong feeling, into which we shall not closely enter. Attention has often been drawn to them. "Ignorance seldom *vaults* into Knowledge, but passes into it through an intermediate state of obscurity . . ." "deep feeling has a tendency to combine with obscure ideas . . ." We shall not well understand them, unless we are keeping in view the fact that Coleridge always has at the back of his mind the idea; that the idea is at the opposite pole to, but not detached from, sense; and that knowledge and acknowledgment of an idea "requires the whole man, the free will no less than the intellect."

At the moment however we are concerned with that all-important line between law and law, which parallels the line between understanding and understanding; the difference—and of course the relation—between the law of nature, which is at the same time an idea, and the so-called law (more properly a "rule") which may be arrived at by generalising the notices of the senses. Must it not have been on that very line that the real function of experiment, and with it the whole conception of scientific method, balanced and faltered in the mind of Francis Bacon? If Coleridge was convinced that the future of mankind depends on its success in grasping the former distinction, he was no less convinced that the future of science depends on its success in grasping the latter.

In the former case we endeavoured to elucidate the consequences of *failure* so to distinguish, by presenting an alternative scale, decapitated by eliminating reason. If we tried the same experiment in the latter, we should get something like the following:

Fancies (=hypostatized notions)
Laws (=rules)
Hypotheses
Sense

and this is in fact ("fancy paramount in physics") what we have largely got.

For that reason Coleridge has not a great many examples to offer of his genuine laws of nature. On one or two occasions he placed beside the law of gravity the principle of Archimedes and Kepler's laws of the planetary motions. He believed that John Hunter was on the verge of arriving at a law of life, as universal as the law of gravity, and it distressed him to see this true *principle* of life (the tendency to individuation) being gratuitously supplemented by the hypostatized notion of a "fluid," just as the true principle of gravitation was being supplemented by the fancied "ether." Above all, however, there was his own discovery, or rediscovery, of polarity as another law of nature no less universal than that of gravitation. The law or idea of polarity was one he had evidently been feeling towards for a long time; the more so, because in this case the artificial split between law aspect and idea aspect cannot so successfully be maintained. In this case understanding and fancy cannot so easily have it their own way. It might indeed be said that a certain "tragic" element in the relation, in the very identity, between idea and law, which he laboured to expose in his paper on the "Prometheus of Aeschylus," is *most* evident in the law of gravity, *least* so in the law of polarity. Much in his letters, and many unpublished notes, show that in his latest years he devoted a good deal of attention to the contrast and relation between the two. But it will be best to consider this in its bearing on the relation between what Coleridge thought and the world of modern science.

M. H. ABRAMS

Coleridge's "A Light in Sound"

After he had finished correcting the proofs for *Sibylline Leaves* [1817], Coleridge sent the printer a list of Errata in which he included, for insertion [in "The Eolian Harp"] immediately after the lines on the birds of paradise, a new quatrain, together with a version of the succeeding passage on the love for all things which he had revised so as to accord with these four new lines. The total insertion, which I reproduce as it was printed in the Errata, constitutes lines 26–33 of the final text:

> O! the one Life, within us and abroad,
> Which meets all Motion and becomes its soul,
> A Light in Sound, a sound-like power in Light,
> Rhythm in all Thought, and Joyance every where—
> Methinks, it should have been impossible
> Not to love all things in a world so fill'd,
> Where the breeze warbles and the mute still Air
> Is Music slumbering on its instrument!

"O! the one Life . . ." The exclamation introduces a moment of vision that every reader feels to be the imaginative climax of the poem. These lines, however, in T. S. Eliot's phrase, communicate before they are understood. In the confidence that they will communicate more subtly and richly after they are understood—and also that to understand them is to understand what

From *The Correspondent Breeze: Essays on English Romanticism.* © 1984 by M. H. Abrams and Jack Stillinger. Norton, 1984. Originally entitled "Coleridge's 'A Light in Sound': Science, Metascience, and Poetic Imagination."

is most distinctive in Coleridge's mature thought and imagination—I shall undertake to explicate the passage by seeking answers to four questions: What did Coleridge mean by his allusion to "a light in sound, a sound-like power in light"? How is this allusion related to "the one Life within us and abroad,/ Which meets all motion"? In what way does the insight into a light in sound justify the sense of "joyance every where"? And what has this entire complex of a light in sound, the one Life, and universal joyance to do with the relation between the human lovers that precedes it and the culminating love for all things that follows it?

I. "A light in sound"

What are we to make of the mysterious reference to "a light in sound, a sound-like power in light"? The figures, technically, are oxymorons, and have usually been interpreted as alluding to synesthesia—the phenomenon in which the stimulation of one sense evokes a response involving a different sense. There had during the preceding century been intense interest, among poets and critics as well as philosophers, in such intersensory phenomena, stimulated in part by Newton's analogies in his *Opticks* between the propagation of light and of sound and between the perception of harmony and discord in musical tones and in colors. Coleridge shared this interest in what he called in the *Biographia Literaria* "the *vestigia communia* of the senses, the latency of all in each, and more especially... the excitement of vision by sound," and the line "A light in sound..." may include the suggestion of such a vestigial common-sensorium as an instance of the universal "latency of all in each" that leads to the poet's invocation of the one Life. But Coleridge's orbit of reference in this line is much wider than the psychology of sense perception, for it involves a total metaphysic of the constitution of the material universe, of the nature of life, and of the relation of the mind to the universe it perceives.

The quatrain of "The Eolian Harp" on a light in sound was added to the text in a list of Errata to *Sibylline Leaves* that Coleridge composed no earlier than the spring of 1816, and possibly as late as the spring of 1817. This places the writing of the quatrain squarely in the middle of the remarkable span of four years or so when, in a sudden burst of intellectual activity, Coleridge composed his most important works on philosophy and science, including the *Biographia Literaria*, the *Theory of Life*, his two *Lay Sermons*, his radically revised and enlarged version of *The Friend*, and the series of *Philosophical Lectures* that he delivered between December 1818 and March 1819. All these works contain passages relevant to Coleridge's theories of the relations between light, sound, and life, and I shall later cite some of them. Most immediately pertinent and revealing, however, are a series of philosophical letters that Coleridge wrote between November 1816 and January 1818—that is, during and soon after the time when he composed the Errata—which show that he was almost obsessively preoccupied with the ideas that underlie the passage added to "The Eolian Harp."

Thus, Coleridge wrote Ludwig Tieck on 4 July 1817, a few weeks before *Sibylline Leaves* was issued, that the positions taken by Newton in his *Opticks* that "*a Ray* of Light" is a "*Thing*," "a physical *synodical Individuum*," and that "the Prism is a mere mechanic Dissector" of "this complex yet divisible Ray," had always appeared to him "monstrous FICTIONS!" Instead he put forward the view—adopted, he said, "probably from Behmen's Aurora, which I had *conjured over* at School"—"that Sound was = Light under the praepotence of Gravitation, and Color = Gravitation under the praepotence of Light." Above all, two letters that Coleridge wrote shortly thereafter to the Swedenborgian, C. A. Tulk, provide decisive clues not only to the line about light and sound but also (as we shall see) to the entire passage we are scrutinizing. In the first letter, written two months after the publication of *Sibylline Leaves*, Coleridge declared that "the two Poles of the material Universe are . . . Light and Gravitation. . . . The Life of Nature consists in the tendency of the Poles to re-unite, and to find themselves in the re-union." Then:

> Color is Gravitation under the power of Light . . . while Sound on the other hand is Light under the power or paramountcy of Gravitation. Hence the analogies of Sound to Light.

"A light in sound, a sound-like power in light"—we find in these letters references to the light, sound, and power alluded to in this line, and to the analogies that the line suggests between sound and light, as well as an indicated relation between these matters and life—"the Life of Nature." But what has all this to do with gravitation, the deficiencies of Newton's theory of light, and the polarity of the material universe, and what are we to make of "praepotence"? At first sight these passages, instead of explaining the mystery of a light in sound, seem to wrap it in an enigma. To explain in turn this enigma, we need to glance at some elements in the world-view that Coleridge was evolving in the period 1815–18.

Coleridge's reference of his views on light and sound to Boehme's *Aurora*, it will appear later, has substantial grounds, but it is misleading nonetheless. Coleridge's immediate precedents for the particular terms and metaphysical constructions in these letters were the writings of the contemporary philosopher Friedrich Schelling and, to a lesser extent, the writings of Schelling's fellow workers in *Naturphilosophie*, especially Henrik Steffens. He had begun to study Schelling intensively in about 1808—his burst of philosophical activity in the 1810s is, in considerable part, a result of the exciting possibilities that Schelling's thought opened out to him. For the sake of brevity I shall attend mainly to Coleridge's own views, with only an occasional glance at the German formulations that he adopted but altered to accord with his prior interests and speculations. Our investigation leads us to the center of Coleridge's philosophy of nature. This is an area of his thought that, until very recently, scholars have either discreetly overlooked or else—assessing it as an attempt to achieve by free fantasy what scientists discover by patient experiment—have rejected as "mere abracadabra," "a bizarre farrago of pretentious nonsense." Such judgments are inevitable if we simply apply to Coleridge's scheme of nature the criteria of the philosophical positivism that Coleridge's scheme was specifically intended to dispossess. If our intent, on the other hand, is not to dismiss but to understand an important development in nineteenth-century intellectual history, then we can do no better than to emulate Coleridge's own procedure, which John Stuart Mill found to be so intellectually liberating. Mill pointed out that by Bentham (the great philosophical positivist of his time), men have been led to ask of an opinion, "Is it true?" By Coleridge, they have been led to ask, "What is the meaning of it?" and to answer this question by trying to look at the opinion "from within."

> The long duration of a belief, [Coleridge] thought, is at least proof of an adaptation in it to some portion or other of the human mind; and if, on digging down to the root, we do not find, as is generally the case, some truth, we shall find some natural want or requirement of human nature which the doctrine in question is fitted to satisfy.

Let us then take Coleridge's vision of nature seriously and try to look at it from within, to see what it undertook to accomplish and what natural want it served to satisfy.

Coleridge's aim was not to replace experimental science by speculative science but instead to develop a countermetaphysic to the metaphysical foundations of modern science; his philosophy of nature, in short, was not science nor anti-science but metascience. By the reference, in his letter to Tieck, to Newton's "monstrous Fictions" in the *Opticks*, he did not mean to oppugn Newton as an experimental physicist, to whose procedures and discoveries he paid spacious tribute. His objection was to Newton as a man whose prestige as a physicist had given impetus to a metaphysics that, in Coleridge's view, permeated and vitiated all areas of thought and culture in the eighteenth century, "the Epoch of the Understanding and the Sense" in philosophy, psychology, politics, religion, and the arts. For despite his reluctance to frame hypotheses, Newton had proposed, in the "Queries" he added to his *Opticks*, that rays of light are "corpuscular," that is, "very small Bodies emitted from shining Substances," and that these bodies in motion excite "Waves of Vibrations, or Tremors" in a hypothetical "aether." This aether, although very "rare and subtile" is nonetheless a material medium that pervades, in varying densities, both space and bodies and serves to explain not only the action at a distance both of light and gravity but also the refraction and reflection of light, as well as the propagation of light and sound from the eye and ear through the nerves "into the place of Sensation" where they are converted into sight and hearing.

This procedure, Coleridge argues, sets up a logical regress, since it undertakes to solve "Phaenomena by Phaenomena that immediately become part of the Problem to be solved." Worse still, Newton in his famed thirty-first Query had put forward the stark image of a universe whose ultimate elements are indivisible particles of matter capable of motion:

> It seems probable to me, that God in the Beginning form'd Matter in solid, massy, hard, impenetrable, moveable Particles, of such Sizes and Figures, and with such other Properties, and in such Proportion to Space, as most conduced to the End for which he form'd them.

And as ultimate reality is thus reduced to masses and motion—for the simple reason that these are the only things that the highly specialized techniques of physical science are capable of managing mathematically—so the Creator of this reality is reconstrued to accord with such a postulated creation. That is, Newton's God is represented as the omnipresent mover of all particles, and also as the infallible seer of the particles in themselves that we are able to see only after they have been translated into the "images" formed by the sense through the intermediation of rays of light. God, Newton says, is "a powerful ever-living Agent, who being in all Places, is . . . able by his Will to move the Bodies within his boundless uniform Sensorium"; he is also the Being

> who in infinite Space, as it were in his Sensory, sees the things themselves intimately . . . wholly by their immediate presence to himself: Of which things the Images only carried through the Organs of Sense into our little Sensoriums, are there seen and beheld by that which in us perceives and thinks.

"Sir Isaac Newton's Deity," Coleridge drily remarked, "seems to be alternately operose and indolent," for he undertakes to do everything, yet delegates so much power to "Vice-regent second causes" as "to make it inconceivable what he can have reserved."

Newton's move, as Coleridge saw it, was an immense extrapolation of a working fiction of physical science—what we now call a "conceptual model"—into a picture of the actual constitution of the universe. The "Mechanic or

Corpuscular Scheme," Coleridge said, "in order to submit the various phenomena of moving bodies to geometrical construction," had to abstract "from corporeal substance all its *positive* properties," leaving it only "figure and mobility. And as a *fiction of science*, it would be difficult to overvalue this invention." But Descartes and later thinkers "propounded it as *truth of fact*: and instead of a World *created* and filled with productive forces by the Almighty *Fiat*, left a lifeless Machine whirled about by the dust of its own Grinding."

To Coleridge this view of the ultimate structure of reality was both incredible to human experience of the world and intolerable to human needs. As no more than a drastic subtraction from the rich diversity of sense phenomena, it remains itself phenomenal, the product of what Coleridge repeatedly described as a "slavery" to the senses, especially to the eye. The "needlepoint pinshead System of the *Atomists*" was a fictional product of that "slavery to the eye" which reduces "the conceivable... within the bounds of the *picturable*," and excludes "all modes of existence which the theorist cannot in imagination, at least, *finger* and *peep* at!" Against this world picture, in the literal sense of "picture" as something that can be visualized, Coleridge again and again brought the charge that it is, precisely speaking, lethal. It has killed the living and habitable world of ordinary experience, as well as the metaphysical world of the pre-Cartesian and pre-Newtonian past, in which the mind of man had recognized an analogon to itself and to its life, purposes, sentiments, values, and needs; a world, therefore, in which man was a participant and could feel thoroughly at home. By the translation of the "scientific calculus" from a profitable fiction into ontology, Coleridge claimed in 1817, "a few brilliant discoveries have been dearly purchased at the loss of all communion with life and the spirit of Nature." And against this "philosophy of death," which leaves only the "relations of unproductive particles to each other," he posed his own philosophy of life, in which "the two component counter-powers actually interpenetrate each other, and generate a higher third, including both the former."

That is, in radical opposition to the picture of a world composed of particles of matter in motion, to whose impact an alien mind is passively receptive, Coleridge sets up what, following Schelling, he calls a "vital," or "dynamic," or "constructive" philosophy. The elements of his philosophy are not moving material particles but inherent energies, or "powers," that polarize into positive and negative "forces" (also called "thesis and antithesis") which operate according to "the universal Law of Polarity or essential Dualism." By this Coleridge means that the generative and sustaining elements of his universe exist only relatively to each other and manifest an irremissive tendency on the one hand to oppose themselves and on the other hand to reunite. These powers and forces are not physical or phenomenal, but metascientific and prephenomenal elements (in Coleridge's terms, they are not "real" but "ideal"), hence they cannot be pictured but only imagined; they do, however, within the phenomenal world which they bring into being, have especially close and revealing analogues that Coleridge calls their "exponents." It is only by their "living and generative interpenetration," or "synthesis," that the polar powers and forces achieve the condition of matter, and so move into the phenomenal realm available to the senses. "In all pure phaenomena," Coleridge says, "we behold only the copula, the balance or indifference of opposite energies," and "matter" is to be considered "a Product—coagulum spiritûs, the pause, by interpenetration, of opposite energies."

We are at length ready to turn back to Coleridge's enigmatic statement, in his letter to C. A. Tulk of September 1817, that "Color is Gravitation under the power of Light. . . while Sound on the other hand is Light under the power or paramountcy of Gravitation." "The two Poles of the material Universe," Coleridge there says, are "Light and Gravitation." Or as he wrote in a manuscript note:

> Well then, I say that all Powers may be reduced, in the first instance, into
>
> Light & Gravity.
>
> But each of these beget two other powers. Under Gravity we place Attraction and Repulsion: and under Light the Powers of Contraction and Dilation.

That is, the two elemental counterpowers that generate the cosmos he calls "light" and "gravity." These are not the light we see nor the weight, or gravitational force, we feel; they exist on a different ontological plane as "speculative" or "ideal" powers of which phenomenal light and weight serve as the closest "exponents" in experience. Each of these two powers evolves two counterforces, constituting a tetrad of forces that Coleridge represents graphically as a north-south line crossed by an east-west line: gravity involves a pull in and its opposite, a push out, while light pulses radially in all directions and at the same time contracts back to its center. The continuous and incremental syntheses of the two counterpowers of gravity and light constitute the material elements and bodies of everything that exists. The innumerable qualitative differences among existing things, hence among the phenomena perceived by the senses, are determined by which of these two elemental powers—at any given level of their synthesis— is "predominant," in a range of ratios that extends from the extreme predominance of gravity, through a midpoint of "indifference" or "neutralization" between the two powers, to the extreme predominance of light. "That a thing *is*," as Coleridge puts it, "is owing to the co-inherence therein of any two powers; but that it is *that* particular thing arises from the proportions in which these powers are co-present, either as predominance or as reciprocal neutralization." (For "predominance," Coleridge elsewhere uses the alternative expressions "praepotence," "dynasty," "under the power of," or "paramountcy.")

The metaphysical enigma has, I trust, become transparent enough so that we can look through it at the initial mystery of "The Eolian Harp," line 28: "A light in sound, a sound-like power in light." Seated in close communion with his bride and luxuriously open to the light and color and sounds of the outer world, the poet, by a leap of imagination, achieves insight to the common prephenomenal powers of which all these phenomena are exponents, and so apprehends the unity within their qualitative diversity—sounds that incorporate the elemental counterpower of light, and light that, appearing as color, incorporates the elemental counterpower of gravity. For as we have seen, the power of gravitation, when predominant over the "co-present" power of light, manifests itself to the senses as sound, and when subordinate to light, manifests itself to the senses as color.

II. "THE ONE LIFE"

In what Coleridge called his "speculative," as opposed to "empirical," science of nature and life, he "constructs" (in the sense of rendering intelligible by reference to a single genetic principle) the total universe. Driven by their inherent stresses of opposition-in-unity, and manifesting in the struggle diverse degrees of relative "predominance," the powers of light and gravity evolve, by the progressive synthesis of prior syntheses, through the several distinctive orders of organization that Coleridge, following Schelling, calls "potences." At each level of organization, entities are linked by correspondences—according to an equivalence in the predominance of light or gravity—to entities on all other levels. On the first level of potence we get magnetism, electricity, and galvanism (which to Coleridge includes chemical combination), then all the forms of the inorganic world, then the forms of the organic world of plants and animals up to the highest stage of organic life, man; at which point mind, or "consciousness," emerges. This culminating achievement is a radical breakthrough in the developmental process, for consciousness is capable of a reflex act by which—in a continuing manifestation of "the universal Law of Polarity" whereby it counterposes, in order to reconcile, the outer world as "object" to itself as "subject"—it reengenders as knowledge the natural world within which it has itself been engendered, and of which it remains an integral part. Thus man's mind closes the evolutionary circle of polar generation by the powers of light and gravitation, the human and the nonhuman world merging at the focal point of consciousness.

We come to the moment in line 26 of "The Eolian Harp"—"O! the one Life within us and abroad." Coleridge's preoccupation with the one Life as a truth manifested in highest human experience but alien to the post-Newtonian world picture, goes back long before 1816 or 1817, when he added this passage to the poem. As early as 1802, for example, he had written to Sotheby that Nature will have her proper interest only to him "who believes & feels, that every Thing has a Life of its own, & that we are all *one Life*." In the Hebrew Psalmists, unlike the mythological poets among the Greeks, you find "genuine Imagination."

> In the Hebrew Poets each Thing has a Life of it's own, & yet they are all one Life. In God they move & live, & *have* their Being—not *had*, as the cold System of Newtonian Theology represents, but *have*.

And in the conversation poems that Coleridge wrote within several years after the 1796 version of "The Eolian Harp," the climax of each meditation on a landscape had been a moment of insight—the sudden awareness of a single Presence behind and within the phenomena of sense. In all these early poems, however, the visionary moment had been described in terms that had long been traditional. In "The Eolian Harp" of 1796, the poet tentatively put forward a latter-day version of the Stoic World-Soul—"one intellectual breeze"—as the principle that makes all animated nature "tremble into thought." In other conversation poems the poet found "religious meanings in the forms of nature!" or discovered that nature was an orthodox "Temple" built by "God" and that the diversified landscape "seem'd like Omnipresence"; or else the landscape manifested itself to be God's veiled self-revelation,

> of such hues
> As veil the Almighty Spirit, when yet he makes
> Spirits perceive his presence;

or (in the concept that had persisted from early Christian exegetes through Bishop Berkeley) the objects and aspects of the landscape were recognized to be *verba visibilia* in God's Book of Nature,

> The lovely shapes and sounds intelligible
> Of that eternal language which thy God
> Utters.

Now, some fifteen years later, the metascience of nature that Coleridge had evolved from German *Naturphilosophie* provided him with a full and detailed conceptual structure to support and articulate his earlier intuitions. In this scheme, in which all matter and spirit are generated by the interplay of the same elemental powers, there is no gap between the living and the lifeless, nature and man, or matter and mind but only a distinction of levels of organization. "What is *not* Life," Coleridge asks, "that really *is*?" For "in the identity of the two counter-powers, Life *sub*sists; in their strife it *con*sists: and in their reconciliation it at once dies and is born again into a new form." This "universal life" of ever-renewing strife and reconciliation pulses through all individual forms and all the orders of being, beginning with "the life of metals"—where in "its utmost *latency*. . . life is one with the elementary powers of mechanism"—up through the progressive levels of "individuation" to the human consciousness, which in its living reciprocity with its specific contrary, nature, is capable of achieving the awareness that there is only one Life within us and abroad.

Hence the statement I quoted earlier from Coleridge's letter to C. A. Tulk that "the Life of Nature" consists in the sustained tendency of the poles of "Light and Gravitation" to separate and reunite. But this same revealing letter, written within a few months of the final version of "The Eolian Harp," makes it plain that Coleridge's intuition of "the one Life within us and abroad" has not merely a metascientific basis but a biblical one as well. It will help to clarify this essential aspect of Coleridge's thought—and of the poem—if we turn back to consider the significance of Coleridge's statement to Tieck, that same year, that he had adopted the idea of the relation of light and gravity to color and sound "probably from Behmen's Aurora, which I had *conjured over* at School."

The Aurora, written in 1611–12, was the first of Jacob Boehme's books; it is incomplete, and even more obscure than Boehme's later expositions of his esoteric but very influential doctrines. Through the fantastic terminology and melodramatic narration, however, we can make out its basic concepts and design. Boehme's undertaking is to elucidate the mystery of the creation of the world and of man, as the initial episode in the history of human and cosmic salvation. He bases his account of the creation on the first chapter of Genesis (which he regards as in fact the story of a second creation, intended to repair the wreck of the angelic world occasioned by the fall of the angel Lucifer) and also upon the commentary on the creation in the Gospel of John (on which Boehme largely relies for his account of the first creation of a perfect world). But Boehme claims that he has been inspired by divine grace infused "in my spirit," and that he is therefore able to decipher the spiritual truths concealed within the esoteric sound-symbolism of the literal biblical narrative. Boehme's symbolic interpretation of the creation (more accurately, of the two creations) turns out, in fact, to be mainly a remarkably elaborated version of the doctrines and terminology he had learned (at this period of his life, at second hand) from the alchemical philosophy of Paracelsus and other Renaissance Hermeticists.

To Boehme, the essential condition for all creativity and progression, both in being and in thinking, is a strenuous tension between contraries, or opposed forces, whose sequential separations and unions give rise to everything that exists. The archetypal struggle in the fallen world is between the contrary forces of good and evil, love and hate, but these are destined to eventuate in the triumph of good and love in the coming redemption. Even the original creation of the angelic world, however, resulted from the energy generated by opponent principles. For God the Father manifests a joyous union of divine powers that Boehme calls, collectively, the "Salliter," or the "Sal-niter." This totality involves seven different *Qualitäten*, which Boehme derives from *Quelle* and *quellen* ("a spring," "to gush forth"), and which are therefore not what we ordinarily call "qualities" but "powers" or "forces" *(Kräfte)*. Each one of these elemental powers is a balance of opposing contraries, and each also has its appropriate counterpower. From the divine Salliter, in the successive unions and renewed oppositions of the diverse opponent powers and forces, issues all that constitutes the world, from stones and metals through plants and animals to the body and spirit of man, who as microcosm is the perfect analogue of the world's body and spirit. In Boehme's world there is thus no gap between animate and inanimate, body and mind, conscient and inconscient—all are an emanation of the powers of the one Deity, and throughout all there surges one life, exhibiting itself in the conflict and interpenetration of the same vital forces.

In this great radiation outward from the divine source of all life and being, Boehme puts by far the greatest stress on the role in creation of two elements, sound and light. The reasons for this emphasis are patent. In the Book of Genesis, God's creation is by word, or sound. His first creative sounds are, "Let there be light," which forthwith become light, and His later creative sounds become all forms of life, including man. And in the first chapter of John we find the creative fiat represented as the Word, which is equated with light, and also with life, and finally becomes itself incarnate:

> In the beginning was the Word, and the Word was with God, and the Word was God. . . .
>
> All things were made by him; and without him was not any thing made that was made.
>
> In him was life; and the life was the light of men.
>
> And the light shineth in darkness; and the darkness comprehended it not.
>
> And the Word was made flesh, and dwelt among us.

Boehme repeatedly echoes these passages from Genesis and John. In his symbolic translation of them into a philosophy of nature, light is represented, not as one of the primal powers, but as something which is generated from the ensemble of the seven powers; as Boehme puts it, light is "perpendicular" to the ontological plane of the powers. This light is equated with the Son, as well as with the sun, the "place" of light in the heavens; while in man, the light constitutes his soul and spirit. Sound, on the other hand, is one of the seven elemental powers within the divine Salliter itself; this power Boehme calls "Mercurius" (that is, Mercury or Hermes Trismegistus, the great magus of the Hermetic philosophers). Boehme identifies this "sound" (*Schall*) with the creative voice and with the harmony of the heavenly music; accordingly, from this "sound, tone, tune or noise. . . ensued *speech*, language, and the *distinction* of everything, as also the ringing melody and *singing* of the holy angels, and therein consisteth for forming or framing of all *colours*, beauty and ornament, as also the heavenly *joyfulness*" (*Aurora*). In its manifestation as speech, sound serves as the vehicle for the expression of spirit, hence as the vehicle (in God's creative fiat) by which the third aspect of God, the Holy Spirit, expresses itself. Sound, in Boehme's intricate system of analogies and identities, thus is equated with the Word, or divine Logos itself, and so is integral with light and life and the Son, as an element in the triune nature of God which manifests itself throughout the creation.

Whatever the extent of his claimed knowledge of *The Aurora* during his schooldays, we know that Coleridge closely studied and copiously annotated this and other books by Boehme, in the English "Law edition," from the year 1807 on, just prior to and collaterally with his immersion in Schelling and other *Naturphilosophen* during the second decade of the nineteenth century. Coleridge's thinking was inveterately organic and genetic, always traveling back to the radical of a view—or as he called it, to the "seminal" idea—which has proved historically capable of growing into a total metaphysic. It should be clear even from my brief summation that he found a great deal in Boehme's dualistic vitalism that suited his own mature "dynamic" philosophy; and in the letter to Ludwig Tieck, as well as in his private annotations, Coleridge tended to impose on Boehme's inchoate views the terms and structure of the metascience he had developed on the basis of contemporary German thinkers. It was in line with this persistent tendency (and not in order to hide his debt to Schelling) that Coleridge interpreted Boehme's arcane statements about the primary roles of light and sound in nature to accord with his own doctrines about the elemental counterpowers of gravitation and light and their relative "predominance" in the diverse phenomena of sound and color.

But what in Boehme's writings made the greatest appeal to Coleridge, as against Schelling's early *Naturphilosophie*, was that Boehme had derived his scheme of nature from the biblical accounts of the creation, although Coleridge feared that Boehme had not entirely avoided the "Pantheism" that he found blatantly manifested in Schelling—the assimilation of a transcendent Creator into a religion of Nature. As far back as the letter to Sotheby of 1802, it will be recalled, Coleridge had discovered the sense of "one Life" within all things, specifically, in "the Hebrew poets" of the Old Testament. Now, in a marginal comment on *The Aurora*, he comments on Boehme's treatment of light in the creation and Incarnation:

> That not Heat but Light is the Heart of Nature is one of those truly profound and pregnant Thoughts that ever and anon astonish me in Boehme's writings. . . . The affinity . . . of the Flesh and Blood generally to Light I trust that I shall make clear in my commentaries on the first and sixth chapters of the Gospel of John. Hence in the Logos (distinctive energy) is *Light*, and the *Light* becomes the *Life* of Man.

The "commentaries" on John to which Coleridge alludes he planned to include in his *Logosophia*, the comprehensive philosophical work on which he labored for decades but never completed. In this "Opus Maximum," the exposition of his own "Dynamic or Constructive Philosophy" was to be "preparatory" to "a detailed Commentary on the Gospel of St. John," in order "to prove that Christianity is true Philosophy"; and this section was in turn to be followed by a treatise on "the Mystics & Pantheists," including Jacob Boehme.

We return to the indispensable letters that Coleridge wrote to C. A. Tulk in 1817 and early 1818. There he begins his "rude and fragmentary" sketch of "the Science of the Construction of *Nature*" with God, who is the absolute "Identity" or "*Pro*thesis" which precedes any polarity between thesis and antithesis; Coleridge comments that to adopt the alternative, the "Lockian, and Newtonian" Creator as "an hypothetical Watch-maker," is in fact to "live without God in the world." And he begins his construction of nature—"the Genesis . . . the *Birth* of Things"—with an interpretation of the opening sentence of the Book of Genesis, "In the beginning God created the Heaven and the Earth." Coleridge's hermeneutics is based on his view that the Bible embodies the ideas of "reason" in the mode of "imagination," hence that it is "a science of realities" expressed in "symbols." His interpretation of the biblical accounts of the creation, therefore, like Boehme's, is symbolic, although on quite different grounds.

I will not reconstruct the exegetic maneuvers by which Coleridge translates "And the Earth was waste and void . . . and Darkness on the Deep" to signify that what first came into existence was "gravitation," which is best designated by "the combination of the Ideas, Darkness & the Deep or Depth." He continues:

> And God said—Let there be *Light*: and there was *Light*. And God divided the *Light* from the *Darkness*—i.e. Light from Gravitation . . . and the two Poles of the material Universe are established, viz. Light and Gravitation. . . . The Life of Nature consists in the tendency of the Poles to re-unite. . . . God is the Sun of the Universe—it's gravitation or Being by his Omnipresence, it's Light by his only-begotten Son . . . Deus alter et idem!

He also conjoins the account of the creation of light in Genesis with the commentary on the creative Logos in the opening chapter of John:

> God SAID, Let there be Light: and there became LIGHT! In the beginning was the Word. All things *became* . . . through the Word, the living and vivific Word . . . whose Life is the *Light* of men. . . . The Light . . . rose up in the Darkness and in the Depth—and in and with it *became* . . . the two Primary Poles of Nature, Light and Gravitation.

On these grounds Coleridge proceeds to "construct" the orders of being and of sense phenomena that make up the universe, including, in the passage which is our central concern, the construction of color as "Gravitation under the power of Light" and of sound as "light under the power or paramountcy of Gravitation."

Coleridge's inserted passage in "The Eolian Harp," then, is only the visible tip of a massive complex of submerged ideas, scientific and metascientific, Scriptural and theological. We know enough of this substructure to recognize now that the poet's moment of vision is also a theophany, and that the oxymorons in which the moment is expressed signify not only the "law of contradiction," or polarity, on which Coleridge's metascience is based but also the central Christian mysteries. For in Coleridge's interwoven universe of correspondences and analogues, of exponents and symbols, "a light in sound" is the distant reflection of the light generated by the primal sound, "Let there be light," while "a sound-like power in light" is the distant echo of the creative Word which became flesh and is the Light as well as the Life both of nature and man.

In line 27, this one Life "meets all motion and becomes its soul." In the Newtonian world picture, motion—as measured by the altering position, through time, of particles of matter in space—had been an elementary postulate. Coleridge, however, by intricate reasoning derives "ideal" (prephenomenal) time and space from his own first premise, or "Prothesis," as the primitive polar opposites whose synthesis constitutes "motion." He conceives motion, that is, as a point moving through space in time, so that it forms, and is represented graphically by, a line; and the bipolar line, in the next synthesis, achieves a third dimension as "depth." Coleridge cryptically summarizes to Tulk the role of these elementary constructs in generating the universe:

> Time × Space = Motion. Attraction × Repulsion = Gravity as Depth.—These are ideal relations. The ideal + real, or rather the Ideal = Real, World arises out of chaos (= Indistinction) or begins, with the creation of Light.

He adds, however, that "a Life, a Power, an *Inside*, must have pre-existed" the ideal dimensions of time, space, motion, and depth, of which "the LIFE *appearing*" in the real, or material, world is the result; and that this process of the "interpenetration of opposite energies," of which matter is a product, sustains itself, as process, to constitute the "spirit" in all matter. Otherwise stated: the elemental rhythm of opposing and interpenetrating polarities in which life consists, when it meets all "ideal" motion, brings it into existence as matter, in which the continuing pulsation of the one Life constitutes the spirit or soul; and this vital outer rhythm, he goes on to say in "The Eolian Harp," has its analogue, in high moments of human consciousness, as a "rhythm in all thought."

III. "JOYANCE"

Now, what of the "joyance every where" in line 29? "Joy" and "joyance" were specialized terms, used by Coleridge as the emotional index to a particular relationship between the conscious self and the outer world. To clarify its significance in "The Eolian Harp," we need to consider again Coleridge's evolving scale of being, at the point at which the reflexive consciousness emerges in man.

Man, Coleridge says in his letters to Tulk, represents the ultimate product of the two contrary "ends" of the life process, namely "Individualization, or apparent detachment from Nature = progressive Organization" and "the reunion with Nature as the apex of Individualization." And since, as he says in the contemporary work, the *Theory of Life*, "the form of polarity" applies at this as at every evolutionary stage, "the intensities must be at once opposite and equal," so that the independence of an individual man should ideally be matched by "interdependence" with other men in the social organization, while "as the ideal genius and the originality [i.e., the highest degree of human autonomy], in the same proportion must be the resignation to the real world, the sympathy and the intercommunion with Nature," which exists "in counterpoint to him." But although man is both product and participant in the universal process of life, he is radically different from the rest of nature, in that by achieving consciousness, he also achieves freedom of the will. As Coleridge puts it in the same passage, man "is referred to himself, delivered up to his own charge"; and here things can go drastically wrong. For an excess in the tendency to individuation—especially when fostered by untoward "hardships" and "circumstances"—can force "a man in upon his little unthinking contemptible self," and so cut the individual consciousness off from the sense of its interdependence with other men and of its intercommunion with outer nature.

To be cut off from all relationship to man and nature, to suffer what he called "the evils of separation and finiteness," was to Coleridge as to other Romantic thinkers and poets the radical affliction of the human condition. This is the state to which the Romantic philosopher Hegel gave the name "alienation," and it is, as Coleridge saw it, the inescapable situation of anyone who accepts the Newtonian world picture, the dead universe of matter in motion, as existential reality. "Joy," on the other hand, is the term Coleridge specifically appropriated to the state of mind in which all alienation is annulled—it is an equipoise of the contrary mental powers, manifested in an inner life so abundant that it breaks through the barrier of self to yield awareness of the one Life that is shared with other selves and with nature. As Coleridge says about "joy" in his *Philosophical Lectures*, with respect to "genius," which is the term he uses for the creative power of the human mind and imagination:

> All genius exists in a participation of a common spirit. In joy individuality is lost. . . . To have a genius is to live in the universal, to know no self but that which is reflected not only from the faces of all around us, our fellow creatures, but reflected from the flowers, the trees, the beasts, yea from the very surface of the [waters and the] sands of the desert.

To this I shall add a contemporary statement by Coleridge in *The Friend* of 1818. This passage, in its context, ascribes the scientific world picture to an alienation of mind from nature, and counters it, as the premise of philosophy, with the primal intuition of an integrity of the self and not-self, mind and nature, of which the sign in human consciousness is the condition called "joy":

> The ground-work, therefore, of all true philosophy is the full apprehension of the difference between . . . that intuition of things which arises when we possess ourselves, as one with the whole . . .

> and that which presents itself when . . . we think of ourselves as separated beings, and place nature in antithesis to the mind, as object to subject, thing to thought, death to life. This is abstract knowledge, or the science of the mere understanding. . . . [The former on the other hand] is an eternal and infinite self-rejoicing, self-loving, with a joy unfathomable, with a love all comprehensive.

IV. "LOVE"

In this intuition of the community of all life, the movement from "a joy unfathomable" to "a love all comprehensive" parallels the movement in "The Eolian Harp" from "joyance every where" to the universal love described in the next lines, which Coleridge revised and integrated with the added passage on the one Life:

> Rhythm in all thought, and joyance every where—
> Methinks, it should have been impossible
> Not to love all things in a world so filled

There remains, in conclusion, to show the relation in Coleridge's thinking at this period between all-comprehensive love and the elemental powers of gravity and light, as these manifest themselves in a light in sound.

In this instance, too, the connection is established in one of his letters to C. A. Tulk. There having "constructed," on both metascientific and biblical grounds, "the two Primary Poles of Nature, Light and Gravitation," he goes on to say that these "correlatives and correspondent Opposites, by and in which the Unity is revealed," are

> (to borrow your happy and most expressive Symbol) the Male and female of the World of Time, in whose wooings, and retirings and nuptial conciliations all other marriages . . . are celebrated inclusively.—These truths it is my Object to enforce in the manner best fitted (alas! how hopeless even the best!) to the present age.

To indicate what lies behind this astonishing attribution of sexuality to all phenomenal nature ("the World of Time") requires another look, from a different vantage point, at Coleridge's metascientific enterprise. The post-Newtonian world picture repelled him because it had been deliberately stripped bare of any correlative to the life of man and any sanction for human purposes and values. While a young man of thirty Coleridge had written to Southey that "a metaphysical Solution, that does not instantly *tell* for something in the Heart, is grievously to be suspected as apocryphal," and in the *Biographia*

Literaria, contemporaneously with the last version of "The Eolian Harp," he extolled Boehme, despite the "delusions" and fantasies he found mixed with his "truths," because he had contributed "to keep alive the *heart* in the *head*; gave me. . . [a] presentiment, that all the products of the mere *reflective* faculty partook of DEATH." Coleridge meant that, as man cannot live by science alone—in his terms, by the evidence of the senses ordered by the "reflective faculty," the "understanding"—neither can he endure a universe constructed to suit the narrow requirements of Newtonian physics rather than the large requirements of human life. Coleridge undertook to develop an alternative world vision that would suffice to the heart as well as the head, by supplementing science with imagination—as he put it in terms of his faculty-philosophy, the phenomena of "the senses," as classed and ordered by "the understanding," are to be "impregnated" by "the imagination," and so reconciled and mediated to the requirements of the supreme and inclusive power of mind, "the reason."

We can translate Coleridge's terms into the idiom of our own time. His prime endeavor, like that of his contemporaries, the great German architects of all-inclusive metaphysical "systems," was to assimilate the findings and hypotheses of contemporary science to the inherent demands and forms of the human imagination, in the kind of inclusive vision of man in the world that Northrop Frye calls a "myth of concern." In this undertaking man is put back into nature, from which the sophisticated logic of science had severed him, by applying the primitive imaginative categories of analogy, correspondence, and identity. Through this procedure nature is once more endowed with the inherent energies of life and with humanly intelligible purposes and values, and so constitutes a milieu in which man can fully live and be at home. And since the cultural myth of concern that Coleridge had inherited was the Judeo-Christian one set forth in the Bible, and since Coleridge felt a greater need than contemporary German philosophers to salvage the essentials of its creed of salvation, he undertook explicitly to ground his world vision on bases common both to the Old and New Testament and to "speculative physics."

No doubt Coleridge would have rejected this description, since it transposes the criterion of his intricately rationalized system from a truth of correspondence to ultimate reality to a truth of correspondence to man's deepest instincts and needs, as these shape the forms of his imagination. But Schelling, I think, might well have accepted it, for Schelling was one of the German philosophers who helped establish the present views, of which Northrop Frye is a distinguished representative, that human needs inevitably compel the creation of a mythology to live by, in civilized no less than in primitive societies. Schelling asserts that in the modern world the mythology of the ancients has been outworn, while "the mythology of Christendom" is unsuitable for valid poetry, so that now "every truly creative individual has to create his own mythology." All these separate creations, however, will prove, in the indeterminate future, to be parts of a single system of myth. The preeminent material for this evolving mythology is contemporary *Naturphilosophie*, such as he has himself developed. It is his conviction, Schelling says, "that in the higher speculative physics is to be sought the possibility of a future mythology and symbolism," which will reconcile the contraries between the pagan and Christian mythologies in one vision of nature; but this achievement, he adds, will be the work not of any one individual, but of "the entire era."

Conspicuous in Schelling's own later *Naturphilosophie* is its tendency to move from abstract concepts to explicitly anthropomorphic and mythical formulations. This tendency is most obvious in the instance of his basic principle of polarity. In his early writings Schelling had based this category on the concepts of bipolarity in recent scientific developments in magnetism and electricity, as well as on Kant's essay of 1786, which undertook a "metaphysical" derivation of the primitive "matter" of Newtonian physics from the elemental "powers" of attraction and repulsion. Coleridge in his turn based his early formulations of the polar-principle on the theory of his scientific friend Humphry Davy that all substances are the product of elementary forces, even before he absorbed the views of Kant and the metaphysical system of Schelling. Coleridge, however, rightly pointed back to a long tradition, from "the Dynamic Theory of the eldest Philosophy" in the pre-Socratic thinkers, through Renaissance Hermeticism, to Jacob Boehme as precedent to Schelling in putting forward "the universal law of polarity." In these earlier thinkers the philosophical representation of an all-originative and sustaining interplay of elemental oppoites had not yet completely emerged from its origins in a cosmic myth of universal bisexuality—the myth of male and female divinities or powers, antithetic and warring yet mutually attractive and necessary, which periodically merge in unions that beget the world and all things in it. In its older forms, in other words, universal polarity had been derived from bisexual procreation as its prototype; and it is the sexual dimension of human nature, we may plausibly conjecture, that gives the myth of cosmic bisexuality its persisting hold on imagination even today, in current forms of the "perennial philosophy." After all, as Schelling remarked, human union and procreation is "the single instance in which we are to a certain extent permitted to be witnesses of an original creation."

In his early writings of 1797, Schelling at times referred to the contrary powers of gravity and light as the feminine or "mother-principle" and the masculine or "procreative principle," which are "represented" or "expressed" in the differentiated sexes of the higher organisms. Increasingly after that he dramatized his metaphysics of polarity by endowing it with anthropomorphic features and relationships. He wrote in 1804, for example, that "made pregnant by light, gravity gives birth to the diverse forms of things and delivers them from her fruitful womb to independent life." Driven by the compulsion to progressive individuation, the powers of gravity and light, at the organic stage of evolution, separate first into the bisexual organs in a single plant, then into the separate sexes of the animal and human realms. Yet every individual remains the product of both powers, and each monosexual individual needs its polar opposite in order to fulfill the contrary compulsion of nature toward identity. "This is the secret of eternal love . . . in that each is a whole, yet desires the other and seeks the other." Hence:

> As the being and life of nature rests on the eternal embrace of light and gravity, so the unions of the two sexes, their begetting and propagation of innummerable species, are nothing else than the celebration of the eternal love of those two [powers] which, when they could have been two, yet wanted to be one, and thereby created all of nature.

Such also are the grounds of Coleridge's statement, in his letter to Tulk, that light and gravitation are "the Male and female of the World of Time, in whose wooings, and retirings and nuptial conciliations all other marriages . . . are celebrated inclusively." Like the German *Naturphilosophen*, Coleridge sometimes mythicized his metascience, to humanize his vision of a natural world whose diverse orders of being are linked by familial correspondences to man and mind, and whose processes are compelled by inconscient analogues of love and hate, of oppositions and marriages. Hence those strange passages in Coleridge's speculative natural history that seem to a casual reader to be merely fantasies based on free association. In a manuscript, for example, he declares that, though all the chemical elements contain the two counterpowers, "Gravity and Light with Warmth as the Indifference," yet because of the differing "predominance of some one, Carbon most represents Gravity, Oxygen Light, and Hydrogen Warmth." When, in the sequential combinations of these chemical elements, nature achieves the plant, we find in its generative organ, the flower, "the qualitative product of Oxygen = Light in the outness and splendor of Colors, the qualitative product of Hydrogen = Warmth in the inwardness and sweetness of Fragrance"; and this fragrance Coleridge interprets as the accompaniment of "gentle love," of which the flower serves as a material symbol. And when—in the continuing genetic process of the "interpenetration" of the primal opposites, gravity and light—we reach the level of birds, we find that the colors of their plumage correspond to the colors of the flower, but that a new phenomenon, birdsong, or sound, has replaced the odors of flowers and taken over their biological function in ensuring fertilization. In birds, then, Coleridge says, we have "light in the form (under the power) of Gravity in Color, and Gravity sub formâ et ditione Lucis subditione"—that is, "gravity subordinated to the form and dominion of light"—in the birdsong. The "Sounds and sweet yearning varied by quiet provoking challenging sounds" are thus "the surrogates of the Vegetable Odors—and like these, are the celebrations of the Nuptial moments, the hours of Love."

Such passages provide a bridge between the "sound-like power in light" and the love of all things in the inserted section of "The Eolian Harp." They provide also a broader perspective though which to review the long evolution of that poem between 1795 and 1817, as I described it at the beginning of this essay. In its first short form "The Eolian Harp" had been a love poem which assimilated the relation of the wind and the strings of the harp to the dalliance, the "wooings, and retirings" of the human lovers. It had next been developed into a marriage poem, and also expanded into a metaphysical speculation about "all of animated nature." In its final form it is still a love poem, but a cosmic love poem, in which the love between the poet and his bride becomes the exponent of a universal relationship—the "union of the individual with the Universe" which, Coleridge said, occurs "through love." It is still a marriage poem, too, but one in which the human union becomes, in Coleridge's technical term, an "exponent" of the primal union in which "all other marriages . . . are celebrated inclusively." For in the lines added in 1817 the poet breaks through sensation into vision, in which the phenomenal aspects of the landscape, its colors, music, and odors, are intuited as products and indices of the first manifestations of the creative Word, gravitation and light, in whose multiform unions all nature and life consist; and he goes on to celebrate the world's song of life and joy, which sounds through the wind harp, in which the silent air is merely music unheard, and of which the subject is the one Life that, in marrying all opposites, also weds the single consciousness to the world without. And however we may judge the metascientific and religious beliefs that engendered the moment of vision, they have in this passage been transformed by the imagination from a creed into the poetry of immediate experience, and so compel our participation independently of either belief or disbelief:

> O! the one Life within us and abroad,
> Which meets all motion and becomes its soul,
> A light in sound, a sound-like power in light,
> Rhythm in all thought, and joyance every where—
> Methinks, it should have been impossible

> Not to love all things in a world so fill'd;
> Where the breeze warbles, and the mute still air
> Is music slumbering on her instrument.

Coleridge, we know, printed this passage as an addendum to a poem already set in type. The insertion throws the whole poetic structure into imbalance by locating the climax of the mediation near the beginning. By 1817, however, Coleridge, though capable of poetic moments, was not capable of sustained poetic endeavor; as he said two years later, "Poeta fuimus," but "the Philosopher, tho' pressing with the weight of an Etna, cannot prevent the Poet from occasionally . . . manifesting his existence by smoke traversed by electrical flashes from the Crater." In succeeding printings of "The Eolian Harp" Coleridge simply transferred the added passage into the text without altering its context. But the poet's retraction of his metaphysical speculations in the original conclusion to the poem had never been at ease with its surroundings either in tone or in idiom, and after this high moment of religious as well as metaphysical imagination, the coda is rendered inconsequent as well as anticlimactic.

ANGUS FLETCHER

"Positive Negation"

PERSONIFICATION AND NEGATIVITY

A new or renewed Renaissance mode of personification would seem to be the main yield of the poetry of threshold. The need to renew personification was inherited directly from most eighteenth-century verse except the greatest. During that period the older, conventional personified abstractions slowly froze to death, and now poets had to bring the statues back to life. Frank Manuel, like Hartman in his studies of genius, has shown that the preromantics could reanimate a daemonic universe in the mode of "the new allegory." From another point of view personifications could come alive again because there were once again adequate conditions of rumination. As Michel Foucault has said, the celebratory religions of an earlier time now gave place to "an empty milieu—that of idleness and remorse, in which the heart of man is abandoned to its own anxiety, in which the passions surrender time to unconcern or to repetition in which, finally, madness can function freely." Madness is complete personification. Poets need not, though some in fact did, descend into this generative void.

Yet the conditions of madness and a renewed animism still demand the appropriate poetic forms, which Coleridge had to invent. As Huizinga has remarked, personification is a kind of mental play, and this ludic strain is strong in Coleridge's makeup. Formally, we can say that personification is the figurative emergent of the liminal scene. In the temple there appear to be personi-

---

From *New Perspectives on Coleridge and Wordsworth: Selected Papers from the English Institute.*

Originally entitled "Personification and Negation" and "The Dramatic Personification."

fied abstractions hard at work, virtues and noble essences, while labyrinths are stocked by an equal and opposite number of vices and personified negations—the lions of the Marquess of Bath. Yet these polar opposites perhaps only gain animate life, if they have it, from their participation in the process of passage. Personifications come alive the moment there is psychological breakthrough, with an accompanying liberation of utterance, which in its radical form is a first deep breath. Poetry seeking a fresh animation is poetry seeking to throw off the "smothering weight" of the "Dejection" Ode. Such a poetry must breathe, showing life coming or going away, as in "Limbo."

This breathing may be explained in part, if we reckon with the inner nature of personification. An active, vital, person-making figure must not be a moral cliché. It must not be a machine in a materialist sense. It cannot simply parody the *daimon*. It must be a "real ghost," like the spectral presence of a drug experience or a nightmare or daydream. Hartman has finely observed: "In fact, whenever the question of persona arises in a radical way, whenever self-choosing, self-identification, becomes a more than personal, indeed, prophetic, decision—which happens when the poet feels himself alien to the genius of country or age and determined to assume an adversary role—poetry renews itself by its contact with what may seem to be archaic forces." *This* personifying author will find himself listening, as well as looking, for phantoms.

Above all the phantom must not exist. It must resist existence. To envision and realize the phantom person poetically the poet must empty his imagery of piety and sense, allowing in their place some measure of daemonic possession. The one necessary poetic act will be to utter, to speak, nothingness. To achieve this defining negativity, the poem "Limbo" typically seeks to *posit* negation as the ultimate daemon. By asserting the life of this final nothingness, the poet has reinvented the Ghost of *Hamlet*, the Witches of *Macbeth*, the daemonic powers that abandon Antony, Hermione's statue that comes alive in *The Winter's Tale*. This is a dramatic reinvention; it enghosts and embodies the persons of a play.

The logic of personification requires a phantom nihilism and a return to the heart of drama. This achievement in the later Coleridge depends upon the liminal scene, which permits the greatest experiential intensity at the very moment when the rite of passage denies or reduces the extensity of either the temple or the labyrinth. Drama gets its personifying nothingness—its phantoms—from the making of continuous threshold-scenes. Because the Elizabethan period had so fully subscribed to the norms of drama, its free use of personification—unlike most eighteenth-century personification—goes quite unnoticed. But there is scarcely a line in a Shakespeare sonnet that does not breathe this language of the personified force. Coleridge, in turning to the theme of nothingness, was trying to get back some of that Renaissance utterancy and dramatic presence. Half-brother to Hamlet, he almost succeeded.

THE DRAMATIC PERSONIFICATION

The dramatic or, perhaps more accurately, the melodramatic aspect of the personified "positive negation" must fit a general theory of figurative language. Of late much has been written about the precise differences between metaphor and metonymy. It should by now be clear that the problem of sequence is also a problem of figurative series.

In the modern era, when not only music, but all the arts, have tried to hold their balance while experiencing the loss of tonal center, poets and novelists have testified to the complete loss of cadence within the figurative structures provided by traditional poetics. Atonalism and even aleatory procedures are natural, in an era such as ours. But before its radical breakdowns had occurred, poets could still employ the ancient figurative structures, by bending them.

Such was the Coleridgean scene, where the figurative aspect of threshold and sequence was traditional enough. For the temple and its "timeless" hypotactic structures of sacred being, there was the normal and normative use of part/whole relations, figured in *synecdoche*. For the labyrinth and its unrelieved parataxis the norms were bound to be *metonymic*, as they are in the modern novel, where life is represented in the naturalistic maze of meaningless eventuality. For the threshold the norms were, as the term itself forces us to believe, *metaphoric*. This was the great Romantic rediscovery.

Metaphor has always been the figure of threshold, of passing over. Its symbolic function has always been transfer, transference, metamorphosis, shifting across, through, and over. Metaphor is a semantic process of balancing at the threshold. Metaphor draws the edge of the limen with surgical exactness. When we ally metaphor and the dramatic, we accept the momentary adoption of *an other self*, which the mask of dramatic *persona* makes possible. Significant human integers—men as unique creatures with endowments of a yet universal nature—demand metaphor, because metaphor provides the freedom (not the chaos) of a momentary masking.

The person-making, personifying, gestures of the dramatic poet thus sink down, or fall, to the level of nothingness and ghosts, because at that level of the *ex nihilo* there is a test of the "too, too solid flesh" of man. If a ghost can exist, then so can the hero. If his father has a ghost, Hamlet can avenge (and destroy) him, and *be* Hamlet. Hamlet must personify his father, as it were, in order to be himself. Admiring Shakespeare and identifying with Hamlet, Coleridge brought the study of figurative language into the modern context, by giving it a psycholinguistic basis. This modern grasp of the metaphoric—which Johnson vaguely anticipated in *The Life of Cowley*—seems to require an awareness of the experiential element in the *discordia concors*, an anxiety and liminal trembling which is the experience of living through a metaphor. I have envisaged this tremor as the emergence of a personification, at a threshold. Perhaps these, too, are "only metaphors." If so, they may illuminate the ludic view of theory-building. Coleridge was in nothing so modern as in his theoretical playfulness.

His instincts naturally led him to center his critical theories on the career of Shakespeare, that is, upon a dramatic or dramatistic center. In part this was bardolatry. But Coleridge had a cosmopolitan range of thought, and in his critical theory of method the dramatic (if not always the drama) has fundamental force. For him the drama is the saving test by which men are discovered in their personhood through dialogue. Essaying a poetry and a critique of the liminal moment, he took up arms against the excessive mass of problems which the modern critic knows only too well—our sea of information. Coleridge wanted to find an All that could be One, believed he found it in the final personification—the Trinity—and failed, if he did fail, because he no more than any other man could prevent life's perverse atomism. If he failed to control the world with his personifying eloquence, we should grant him that person and metaphor are the utterance of the gateway, and most men do not want to be standing in gateways. They would rather be inside, or out in the street.

E. S. SHAFFER

The Oriental Idyll

The romantic epic is the "little epic," the pastoral or "minor epic" to which Porphyry in "The Cave of the Nymphs" had assigned a higher, theological level of meaning. It is concerned with the cosmic aetiological drama that is one form of myth. That this level of meaning has been so impressively represented in modern poetry is owing in large part to the reformulation of the significance of myth in the Christian context carried out by the Biblical critics in the 1790s. "Kubla Khan" is one of the first poems to represent the new views of myth and so to usher in a new poetic age.

Lent impetus by Greek studies, the idyll became the most popular form of the eighteenth century, and aesthetic theory confirmed its position. Even major epics, major in length, scope, and intention, tended to have an idyllic core. Schiller spoke of idyll as one of the most characteristic forms of modern poetry, praising Milton's depiction of Adam and Eve as the finest example of it. Its excellence depended not simply on "primaeval communion with the springs of Being," but on suggesting the progress, refinement, and end of Being as well. Schiller suggested the range of the modern poet of idyll:

> Let him [the modern poet] make it his task to create an idyll which carries out that pastoral innocence also in subjects of culture and in all conditions of the most active, passionate life, the most strenuous thought, the most subtle art, the highest social refinement, which, in short, leads man, who cannot any longer return to Arcadia, forwards to Elysium.

From *"Kubla Khan" and the Fall of Jerusalem: The Mythological School in Biblical Criticism and Secular Literature 1770–1880.* The author cited original sources and provided translations. We have deleted the foreign quotations.

The romantic epic operates through a "picture" technique. This was at first tied to the painterly picturesque, as in Lessing's *Laokoon* and in Uvedale Price's theory, well-known in England in the 1790s; but it rapidly acquired greater freedom.

Coleridge was very familiar with these developments, and practised the picturesque method of Gilpin in his notebook descriptions of Germany. A recent critic has commented:

> The picturesque artists' was the wider range of experience that could be managed by discontinuity and planned irregularity, but they kept to the picture-like single perspective. The interior landscape, however, moves naturally towards the principle of multiple perspectives, as in the first two lines of "The Waste Land," where the Christian Chaucer, Sir James Frazer, and Jessie Weston are simultaneously present.

In fact, the exterior landscape, becoming a mobile location, mobile in time and space, developed "multiple perspectives" and so became capable of serving as an interior landscape. The accomplished interchangeability of exterior and interior landscapes is perhaps the most significant achievement of Biblical Orientalism for poetry in the nineteenth century.

The idyll was indeed to be a major nineteenth-century form; one need think only of those two Victorian "apocalyptic epics," Tennyson's *Idylls of the King* and Hopkins's *The Wreck of the Deutschland*. If Tennyson's idyll is the "miniature epic in a luxuriant natural background," as Douglas Bush puts it, Coleridge's is the most miniature epic in the most luxuriant natural background of all. Coleridge's syncretist use of myth, moreover, is echoed everywhere in Victorian poetry not in direct emulation but as a response to the same movements of thought. "Kubla Khan" accomplishes the poetic revolution that in France occupied the period from Chénier's Orphic epic to the "Parnasse." In Germany, not surprisingly, the step from Hölderlin to Rilke scarcely seems to need the mediation of a century.

The visionary tradition had a picturesque perspective built into it. Eichhorn could with justification interpret the Apocalypse as a drama, for in theory, the visionary prophet is actually seeing the events played out in the heavens, as all events are rehearsed before they take place on earth. The heavens are a stage on which he sees the drama unroll:

> But that in these descriptions of visions, prophets, rapt into heaven in ecstatic state, were read to have beheld with their own eyes things to come, realized and represented before the event—this had the power and effect that from it could be concluded, nothing

> happens in the universe which is not first given to be played and watched in the celestial theatre in the presence of God and the heavenly assembly

The mythological Bible critics adapted the visionary theatre, in which the seer was to see the future, to the historian's view of the past. As Strauss put it,

> In the absence of any more genuine account which would serve as a correcting parallel, [the historian] must transplant himself in imagination upon the theatre of action, and strive to the utmost to contemplate the events by the light of the age in which they occurred.

Coleridge's marginalia on Eichhorn's *Commentarius* cluster about the climactic point in the history, that is, around Rev. 9, 13–15, the second of the three woes, when the sixth angel sounds its trumpet. Here the Roman army invades the centre of the city; the destruction of the Temple is imminent, though not to be accomplished until the blaring of the seventh trumpet: "But in the days of the voice of the seventh angel, when he shall begin to sound, the mystery of God should be finished, as he hath declared to his servants the prophets" (Rev. 10, 7).

This moment in the Book of Revelation—

> "And the sixth angel sounded, and I heard a voice from the four horns of the golden altar which is before God,
>
> "Saying to the sixth angel which had the Trumpet, Loose the four angels which are bound in the great river Euphrates"

—is the "pregnant moment" of Lessing's "picture" technique, when the prophetic Laocoön and his sons are seen not in their death agony but calm in the very toils of the serpents. We do not see Troy burn; we are not aware that it will burn, though after the fact the fate of Laocoön is an unmistakable portent. So here, the world is for the first and last time on the brink of a destruction that has been accomplished again and again.

At this idyllic moment in the "little epic" vision of Revelation we see the geography of the city whole—its vertical as well as its cross section—the corrupt city, the place of the imprisonment of the demons and the dead; the Holy City of men; and the celestial city of the New Jerusalem, which Zechariah and Ezekiel envisioned as preexisting and descending into the earthly city with the Messiah's coming. They are united as never before, yet separating out at the trumpet call to judgement, and signalling their final reunion, the single tripartite cosmos of Dante.

As in Shelley's *Prometheus*, a critic tells us, it is the "fusion of outer and mental worlds that become the Romantic substitute for little epic narrative. For them the arresting of a vivid moment of experience, or 'spot of time' in Wordsworth's phrase, took precedence over any ritual order of events." But in "Kubla" we see that the romantics did not "substitute" for the little epic narrative – such a substitution would be inexplicable – but transformed the epic narrative itself into a spot of time that stood for and absorbed the whole. Ritual is not so much abandoned as transfixed at the gesture that implies the necessity of its past and future repetition.

Eichhorn's interpretation of these verses, and Coleridge's dissent from it, carry us from the neoclassic epic and the apocalyptic lay to the centre of the sacred geography of "Kubla." Eichhorn gives the historical interpretation: the Roman army enter the *theatrum* and find the "demon" enemy, some of whom they imprison. ("Angel" may be "demon" in Hebrew folklore.) The Jews, then, are imprisoned. In the Euphrates? Eichhorn comments,

> The place of imprisonment we owe solely to the fancy of the poet, and it allows of no interpretation in accordance with the historical destruction of Jerusalem. Indeed, prophetic poetry postulates that each thing to be declared in the song must be related to specific places and people. Which ones? The Roman army could not be said to have proceeded to surround the Jews from the Euphrates; for it had set out from Achaia, reached Alexandria, and, increased by legions of Ptolemais and of Caesarea, invaded Judea. (See Josephus, *The Jewish War*, Book 3, chap. 1.3.)

He points out that in Old Testament passages "the Euphrates" appears in apposition with "the great river" (Genesis 15, 18; Deut. 1, 7; Jos. 1, 4).

Coleridge condemns the method that makes Eichhorn impotent to interpret this and a variety of other passages: "Eichhorn's great error is in carrying his general meanings, & his resolutions of particular passages into mere poetic garnish, to an excess."

Eichhorn, in short, allegorizes too fully in a historical sense, and when allegory fails him, he gives up, and attributes the passage to mere poetic fancy. This misses the real sense and significance of the apocalyptic style.

Coleridge justifies the apocalyptic poet's imagination. He protests:

> I wonder at this assertion from so acute and ingenious a Man as Eichhorn.
>
> First, as I have noted – as Rome was to be symbolized as *Babylon*, the River must be Euphrates. But that the four mighty Destroyers were bound in the great River "up a great River, great as any Sea"

> is according to the code of popular Beliefs—the bad Spirits are sent bound to the bottom of the Red *Sea*—But a *Sea* would not have been appropriate or designative of the Roman Power—while the Tyber was a perfect Synonime of Rome, and the trite poetic exponent of the Roman Empire—Now the Tyber could not but be changed into the Euphrates—Therefore the ἐπὶ τῷ ποτάμῷ τῷ μεγάλῳ Ἐυφϱάτῃ is no mere poetic ornature, but a very significant & requisite amplification.
>
> Four giant Daemons could not be imagined bound or chained up in a vast *City*—this would have been far too indefinite—But neither in any Dungeon or Tower in Babylon—That would have been as much too narrow, & besides too gross an outrage to probability, & above all, too little ghostliness—with great judgement therefore the sublime Seer transfers their prison to the River but amplifies the River into all the magnificence of a Sea for the imagination of the Readers. Only read the Greek words aloud ore rotundo: and you will feel the effect.—Add to this the Hebrew Associations with the Euphrates—Captivity after bloody Wars, and the Siege, Sack, and utter Destruction of their chief City & Temple!—Is it not, I again say, wonderful that Eichhorn should overlook all these so striking and exquisite proprieties in a "soli debetur poetae ingenio"!!

Now it is not impossible that Eichhorn is right. But what Coleridge does here is characteristic of the symbolism of "Kubla." First, the three great sacred cities—Jerusalem, Babylon, and Rome—are blended; the symbolism is not sequential, as in Eichhorn's scheme, but simultaneous. Because Rome, too, must fall, and the city of wickedness is Babylon, the captive demons in Jerusalem may be imprisoned in "the Euphrates." Coleridge's note exclaims: "As Rome was to be Babylon, the River must of course be Euphrates!" The references are interchangeable, they flow in and out of each other. Geographical mobility is uncannily combined with exact location, timelessness with precise and known history The superimposition and blending of meaning is perfect.

Nor is the method far from Revelation itself: "And their dead bodies shall lie in the street of the great city, which spiritually is called Sodom and Egypt, where also our Lord was crucified" (Rev 11, 8). All great cities are places of corruption, and may be called by their names; and in all places of corruption was, and is, the Lord crucified. This is unstated typology of immense extent.

Especially characteristic of "Kubla" is the way the river expands at a touch into a sea—size is as immaterial as place and time—while retaining all the connotations of that particular named river and acquiring all those of the sea. Both river and sea are prominent in the Apocalypse. Babylon's seat is also "upon many waters" (Jeremiah 51, 13). As Farrer remarks, "we may suppose the side-streams and canals of Euphrates spreading around her." Farrer points out, too, that John's river of blood at the time of the destruction "even unto the horses' bridles" is a reference to Ezekiel 47 and 48, 20 where in the vision of Jerusalem the river of life issuing from it is measured, on all four sides equally, by the depth of the stream on the body of a man trying to ford it.

The sea is of course, as Lowth put it, the "place where the wicked after death were supposed to be confined; and which, from the destruction of the old world by the deluge, the covering of the Asphaltic vale with the Dead Sea, etc. was believed to be situated *under the waters*." Moreover, the sea is a "ritual name." John's vision begins with a presentation of the great "Sea" of the heavenly temple (Rev. 4, 6) which refers to the laver in the Temple, and, in Christianity, to baptism: "Baptism is a 'sea,' indeed, it is the Red Sea water through which the people of God are saved, and separated from heathen Egypt" (I Cor. 10, 1–2).

The Old Testament context of "caves of ice" is even more striking. In the fourth of Herder's *Oriental Dialogues*, which marks the high point in his splendid dithyramb on nature in Oriental poetry, and its dependence on the One God, he shows the connection of God's creativity with His destructive powers, using the Book of Job as his text. The abyss, the unfathomable ocean, is both the place of the dead and the vast region of the unborn. The abyss, or destruction, "hath no covering before Him." "The abyss where light had never pierced, stands uncovered—this is the awful, the dark moment, when CREATION begins." Herder follows the steps of the creation in Job 38: first the founding of the earth, then the formation of the sea:

> The earth is represented as an edifice, founded and measured by the Almighty; and no sooner are its foundations laid, and the corner-stone fixed, than all the *sons* of God and the *morning-stars* raise an acclamation of joy and a song of praise to the great Creator. Now comes the formation of the ocean:
>
> Who shut up the sea within doors,
> When it brake forth, as it were, from the womb?

Herder cites the passage, "Hast thou entered into the springs of the sea? . . . Hast thou entered into the treasures of the snow?"

Hath the rain a father?

> The drops of the dew, who hath begotten them?
> Out of whose womb cometh forth the ice?
>
> The waters rise into mountains, and become as stone,
> And the surface of the waves is bound in frost.

Herder glosses the passage:

> Above, the light comes forth in streams, and the east-wind carries them over the land: the Father of heaven and the earth forms canals for the rain and marks out a course for the clouds. Below, the waters become a rock, and the waves of the sea are held in chains of ice.

The "caves of ice," then, mark a most dramatic moment in the creation: the emergence at once of solidity and variety out of the sea's abyss. The primaeval relation between creation and destruction is the main formal principle of Revelation, as well as of "Kubla." Coleridge, of course, had no need of Herder to remind him of these passages from the Book of Job. But Herder sets Coleridge's enterprise in its context, even ending his chapter with poems of Ossian: "To the Setting Sun," "To the Morning Sun," "To the Moon," "Address to the Evening Star."

And of course one could go on in this vein: a woman presides over each phase of Revelation, and in each of her incarnations she is familiar in the annals of the Old Testament. Jerusalem wails for her imprisoned "demon" leaders (no mere "Gothick" touch this, although "demon-lover" undoubtedly owes something to the vogue for Bürger and perhaps Wieland). In the note previously quoted referring to the Jewish leaders, Coleridge spoke of the Hebrew "Amarus," a link to the "Amahra" of the first draft of "Kubla" and to Milton's Mt. Amara, which critics have agreed was a major reference point for "Kubla" (though no such link is needed), as well as connecting with the sea itself, the bitter waters. The "cedarn" cover of the sacred mountain of Lebanon is proverbial. The "ancestral voices prophesying war" are not a trivial detail filched from Purchas about the priests of the Khan, but the heart of the apocalyptic warning of the seer echoing his great prophetic forbears Jeremiah and Ezekiel, distant and unattended.

The number symbolism which is so conspicuous a feature of Oriental systems was also given a Biblical origin or at least sanction: through one verse from the Apocrypha, Wisdom of Solomon 11, 21: "number was sanctified as a form-bestowing factor in the divine work of creation." The very idea of the Bible as containing all wisdom is a recommendation of brevity. Again the range is from the popular-sententious—like the numerical apothegm from the

Arabian Nights, "Always use the toothpick for two and seventy virtues lie therein"—to the systematic holy mystification of the prophets. "Kubla Khan" contains a considerable amount of sacred numerology, though in a very refined form. The main examples—"So twice five miles of fertile ground/With walls and towers were girdled round" and "Five miles meandering with a mazy motion"—may well have been suggested by Ezekiel's measurements of the Holy City.

In apocalyptic mysticism, the Book of Ezekiel, with its vision of the throne-chariot in the first chapter, and its measurements of the celestial city in the last, was of particular importance. Indeed, St. Jerome mentions a Jewish tradition which forbids the study of the beginning and the end of the Book of Ezekiel before the completion of the thirtieth year. It is, of course, the model for the New Jerusalem of Revelation. In Coleridge's Notebooks for May 1799 appears the significant collocation of "The Tarter Chan" and "The Fable of the Four Wheels," that is, the chariot from Ezekiel.

> [Y]e shall offer an oblation unto the Lord, an holy portion of the land: the length shall be the length of five and twenty thousand reeds, and the breadth shall be ten thousand. This shall be holy in all the borders thereof round about.
>
> 2. Of this there shall be for the sanctuary five hundred in length, with five hundred in breadth, square round about; and fifty cubits round about for the suburbs thereof.
>
> 3. And of this measure shalt thou measure the length of five and twenty thousand, and the breadth of ten thousand: and in it shall be the sanctuary and the most holy place (45, 1–3).

The incantatory numbers, based on five, continue throughout the measuring of the sacred river waters on the body of the prophet:

> 15. And the five thousand, that are left in the breadth over against the five and twenty thousand, shall be a profane place for the city, for dwelling, and for suburbs: and the city shall be in the midst thereof.
>
> 20. All the oblation shall be five and twenty thousand by five and twenty thousand: ye shall offer the holy oblation foursquare, with the possession of the city.
>
> 21. And the residue shall be for the prince, on the one side and

> on the other of the holy oblation, and of the possession of the city, over against the five and twenty thousand of the oblation toward the east border, and westward over against the five and twenty thousand toward the west border, over against the portions for the prince: and it shall be the holy oblation; and the sanctuary of the house shall be in the midst thereof (48, 15–21).

It is not surprising that this obsessive five, a holy number, ambiguously indicating the sanctuary and in the centre the most holy place, the city and the suburbs, and then the entire surrounding area of land, in the prophet who provided the pattern for the Book of Revelation, should be used by Coleridge as a sign of the tradition of the coming of the New Jerusalem.

To go on allegorizing "Kubla" in this vein would not be quite futile, for the Christianized Old Testament context was certainly the primary one for Coleridge. Nevertheless, it is inadequate to the poem, as all interpretations of "Kubla" have been, for it fails to take account of the method of simultaneous Oriental contexts developed in half a century of Biblical and literary studies. In rejecting our simple allegory of Revelation, we shall see the process by which the renascence of allegory in Biblical criticism modulated into romantic symbolism.

The impetus to a new mythological understanding came from many sides: from explorers' and travellers' reports, from Sir William Jones's *Asiatick Researches*, from the *philosophes*' speculations on the nature of primitive man. But the most profound alteration in attitudes and ideas was brought about when Christianity faced the fact of its own mythological character. The Biblical critics' new views of myth, clearly stated by Eichhorn and Gabler in the 1790s, represent the most subtle and influential, if desperate, Christian apologetics. In myth, the legendary, the monstrous, and the traditional could be accommodated by historical scholarship; in myth, "fact" and "fiction" could be merged into a new form of truth.

The visionary Oriental landscape of poetry bears the traces of this whole difficult history; it emerges at the end of the century in a new form, nowhere so fully or so gracefully achieved as in "Kubla Khan." Far from reflecting ignorance about the Orient, far from any mere search for the exotic, the ornamental, or the artificial, far from being a mere "expressive" reaction in favour of the primitive, the new mythical landscape has absorbed the vast quantity of new information and the insights of an Oriental scholarship gradually freed, almost against its will, from the literalism both of inherited tradition and of rationalist historicizing.

As the new view of myth began to emerge, the Edenic scene intensified in significance through the multiplication of simultaneous reference: the primordial myths persist not only through all the stages of Christian thought, dressed up anew at each major religious metamorphosis, they appear in all religions and nations. "Kubla" represents in its eighteenth-century form the great primordial myth of the origin and end of civilization in the religious spirit of man.

What "spot" is it we actually see in "Kubla" at the pregnant visionary moment? The landscape of Revelation is there, certainly: the sacred river, the fountain, the sea where the forces of darkness are imprisoned, the woman both holy and demonic, the sacred enclosure of the Temple. But the immediate impression is, of course, primarily pastoral, paradisaical, and Oriental, and the imagery has always been felt, rightly, to have been displaced from the undeniable Biblical base. Yet the first clues are in the Bible. Goethe reminds us that "in speaking of Oriental poetry, we must take note of the Bible, as the oldest collection." One of Goethe's favourite books of the Bible was the Book of Ruth, "the most charming little unity, epic and idyll, that has been handed down to us."

One of the most charming little epic-idylls of the eighteenth century was the pastoral poet Salomon Gessner's *Der Tod Abels, The Death of Abel*, a poem to which Coleridge often referred admiringly. It is a good poem, deserving of the vast popularity it enjoyed in Germany and in England; even in the poor English translation by Mrs Collyer, in its ninth edition by 1768, something of its virtue is preserved. Gessner made a skilful fusion of the religious epic, the idyll, and the Oriental setting.

Just before the most likely date for the composition of "Kubla Khan," 18 November 1797, Coleridge and Wordsworth on their walking tour planned to make the Valley of Stones the scene of a prose tale in the manner of Gessner's *Death of Abel*, and probably within a few days *The Wanderings of Cain* was begun and, as a collaborative enterprise, abandoned. At the same time, certainly in the course of the tour, the idea of the *Lyrical Ballads* was conceived. Coleridge retired to the farm between Porlock and Linton with the setting of the Biblical idyll and the idea of the lyrical ballad uppermost in his mind.

The setting has much in common with that of the Song of Songs, as Goethe described it (and for that matter with the Book of Ruth):

> Through and through the poem wafts the mild breeze of the loveliest district of Canaan; rural circumstances of mutual trust, vineyards, gardens, groves of spices, something of urban confinement too, but then a king's court with its formal splendours in the background. The main theme nevertheless remains the burning love of

> two young hearts, who seek, find, repel, and attract one another amid circumstances of exceedingly great simplicity

This landscape, at once rural arcadia, city, and court, is an archetype of Oriental poetry.

These descriptions of the small "city-kingdom" (Newton's phrase) are a commonplace of the numerous eighteenth-century efforts to write a complete universal history of civilization, sacred and profane. Newton, Vico, Boulainvilliers began with a universal prehistory based on the old notion of "the four ages of the world." They mused on the condition of the first men after the Flood, prior to the founding of cities.

> The first men after the flood lived in caves of the earth & woods & planes well watered by rivers for feeding their herds & flocks, such as were the planes of Babylonia, Assyria, & Egypt. By degrees they cut down the woods & learnt to build houses & towns of brick in the planes of Assyria, Babylonia & Egypt. Thence men spread into places less fertile.

They described the gradual formation of human communities, from the isolated units of the mobile desert patriarchs through the establishment of religious centres and the agglomeration into larger urban, national, and finally the vast imperial monarchies of Egypt, Assyria, Persia, and Greece. All empires were held to have shown the same pattern of growth. Newton, equally interested in precise calculations and in general laws of development, tried to plot the size of the ancient city-kingdoms, and he held them to have been very small, comparable with contemporary English villages and corporation towns. He computed that before the victory of the Israelites there had been about 1000 walled cities in the land, the large number indicative of their puny dimensions. He illustrates the particulate origin of empires by "the small size of the army, hardly more than a collection of retainers, that Father Abraham had arrayed against the kings of Sodom and Gomorrah."

On the one hand, these were scientific descriptions, laws of growth, intended as a counterpart to the physical history of the world; on the other, they were celebrated, as De Bougainville, secretary of the Académie des Inscriptions et Belles-Lettres, celebrated Newton's, as "l'histoire de l'esprit humain." A modern treatment like Lewis Mumford's *The City in History* is remarkably similar in spirit and in detail to its eighteenth-century forerunners.

In Gessner's poem, we find the ancient city-kingdom described at the point of its Biblical origin: the settlement built by Adam and Eve after their expulsion from Eden. We are shown the still lovely landscape of a holy mountain, reminiscent of Eden, still visited by spirits, yet new and bleak, a wholly human settlement, a raw stockade barely maintained against the wilderness, an altar visited as much in despair as in reverence. Adam and Eve echo their situation, wonderfully combining their original patriarchal dignity, simplicity and virtue with new labours, plaints, and pains. Gessner with great success and delicacy created a world half original paradise, half fallen nature.

Just this landscape, combining still-remembered paradise, wilderness, enclosed city, and cultivated court, is captured in "Kubla." City and country, rural yet populous, idyllic yet threatening, holy yet secular, sacred yet fallen, court and cot–it is tempting to see the stereotypes of the eighteenth century merging into those that will dominate the nineteenth. Just for this moment, in this exotic setting, they exist simultaneously, and express a permanent condition of man.

In the Biblical poems of the eighteenth century, this primeval Oriental scene recurs in a dazzling variety of forms. "Eden" was an immensely diversified scene, a mobile location, not merely of the Creation and the Fall but of that characteristically eighteenth-century topos, the founding state of civilization in general, the centre of *Urmonotheismus*, archetypal monotheism. Typically, as in Gessner, the scene was paradise displaced, paradise already lost though still visible, paradise beset by the ambiguities of human culture. Only with the Fall could civilization begin and develop. Eden had taken on new significance for a century that liked to believe in the progress of civilization and yet profoundly knew its corruption.

After the first night spent outside Paradise, Adam gathers new courage:

> Seest thou, EVE, that river, which, like a huge serpent, winds in bright slopes through the meadows? The hill on its bank, seems, at this distance, like a garden full of trees, and its top is cover'd with verdure.

Adam and Eve approach the brilliant scene:

> We now advanc'd to the eminence. Its gentle ascent was almost cover'd with bushes and fertile shrubs. On the summit, in the midst of fruit-trees, grew a lofty cedar, whose thick branches form'd an extensive shade, which was render'd more cool and delightful, by a limpid brook, that ran in various windings among the flowers. This spot afforded a prospect so immense, that the sky was only bounded by the dusky air; the sky forming a concave around us, that appear'd wherever we turn'd, to touch the distant mountains.

Here, then, are two natural domes, suggesting the presence of a celestial infinity, in a spot which, as Adam says, is "a faint shadow of Paradise, whose blissful bowers we must never more behold." He concludes: "Receive us, majestic cedar, under thy shade." Coleridge had a wealth of fully developed and directly relevant poetic description of fallen paradises at hand.

If Gessner maintained a sense of the patriarchal dignity of Adam and Eve even in their fallen state, Klopstock in *Der Tod Adams, The Death of Adam*, made palpable the fear of what must happen to the race when the memory of paradise is finally extinguished. In the morning the Angel of Death appears to Adam and tells him that he will die that day when the sun sinks onto the cedar forest that covers the slopes of Eden. The geography is exactly and imposingly generalized: on one of the mountain peaks surrounding that of Eden, the altars of the fallen Adam and Even still face, over the chasm, a dimming Eden. Adam addresses Seth:

> How dreadful looks this earth, my son! no more
> That fertile earth, which I of late beheld
> O'erspread with roses, or in whose deep bosom
> The branching cedars struck fantastic root.

Adam looks in the direction of Eden, no longer able to see it.

> O ye happy plains,
> Ye lofty mountains, where a thousand springs
> Rise; and, with streams luxurious, pour down
> The steep declivities; ye vales eternal,
> With cooling shades and laughing verdure crown'd
> Let us depart,
> My son; my feeble sight can scarce discern
> Distinctly ought, nor from the river's stream
> Knows the firm earth.

These "Forests elder than the Sun," as Coleridge called them, become an obsessive image in the poem. Adam, looking in the direction of Eden:

> *Adam.* Alas, my child,
> I see them not. The sun perhaps with clouds
> Is darken'd o'er.
> *Seth.* The clouds are thick; yet shade not
> All the sun's brightness.
> *Adam.* From the cedar's forest,
> Seems it far distant yet?

Again, in Act III, Seth looks out towards Eden:

> *Seth*. The sun declines apace and the tall cedars
> Fade on the eye:—oh father, father, bless us.
> *Adam*. The sun already at the cedar's forest!

Thus Eden, now screened by the cedars' cover and veiled by failing vision, becomes the seal of death for the fallen Adam.

This mountainous, cedar-covered scene is, of course, the Hebraic, the Palestinian paradise reflected in Coleridge's lines:

> And here were forests ancient as the hills
> Enfolding sunny spots of greenery.
>
> But oh! that deep romantic chasm which slanted
> Down the green hill athwart a cedarn cover!

As popular as the creation story was its repetition in reverse at the time of the Flood, when degraded civilization was destroyed and patriarchal simplicity restored. More than one theorist of the origins of religion chose this as the crucial historical moment: whether in Vico's compelling descriptions of the distressed state of postdiluvian man, out of which rose his worship of ferocious gods, or in Boulanger's mild, suffering, melancholy, and beneficent postdiluvian primitive, this second Fall seemed to usher history in, to be a testing-place for man's secular psychology when the last authentic memory of prelapsarian Eden had been dispersed. "Kubla," with its perfected simultaneities of reference, shows us both: the Eden of the first creation and the Eden of God's wrath on the rising verge of the Flood waters, where the ancestral voices prophesy in vain.

Although [Sir William] Jones opted for Iran [as the center from which all other civilizations radiated], his own remarks support another possibility: Abyssinia, the scene of Milton's false paradise, Mt. Amara. "Ethiopia and Hindustan were peopled or colonized by the same extraordinary race," the people said by Apuleius to have "received the first light of the rising sun." Jones cites the tradition (treated by D'Herbelot as a fable, but by Newton as genuine) that colonists from Edom had carried the arts and sciences of astronomy, navigation, and letters into Italy; and since the invention and propagation of letters and astronomy were widely agreed to be of Indian origin, the Idumeans must have been a branch of the Hindu race. The "goddess with many arms," representing the powers of Nature, dominated both Egypt (as Isis) and Bengal (as Isani).

Abyssinia was noted for its wisdom; Aesop was an Abyssinian, and his apologues are related to the Hindu. Lowth and Eichhorn both credited the great culture of the Book of Job to its origin in Idumea, as Eichhorn put it, "from time immemorial the seat of Oriental sages." The links of Abyssinia with the Bible were stronger still: for many had argued in the eighteenth century, among them Bishop Warburton, that Moses, for better or for worse, had gleaned all his wisdom from the Egyptian priests. Jones adduces a linguistic connection as well, holding that "the Jews and Arabs, the Assyrians, or second Persian race, the people who spoke Syraick, and a numerous tribe of Abyssinians, used one primitive dialect" which was wholly distinct from that of the first race of Persians and Indians, Romans, Greeks, Goths, Egyptians (or Ethiopians).

If, then, one were seeking a geographical centre of Oriental civilization as closely linked with Mosaic history as possible, Abyssinia would be a more attractive choice than Iran. Coleridge in "Kubla Khan" distributes his favours almost equally between the icy Tartary of the Khan and the Abyssinia of the "damsel with the dulcimer", Abyssinia as the only actual place named in the poem carries the day. The Christian implication is still uppermost, though deliberately obscured and merged with its equivalent myths:

> A damsel with a dulcimer
> In a vision once I saw·
> It was an Abyssinian maid,
> And on her dulcimer she played,
> Singing of Mount Abora.

The Nile and India were thus connected by a stronger link than "a hook of memory" between two isolated passages of Coleridge's reading; Jones even pays tribute to Bruce's modern description of the Nile, in the course of his discussion of the primal origin of civilization and the reasons for universal moon worship. Coleridge had no need to make "free associations" in the manner of Lowes: the context was well established.

Coleridge's syncretism, even working within the bounds of Christianity, gave him a range and depth and sympathy hardly to be found in any orthodoxy. It is just possible that a Buddhist might have a vision of the Virgin Mary—or of an Abyssinian maid. In that primitive yet cosmopolitan dawn just before the beginning of the nineteenth century it was not so evidently necessary that "The gods of China are always Chinese," as Wallace Stevens put it for our own tribal times in "Two or Three Ideas." Coleridge's transcendental enterprise was to lay bare the source of mythology, the sense for a God in the human race. In "Kubla Khan" we see the enterprise making its earliest and most attractive appearance, as we find there the sense for a God in its first pristine form, before articulation, before all tradition. It is first revelation, as it is last.

KATHLEEN COBURN

Experience into Thought

It is my main concern here to show that Coleridge *experienced* what he thought and *thought* only what he experienced. When he met his own thought or a similar experience in a book, as in a friend, he jumped for joy. In reading, as in experiencing, his was the great art of recognition, a surprisingly rare gift that goes with acute logicality.

The autobiographical entry makes evident Coleridge's own awareness of a split in his childhood experiences—at least one split. On the one hand, there was the sense of the outer human world, largely painful, and very lonely—to the point of depriving him of many of the sheer physical sunshine joys of childhood. On the other, there were the traumas of inner states, both painful and pleasant, from fantasies and daydreams.

His own accounts make it clear that Coleridge's mental life in childhood was precocious, far in advance of his sensory experiences. When those did (rarely) come, they were rapturous:

> I remember, that at eight years old I walked with him (my father) one winter evening from a farmer's house, a mile from Ottery—& he told me the names of the stars—and how Jupiter was a thousand times larger than our world—and that the other twinkling stars were Suns that had worlds rolling round them—& when I came home, he shewed me how they rolled round—/. I heard him with a profound delight & admiration; but without the least mixture of wonder or incredulity. For from my early reading of Faery Tales,

From *Experience into Thought: Perspectives in the Coleridge Notebooks*. Originally entitled "Lecture One."

> & Genii &c &c—my mind had been habituated *to the Vast*—& I never regarded *my senses* in any way as the criteria of my belief.

But then there came in his sixteenth year the effect of making friends for the first time—"a bursting forth from misery & mopery" into the physical world the sensations of which were all the more exuberant for having been so long dammed up, so acute that to a conscience predisposed to guilt they were almost unbearable. By the time he was twenty-two he was writing to a friend: "I would to God, that I too possessed the tender irritableness of unhandled [?unbridled] Sensibility—mine is a sensibility gangrened with inward corruption"—and "the keen searching of the air from without!" (Where the punctuation appears to be misleading: I have substituted a dash for a comma.)

That the stresses of inner conflict did not destroy him was owing in the main, I believe, to two characteristics that help to make him interesting now, as they did to his friends in his own time. His rebellion against the intellectual complacency and social corruption of his day, hardened as the social "cake of custom" was in the seemingly endless reign of George III, his distrust of the disparity between outer appearance and living reality, made him an original and independent critic of that society on every front. It is a mistake to think of Coleridge as a rebel only in his youth; he was in some respects radical all his life. The radicalism of his Cambridge days, wildly idealistic and unrealistic though it may have been, probably helped to stabilize his sanity. It gave an overintrospective lad those saving outward thrusts of mind, from sympathy towards the unconforming, the martyrs, the unrespected outcasts of various hues and times.

The other, less conspicuous but very potent characteristic (it had its dark underside) was a gift for minute and searching observation, an intellectual but not merely cerebral exercise that gave the mental and emotional thrusts inward a quality such as the world has seldom seen, even among poets. It is impossible to exaggerate Coleridge's uncertainties about himself and equally impossible to understand how, by what mental and physical powers he was able, in the swirling waters of self-doubt of which he was the vortex, to maintain the degree and range of curiosity, psychological insight, and a peculiarly objective introspection necessary to him as poet, critic, and philosopher. We look at it not as at an interesting case study but because out of this self-scepticism and critical observation Coleridge built a poetry and a philosophy; and from it he reached out to other minds in which he saw similar struggles behind quite different achievements.

It is difficult in our post-Freud times to conceive what it was like two hundred years ago to think about mental anxieties and illnesses. Dr. Battie's *Treatise on Madness* (1738) and his treatment of the mentally ill in asylums and "mad houses" were still so little understood for decades as to give his name,

Battie, in cruel popular usage, to his patients. What did it mean then to inquire "how much lies *below* [man's] own Consciousness," a concept not easily grasped at any time? Yet in 1794 Coleridge referred to "depths of Being, below, & radicative of, all Consciousness." Such inquiries came out of his own experiences, including the horrors of the night. In the following notebook entry Coleridge is writing about marital unhappiness, and the frightening combined effect in sleep of "Despair" and "Hope," and "Guilt." Something a bit like Macbeth's vision of Banquo's ghost, or Hamlet's of his father, seems to be present.

> Hence even in dreams of Sleep the Soul never *is*, because it either cannot or dare not be, any <ONE> THING; but lives in *approaches* —touched by the outgoing pre-existent Ghosts of many feelings—It feels for ever as a blind man with his protended Staff dimly thro' the medium of the instrument by which it pushes off, & in the act of repulsion, O for the eloquence of Shakspeare, who alone could feel & yet know how to embody these conceptions, with as curious a felicity as the thoughts are subtle. As if the finger which I saw with eyes had, as it were, another finger invisible—Touching me with a ghostly touch, even while I feared the real Touch from it. What if in certain cases Touch acted by itself, co-present with vision, yet not coalescing—then I should see the finger as at a distance, and yet feel a finger touching which was nothing but it & yet was not it/ the two senses cannot co-exist without a sense of causation/the *touch* must be the effect of that Finger, I see, yet it's not yet near to me, <and therefore it is not it; & yet it is it. Why,> it is it in an imaginary preduplication. N.B. there is a passage in the second Part of Wallenstein, expressing not explaining the same feeling—The Spirits of great Events Stride on before the events—it is in one of the last two or 3 Scenes.
>
> How few would read this Note—nay, *any one?*/and not think the writer mad or drunk!

The richness and variety of Coleridge's notes on sleep and dreaming, as seen in the notebooks, is a subject in itself for an experienced analyst with the soul of a poet and a wide reading equal to Coleridge's own. No wonder no one has explored it. One can scarcely imagine what it was like to write or think like this about dreams at a time when dreams were treated in the context of prophecy, foreboding, tabus, and ghosts. Astonishingly prescient about what he called "the afflictions of sleep," Coleridge said, "Every Dream has its scheme," contrasting dream with delirium in this respect. What are the links with such feelings as fear, terror, and rage, he wonders. The "Dreamatis

Personae are combined with *motives*, generally suggested by the Passions." Again he compares dreams with nightmare and with reverie. He had asserted the dogma, he says, that "the Forms & Feelings of sleep are *always* the reflections & confused Echoes of our waking Thoughts & Experiences" but now he wonders if this is so. He has also been curious about the link between bodily pain, a cramp, any physical sensation, and nightmares; he concludes that "the Terror does not arise out of a painful Sensation but is itself a specific sensation." He asks, whence the weeping and self-pity in dreams? He is aware of sexual elements. And he wonders why certain kinds of dreams of fear and anger regularly go back to school days and Christ's Hospital. But there are about three hundred entries on dreams and sleep, in which the very questions he asks himself point to the slenderness of our knowledge of our inner life.

I turn here to some other kinds of self-examination, also typical. Many of us can recognize this one:

> If one thought leads to another, so often does it blot out another—This I find, when having lain musing on my Sopha, a number of interesting Thoughts have suggested themselves, I conquer my bodily indolence & rise to record them in these books, alas! my only Confidants.—The first Thought leads me on indeed to new ones; but nothing but the faint memory of having had them remains of the others, which had been even more interesting to me.—I do not know, whether this be an idiosyncracy, a peculiar disease, or *my* particular memory—but so it is with *me*—My Thoughts crowd each other to death.

That was written in 1808 when Coleridge was thirty years old, and already, Hamlet-like, applying the word *disease* to himself.

Three years earlier he had jotted down an example of this form of forgetfulness:

> What is the right, the virtuous Feeling, and consequent action, when a man having long meditated & perceived a certain Truth finds another & a foreign Writer, who has handled the same with an approximation to the Truth, as he <had previously> conceived it?—Joy!—Let Truth make her Voice *audible!* While I was preparing the pen to write this remark, I lost the train of Thought which had led me to it. I meant to have asked something else, now forgotten: for the above answers itself—it needed no new answer, I trust, in my Heart. 14 April, 1805—

In fact I suspect the "train of Thought" he lost track of was in the observation immediately preceding on the page overleaf!

> Saturday Night, April 14, 1805—In looking at objects of Nature while I am thinking, as at yonder moon dim-glimmering thro' the dewy window-pane, I seem rather to be seeking, as it were *asking*, a symbolical language for something within me that already and forever exists, than observing any thing new. Even when that latter is the case, yet still I have always an obscure feeling as if that new phaenomenon were the dim Awaking of a forgotten or hidden Truth of my inner Nature/It is still interesting as a Word, a Symbol! It is Λογος, the Creator! <and the Evolver!>

The active participating response to the book of nature is both projective and receptive: inner and outer worlds come together in the Word, the Symbol. Perhaps the daring application of the word Logos to himself made him drop the subject, in fright.

He reflects on the nature of *habit* on which he had once proposed to write an essay:

> Of *Habit*—O how miserable this makes me, not only as recalling an evil *habit*, but as recalling one of its consequences—what glorious, original Notions I had of this untreated of subject 5 years ago—& nothing done:—& I understand it less now by far, than I did then—All the dim Analoga of Habit in Inanimate forms [are] either the Effect of some actual alteration in the substance of the thing—ex. gr. an old Violin as giving a mellower sound than new wood—or act only defectively, as the rumple in a Leaf of long continuance—None of these seem even to give a decent *Simile* for the increase (almost indefinite) of *Power* by Practice in a vital Being—the muscular motions of a capital Performress on the Piano Forte, or (O bless the fair white arms of dear departed Laura Montague!) on the Pedal Harp—&c &c &c.—

(It would be cheating to spare you the comedy of some of Coleridge's sentimental illustrations.)

Clearly he knew he was blocked by his own emotions connected with this subject of habit. The introspective initiative is patently clear, but notice how it moves outwards, to the more objective general question of the physiology of habit—and how does practice increase *power*—even muscularly? If only he could understand—*and* apply that!

The sense of contradiction then, between the world within him and the world without, was there from earliest days and seems to have fostered a capacity for asking questions that went on developing throughout his life. Sometimes simply inquisitive, sometimes rebellious, spontaneous inquiry of all sorts was second nature to Coleridge; it brought some kind of focusing of the sensory, the mental, the physical, the personal restlessness. Nothing is too minute or trivial; nothing too fundamental or vast.

> 1. Feb. 1805. Friday. Malta. Of the Millions that use the Pen, how many (quere) understand the theory of this simple machine, the action of the Slit, Etc?—I confess, ridiculous as it must appear to those who do understand it, that I have not been able to answer the question off-hand to myself, having only this moment thought of it.

One cold damp Malta morning in January 1805 having just recorded that he has been appointed Public Secretary pro tem he reflects on the wood fire in his fireplace:

> On a heap of glowing wood embers throw a quantity of large and small Chips and Shavings—& they will all quietly and moulderingly change into the substance of fire—but apply even the smallest Match with the faintest blue *flame* and tho' with a thousandfold less Heat it will set the whole instantly on flame.—A good Simile for sympathy of a predisposed multitude with the courage of some Massaniello [a seventeenth-century Spanish demagogue who led a revolt]—but physically, what is the reason of this phaenomenon! that flame is ignited vapor says nothing till one knows what it is that ignites vapor. Can it be supposed that the tapering blue flame of a match or even of a bit of phosphorus is more intense† than that of a whole Hearth of glowing Embers?—Is not some business of affinity concerned here/the heat in the flame existing in a state of greater *repulsion* & therefore more eager to combine with bodies out of itself—

Then he puts a footnote to the word *intense:*† "a bit of phosphorus is more intense than that of a whole Hearth of glowing Embers?" saying to himself, "Yes! than equal space of embers."

The physics of his answer may be dubious but the question is the thing. The phenomenon fascinated him first as a juxtaposition of opposites, then as a simile for mob psychology (the demagogue match and the mass of embers ready to be inflamed). But from there he takes off and pursues the subject of flame (the triangular symbol of his personal seal is among other things a flame symbol). "What *is* inflammability?" had been a theme in Humphry Davy's first chemistry lectures in the Royal Institution in 1802. Here Coleridge's notebook question to himself comes with a touch of irony—the single little match and the whole bed of embers. What is the principle here, governing the relation between bodies? Affinity? Repulsion? Is the phrase, "and therefore more *eager* to combine with bodies out of itself" merely an example of pathetic fallacy, or is it an unconscious personal metaphor? *Eager* is surely an emotive word.

This is one aspect of what I mean by suggesting that Coleridge's thinking is rooted in personal experience, the minutiae as well as the wider arcs. His curiosity arises from a combination of mental concentration, observation, and an inexplicable personal drive. The directions it takes are not necessarily personal; they may well be an escape from the personal, for much of that from childhood onwards was painful and introspective. Yet Coleridge's sense of isolation did not destroy him. It fostered creative activity.

It has more than once been said that among English poets Coleridge was the great poet of childhood, and of love. That Coleridge understood these out of pain rather than pleasure did not block the detachment necessary to articulate them. He is also the poet of loneliness, the emotional setting of many of his finest poems, including the greatest lyrical ballad of loneliness in the language. His lonely characters may be seen sharply in contrast with Wordsworth's solitaries—those much more self-possessed and harmonious Leech Gatherers and Solitary Reapers. Coleridge's Ancient Mariner and Christabel are sufferers, incomplete in their relation to life, searching for someone to talk to. Like their creator. Hence the dialogue, actual or implicit in so many of the poems. Hence the need (faute de mieux) to make the notebooks his confidants. Coleridge was lonely because he was a warmly gregarious man.

A line in quotation marks, buried in a notebook entry, gave me many a fruitless search. "I am not a god that I should stand alone." Finally after about two decades of hunting, up many blind alleys, it appeared in a Coleridge sale; he quoted it casually in a manuscript letter as from an unpublished poem *of his own*! His deep personal sense of the godlike and ungodlike in loneliness refined his insights, e.g. into Shakespeare's tragic heroes as they endure or do not endure their isolation; it is part of his painful critical sense of the imagination as creator. To be free to initiate it must be free enough to stand alone. He had no confidence that he himself could do so, yet it is, I believe, an overlooked nobility in Coleridge—his frailties are more obvious—that he was able so often to turn his personal loneliness to creative use. The poems, the literary criticism, the philosophy, all were wrenched out of a complex total experience. Failure to understand this is failure to come anywhere near the truth about Coleridge. To understand it makes most of the charges against him trivial. The basis of his strength seems to me to be his awareness of the difficulties of reconciling everywhere those opposites which he first met within himself.

THOMAS McFARLAND

The Origin and Significance of Coleridge's Theory of Secondary Imagination

Coleridge refers to the secondary imagination only once in his published writings. The place is, of course, the end of the thirteenth chapter of the *Biographia Literaria*.

> The IMAGINATION then, I consider either as primary, or secondary. The primary IMAGINATION I hold to be the living Power and prime Agent of all human Perception, and as a repetition in the finite mind of the eternal act of creation in the infinite I AM. The secondary I consider as an echo of the former, co-existing with the conscious will, yet still as identical with the primary in the *kind* of its agency, and differing only in *degree*, and in the *mode* of its operation. It dissolves, diffuses, dissipates, in order to re-create; or where this process is rendered impossible, yet still at all events it struggles to idealize and to unify. It is essentially *vital*, even as all objects (*as* objects) are essentially fixed and dead.
>
> FANCY, on the contrary, has no other counters to play with, but fixities and definites. The Fancy is indeed no other than a mode of Memory emancipated from the order of time and space; and blended with, and modified by that empirical phenomenon of the will, which we express by the word CHOICE. But equally with the ordinary memory it must receive all its materials ready made from the law of association.

It is probably fair to say that this is both one of the most famous passages in all of English prose and one of the least satisfactorily understood. Up until about the middle of this century or shortly afterward, indeed, scholars usually approached it with an almost reverential regard, at the same time that a feeble and redundant gloss was all they could supply by way of commentary. A favorite question on viva voce examinations was a request to distinguish Coleridge's conceptions of primary imagination, secondary imagination, and fancy; and the ritual answer, which invariably satisfied the examiners in full, was simply to repeat the puzzling words.

Where there was not merely ritualistic citation, there was apt to be a certain disgruntlement. To cite a single instance, W. J. Bate, in 1950, said that "this rather artificial distinction between 'primary' and 'secondary' imagination is not among Coleridge's more lucid contributions to aesthetics. . . . The passage may be regarded as simply a cryptic phrasing of what one may discover in other ways to be Coleridge's general theory of the imagination. . . . Whatever its meaning, Coleridge does not dwell upon it elsewhere. As it now stands, it is neither clear nor particularly helpful."

It is easy to sympathize with such objections. Not only is there no preparation for the threefold distinction of chapter 13 in Coleridge's previous writings, there is none even in the *Biographia*. In chapter 4 of that work Coleridge states his conviction that "fancy and imagination" are "two distinct and widely different faculties," illustrates the difference by the examples of Cowley and Milton, and says that it is his object "to investigate the seminal principle" of the distinction. Nowhere is there any mention of, or preparation for, any additional differentiation. When, in chapter 12, he comes nearer to the promised discussion, it is to assert that he will "now proceed to the nature and genesis of the imagination"—still with no foreshadowing of a "secondary" imagination. And in chapter 13 itself, in an astonishing volte-face, he writes himself a letter in which he says: "I see clearly that you have done too much, and yet not enough. You have been obliged to omit so many links, from the necessity of compression, that what remains, looks . . . like the fragments of the winding steps of an old ruined tower." While the reader who has lasted thus far is still bemused by the phrase about the "necessity of compression," Coleridge proceeds simply to dump upon him the threefold distinction, or as the book more elaborately puts it, to "content myself for the present with stating the main result of the Chapter, which I have reserved for that future publication"—that is, for the magnum opus.

Not having the magnum opus to clarify matters, we must accordingly supply our own account of the "nature and genesis of the imagination," and such an account must necessarily be a tracing backward more than a forward progression from first principles. I shall attempt here to supply the essentials of such an account by addressing myself to three questions. First of all, why is the threefold distinction simply deposited rather than deduced? Secondly, where in Coleridge's thought or reading does the secondary imagination originate? And thirdly, what is the context in which we should consider the secondary imagination?

We need not linger over the answer to the first of our questions, that is, Why is the threefold distinction deposited rather than deduced? Briefly, the matter seems to stand this way: Coleridge had been following Schelling's line of reasoning, found himself unable to reconcile it with the threefold distinction—which neither comes from nor is paralleled by anything in Schelling—and so wrote himself a letter promising a later rethinking, while leaving as a down payment, as it were, the statements about primary imagination, secondary imagination, and fancy.

Coleridge had been involved in chapter 12 with an attempt to reconcile the subjective and the objective, which, transposed into his own terms of "I am" and "it is," was the consuming goal of his philosophical activity. To this end he had translated substantial passages from Schelling's *System of Transcendental Idealism*, which seemed to promise such a reconciliation. Coleridge had here accepted the thoroughly Schellingian notion that "the true system of natural philosophy places the sole reality of things in an ABSOLUTE . . . in the absolute identity of subject and object, which it calls nature, and which in its highest power is nothing else than self-conscious will or intelligence."

In chapter 13, still following Schelling, who had been following Kant, Coleridge says that "the transcendental philosophy demands; first, that two forces should be conceived which counteract each other by their essential nature." He goes on to speak of "this one power with its two inherent indestructible yet counteracting forces, and the results or generations to which their inter-penetration gives existence," and moves ever closer to Schelling's own, pantheistic, theory of imagination. Coleridge's last statement, before breaking off and writing himself his explanatory letter, trembles on the very brink of pantheism. "Now this tertium aliquid [God] can be no other than an inter-penetration of the counteracting powers, partaking of both." Coleridge is here only a step from Schelling's openly pantheistic theses that "the system of Nature is at the same time the system of our Spirit," and that "one might explain imagination as the power of transposing itself through complete self-activity into complete passivity."

To Coleridge, whose entire intellectual life was bound up with the necessity of avoiding pantheism, such a reconciliation of subjective and objective came at too high a price. And so he abruptly refuses to press forward. "Thus far had the work been transcribed for the press," he interrupts, "when I received the following letter from a friend."

There is perhaps an additional reason for Coleridge's merely depositing the threefold distinction. By doing so he makes his description, as Bate says, "cryptic"; and he probably was almost as content with this effect as he would have been with a clear demonstration. In any event, his letter's reference to the "many to whose *unprepared* minds your speculations on the esemplastic power would be utterly unintelligible" seems almost to imply the Plotinian view that "holy things may not be uncovered to the stranger." In general, by Coleridge, as by other Romantic thinkers, the faculty of imagination was treasured as something mysterious and unfathomable. Wordsworth refers to it as an "awful Power" that rises "from the mind's abyss." Schelling calls it a "wonderful faculty." Baader says that it is "a wonder of wonders," which is "no mere word, but a microcosmos of secret forces within us." Coleridge, for his part, calls it a "magical power" and says that his investigation of its principle will follow the faculty to its "roots" only "as far as they lift themselves above ground, and are visible to the naked eye of our common consciousness."

Such imprecision and emotional loading of the term in the late eighteenth and early nineteenth centuries were results of a protest against the mechanism and rationalism of Newton, Locke, and what Coleridge calls the "impious and pernicious tenets" of the "French fatalists or necessitarians." As a principle that stood against the passivity of mind, and against the soul's domination by dead outer things, the imagination possessed an importance that seemed actually to be enhanced by a certain obscurity. For obscurity allowed a sense of vastness, mysteriousness, and incommensurability that precision and demonstration tended to reduce. Coleridge honors such predilection for a *je ne sais quoi* in the concept of imagination when he says that "Imagination, Fancy &c." are "all poor & inadequate Terms" for "the sensuous Einbildungskraft." We see the same sense of mysterious expansion, coupled with imprecision, in Herder's reference to "*die Einbildungskraft*, or whatever we want to call this sea of inner sensibility." Indeed, Kant himself was content to be vague on this issue. Jacobi rightly notes that Kant's *Einbildungskraft* is "a blind forward and backward connecting faculty" that rests upon "a spontaneity of our being, whose principle is entirely unknown to us." As De Vleeschauwer says:

> Kant complicates the solution, so simple in its dualistic structure, by introducing imagination as an intermediary and mediating factor. It is the third element between the two original elements. It is capable of adopting this role because its nature is itself uncertain: Kant brings it into relation sometimes with sensibility, sometimes with understanding, and the schematism erects this confusion into a principle by making imagination participate both in sensibility and in understanding. Because of its confused nature the function delegated to it is not everywhere the same.

Coleridge shows both his understanding of Kant's position and his ready acceptance of obscurities in the imagination by saying that "Fancy and Imagination are Oscillations, *this* connecting Reason and Understanding; *that* connecting Sense and Understanding."

The word *connecting* in this last statement is significant both for Coleridge's breaking off of argument and for the function of imagination itself. For it seems clear that to Coleridge the imagination is less necessary as an element in an a priori theory of poetry than as a means of connecting poetic, philosophical, and theological interests. Most of all, it connects the inner world of "I am" with the outer world of "it is."

The importance of systematic connection for Coleridge can scarcely be overemphasized. Indeed, as L. C. Knights has observed, "in the Coleridgean world everything is connected with everything else." So in chapter 9 of the *Biographia Literaria* Coleridge asserts his need for an "abiding place for my reason," and it is evident that this could be found only in system. "I began to ask myself; is a system of philosophy, as different from mere history and historic classification, possible?" To abandon the concept of system was, he then says, a "wilful resignation of intellect" against which "human nature itself fought." And at the end of chapter 12, just before a reference to "the imagination, or shaping and modifying power; the fancy, or the aggregative and associative power," he speaks against those who dismiss "not only all system, but all logical connection." "This, alas!," Coleridge continues, "is an irremediable disease, for it brings with it, not so much an indisposition to any particular system, but an utter loss of taste and faculty for all system and for all philosophy."

Imagination is therefore primarily a connective developed because of Coleridge's commitment to systematic philosophizing. It would not appear to be rewarding, accordingly, to try to make very much critically of its presence in particular poems. But that is not to say that knowledge of the threefold distinction is wholly without value in the understanding of Coleridge's poetry As a single illustration, which I shall try not to labor unduly, the widely held view that "Kubla Khan" is a poem about poetic or imaginative creation, in which the major images are symbolic, would, in the light of the threefold distinction and Coleridge's systematic concerns, seem to be an un-Coleridgean reading, or at least only a partial reading.

"Kubla Khan" is, to be sure, an outstanding example of the secondary imagination at work. Furthermore, not only does the poem possess an unconscious but to us unmistakable undercurrent of sexual reference, but it would also certainly be Coleridgean to think of it as containing a consciously symbolic statement. Indeed, as Coleridge says in *The Stateman's Manual*, the imagination, "incorporating the Reason in Images of the Sense," gives birth to "a system of symbols."

Bate has argued, however, in his sensitive volume in the Masters of World Literature series, that theological preoccupations subsume all Coleridge's other concerns. It is not merely idle chatter for Coleridge to say that "the primary IMAGINATION" is "a repetition in the finite mind of the eternal act of creation in the infinite I AM." The controlling symbolism of "Kubla Khan" is, I think, anagogic; it refers to the "eternal act"—which alone, in Coleridge's scheme, could be called an idea of "reason"—not to the repetitive act in the finite mind nor to the echoes of that act. A poem written by Coleridge that ends with the word "Paradise" and begins with the creation of a garden should be interpreted, I believe, as a poem about God and Eden. The loss of the garden affirms, as Coleridge said in 1815 that he had wanted Wordsworth's poetry to affirm, "a Fall in some sense, as a fact . . . the reality of which is attested by Experience & Conscience." The Khan, wonderful, powerful, remote in space and time, heard about rather than seen, is what Sidney might call "a notable *prosopopeias*" that represents God himself. Although the words in Purchas say that "*In Xamdu did Cublai Can* build *a stately* Palace," Coleridge's Khan does not build, rather he creates by decree—that is, by a word, or divine fiat. And the garden, like Milton's Eden, is menaced from its beginning by conflicts arising from an ancestral past.

Such a reading could be bulwarked by considerations drawn from the extensive literature of commentary on the poem. Geoffrey Yarlott, for instance, suggests that "Alph, the sacred river," instead of being the Nile or the Alpheus, could "derive from 'Alpha,' the beginning—the sacred source of all things." And the part of the poem that does seem to be about poetic creation, that is, where the speaker will revive within him the Abyssinian maid's "symphony and song" so as to rebuild the dome in air, and thereby show that he had "drunk the milk of Paradise," is, as Elisabeth Schneider has pointed out, an echo of the *Ion*, which is the *locus classicus* for the connection of poetic act with divine things.

In any case, and whether one agrees or disagrees with an interpretation of the poem that transfers the emphasis from imaginative creation to theology, it should be evident that the imagination, though it cannot be dismissed in the consideration of Coleridge's poetry, is a tool of only limited critical use. To a considerable extent it functions simply as another name for that which is poetic about a poem. Whatever that may happen to be, however, can be approached by general methods available to any critic. In the *Biographia Literaria*, a book that is largely about poetry, the definition of the secondary imagination emphasizes and honors poetic creation. But it operates more as a link between its author's poetic and his systematic theological and philosophical interests than as a program for how poetry should be written.

Perhaps this role can be more fully understood if we turn to the second of our stipulated questions, that is, Where in Coleridge's thought or reading did the secondary imagination originate? With regard to the answer, a passage published by Ernest Hartley Coleridge in the *Anima Poetae* in 1895 is instructive, both in its own right and for what it indicates about the textual difficulties that have hindered Coleridgean interpretation.

> In the preface of my metaphysical works, I should say—"Once for all, read Kant, Fichte, &c., and then you will trace, or, if you are on the hunt, track me." Why, then, not acknowledge your obligations step by step? Because I could not do so in a multitude of glaring resemblances without a lie, for they had been mine, formed and full-formed, before I had ever heard of these writers, because to have fixed on the particular instances in which I have really been indebted to these writers would have been hard, if possible, to me who read for truth and self-satisfaction, and not to make a book, and who always rejoiced and was jubilant when I found my own ideas well expressed by others—and, lastly, let my say, because. I seem to know that much of the *matter* remains my own, and that the *soul* is mine. I fear not him for a critic who can confound a fellow-thinker with a compiler.

The statement, written in 1804, is clearly central to the whole question of Coleridge's intellectual indebtedness and constitutes both a proud testament to his own mental vitality and also, more ambivalently, perhaps something of a license to engage in the borrowings or plagiarisms that he embarked upon during his period of dejection.

But the editor of *Anima Poetae* did not transcribe the passage correctly. When it was republished in 1961, in the second volume of Kathleen Coburn's monumental edition of the *Notebooks*, numerous changes in punctuation and spelling appeared. More importantly, an interloper appeared as well. Where earlier "Kant, Fichte, &c." had been acknowledged by Coleridge as the masters of his thought, the opening sentence now read,

> In the Preface of my Metaphys. Works I should say—Once & all read Tetens, Kant, Fichte, &c—& there you will trace or if you are on the hunt, track me.

We almost sympathize with Ernest Hartley Coleridge's discarding of the name. For who on earth was Tetens? And what conceivably did he have to do with Coleridge?

To answer the latter question first, Tetens was the thinker to whom we may trace or track Coleridge's theory of secondary imagination. For the rest, he was the most important German psychologist of the *Aufklärung*, exerted a major influence on the formation of Kant's *Critique of Pure Reason*, was for a time professor at the University of Kiel, and from there was given in 1789 a royal commission as a high official of state finance in Copenhagen. He was born, according to varying accounts, on 16 September 1736, or 5 November 1738, and he died in 1807 on 15 August (Danish reckoning) or 19 August (German reckoning).

Although Tetens wrote a number of treatises, some of them in Latin, his fame and significance rest almost exclusively upon a two-volume work published in Leipzig in 1777 and entitled *Philosophische Versuche über die menschliche Natur und ihre Entwickelung*. Coleridge, the "library-cormorant," annotated both volumes, and his copies are at present in the British Library. It seems likely that he studied Tetens over a considerable time, for the notebook entry in 1804 indicates enough enthusiasm to suggest a substantial period of prior reading, and a crossed-out statement on the flyleaf of the first volume, in which he laments his separation from the Wordsworths, seems to have been written not only during his Malta sojourn but also after he learned, in the spring of 1805, of John Wordsworth's death. "O shall I ever see them again? he asks, and then he exclaims, "O dear John! Would I had been thy substitute!"

Indeed, such is the length of Tetens's volumes that reading them over a substantial period of time would be a normal procedure. Kant, who, according to De Vleeschauwer, delayed his first *Critique* in order to complete a study of Tetens, says in a gentle gibe that Tetens, in his "long essay on freedom in the second volume," was hoping as he wrote that with the aid of uncertainly sketched ideas he would find his way out of "this labyrinth," but "after he had wearied himself and his reader," the matter remained the same as before. And Coleridge, in a friendly note on the last page of the preface, seems obliquely to record as much dismay as anticipation about the rest of the work. "Would to Heaven," he writes, "that all Folios & Quartos contained in their 7 or 800 pages as much meaning & good sense, as these 36 pages octavo in large type." As Tetens's first volume, exclusive of preliminary material, is 784 pages, and his second 834 pages, Coleridge's statement about "7 or 800" pages seems to apply very much to matters at hand.

But I suspect he read every word. Both volumes are annotated, although not copiously; the subject of freedom in the second volume, which elicited Kant's gibe to Markus Herz, receives a Coleridgean comment; most of all, however, I trust my own sense of how Coleridge read, built up from tracing or tracking him through numerous treatises. Quite in opposition to earlier views that had him dipping and skimming through works he barely understood, we must see him now as a man who was able to read when he was able to do nothing else. He read the works of Kant, for instance, with an almost unholy attentiveness, and was able to do so straight through the most severe periods of his opium addiction.

In any event, what he needed in Tetens he could find within the first quarter of the first volume. And what was there to be found was not only the formulation of the theory of secondary imagination but also the entire threefold division of the imaginative faculty that he deposits at the end of the thirteenth chapter of the *Biographia Literaria*.

The significance of this aspect of Coleridge's use of Tetens has not, I believe, been fully realized as yet. E. L. Stahl, in an article on Coleridge and Goethe that appeared in 1952 in the *Festgabe* for Fritz Strich, broached the possibility of Tetens (along with Maass) as an influence on Coleridge's theory of imagination. In 1955, René Wellek likewise mentioned the possibility. And although Stahl did not see the full situation, and Wellek contented himself with part of a single sentence, an article by Walter Greiner, which appeared in *Die neueren Sprachen* in 1960, identified both the secondary imagination and the threefold distinction of chapter 13 as stemming from Tetens. Greiner, however, could not know the passage in the *Notebooks* that so conclusively points to Tetens as a Coleridgean source, nor was he, as a doctoral candidate, equipped to assess the meaning of his discovery. His article made no impression on established Coleridge scholarship.

Now Tetens, like Coleridge, and indeed almost everyone who has thought about the matter, initially dichotomizes the power of representation. He explains that "we ascribe to the psyche (*Seele*) not only a power to produce representations in themselves . . . but also a power of calling them forth again, a re-representing power, which is customarily termed fancy [*Phantasie*] or imagination [*Einbildungskraft*]." As to these two latter terms, although Tetens says that *imagination* more truly indicates the rerepresenting power "in so far as it renews imagistic representations of sensation," the words remain for him synonymous, and in his actual practice he seems to prefer the word *fancy*. He is not satisfied, however, with the twofold division of *perceiving faculty* and *fancy*. In a radical departure from previous psychologizing, he adds a third entity, which he calls *Dichtungsvermögen*—that is, the power of joining together, and also, ambivalently, the power of poetry. "The activities of representation," he now says,

> can be conceived under three headings. *First* we produce original representations out of the sensations within us . . . this is *perception*.

> . . . Secondly, this power of sensation is reproduced even when those first sensations have ceased. . . . This effect is commonly ascribed to the . . . fancy. . . .
>
> *Thirdly*. This reproduction of the ideas is still not all, however, that the human power of representation does with them. It does not merely reproduce them, it does not merely alter their previous coexistence . . . but it also creates new images and representations. . . . The soul is able not only to arrange and order its representations, like the curator of a gallery of paintings, but is itself a painter, and invents and constructs new paintings.
>
> These achievements belong to the *Dichtungsvermögen*, a creative power, whose sphere of activity seems to have a great scope. . . . It is the self-active fancy. . . and without doubt an essential ingredient of genius.

Tetens's threefold division of the representing power or *Vorstellungskraft* into *Perceptionsvermögen, Dichtungsvermögen*, and *Phantasie* is paralleled by Coleridges's threefold division of the imaginative powers into primary imagination, secondary imagination, and fancy. Moreover, there are striking similarities between Tetens's *Perceptionsvermögen* and Coleridge's primary imagination. To Coleridge, primary imagination is the "prime Agent of all human Perception"; to Tetens, the *Perceptionsvermögen* is the "facultas percipiendi" or faculty of perceiving. Coleridge's faculty is a repetition of the "eternal act of creation"; Tetens's is called the "constituting power" ("Fassungskraft"). It "produces the original representations out of the sensations in us, and maintains them during after-perceiving, and we preserve these after-perceptions as reproductions of the sensed objects in us."

The similarities extend also to Coleridge's fancy and Tetens's fancy. For Coleridge, fancy "must receive all its materials ready made from the law of association"; for Tetens, fancy operates "nach der Regel der Association"—"according to the rule of association." For Coleridge, fancy is "the aggregative and associative power"; for Tetens, fancy reproduces sensations either according to "their previous coexistence in the senses" or according to the rule that "similar representations group themselves with one another." This, he says, is "the law of the association of ideas."

Tetens's new third entity, the *Dichtungsvermögen*, intrudes into the activities of the law of association. Representations, says Tetens, would occur strictly according to the "true association of ideas," that is, according to their similarity or their coexistence, "if nothing comes in between." But this "if," he says, is "an if that permits exception." "The self-active *Dichtungsvermögen* comes between, and creates new representations out of those already there, makes new points of union, new connections, and new series. The power of thought discovers new relationships, new similarities, new coexistences, and new dependences . and makes in this manner new channels of communication among ideas."

The intruding *Dichtungsvermögen* is the source of an activity that Tetens calls *Dichtkraft*, and *Dichtkraft* seems to be neither more nor less than Coleridge's secondary imagination. Chapter 14 of Tetens's first essay is called "Concerning the Law of the Association of Ideas," and the rubric continues with the assurance that the "law of association" is "only a law of the fancy in the reproduction of sensations: it is no law for the combination of ideas in new series." And then chapter 15 which is called "Von der bildenden Dichtkraft"—that is, "On the plastic joining or poetic power"—begins to discuss how new series are formed. The ten sections of the discussion are indicated just below the title of the chapter and include such headings as "laws of the creative *Dichtkraft*," "influence of the *Dichtkraft* on the order in which the reproductions of the fancy follow," and "the *Dichtkraft's* effecting power extends through all classes of representations."

In the discussion itself are to be found repeatedly the exact words used by Coleridge. Coleridge says that the secondary imagination "dissolves, diffuses, dissipates," that it struggles "to unify", and elsewhere he says that imagination "blends, and (as it were) *fuses*." Tetens says that *Dichtkraft* is characterized by activities of "dissolving" ("Auflösen") and "reuniting" ("Wiedervereinigen"), "diffusing" in the sense of intermingling ("Ineinandertreiben") and "blending" ("Vermischen").

The similarities do not end here. In chapter 13 of the *Biographia Literaria*, just before his threefold formulation, Coleridge refers to the imagination as "*the esemplastic power*", and at the beginning of chapter 10 he opens with the famous statement: "*Esemplastic. The word is not in Johnson, nor have I met with it elsewhere.*" Esemplastic, Coleridge then says, means "to shape into one," which is a "new sense" of the word "imagination." The *Dichtkraft*, likewise, is not only a *bildende*—that is, shaping—power; it is also one whose "first law," Tetens says, is that "several simple representations" be "united into one" ("in Eine vereiniget").

By way of illustrating the difference between fancy and *Dichtkraft*, Tetens invokes the example of Linnaeus, on the one hand, and of Milton and Klopstock, on the other. For Tetens, Linnaeus has, as Coleridge said of Cowley, a fanciful mind; the imagination of Linnaeus, says Tetens, "conceives a countless multitude of clear representations of sensation from bodily objects, and a like multitude of heard and gathered shades and tones; receives them in their clarity and reproduces them." The work of Milton, on the other hand, for Tetens as for Coleridge, is characterized by a different order of imagination—by *Dichtkraft*, which "with inner intensity reworks the imaginings, dissolves and blends, separates and draws together again, and creates new forms and appearances."

Such passages could be adduced in great number, but perhaps these few serve to show that the plastic, shaping *Dichtkraft*, with its emphasis on dissolving, diffusing, blending, reuniting, and forming into one, and its introduction as a third entity into a spectrum made up of a psychological theory of perception and rerepresentation, is clearly an important source of the theory of secondary imagination.

We may approach the third and last of our stipulated questions from the perspective of this fact. What is the context in which we should consider the secondary imagination? Actually, the question might almost better be phrased: What is the context for the primary imagination? For the secondary imagination, although named as such only in chapter 13, seems really to be the imagination Coleridge customarily talks about elsewhere and to be called secondary only because of the primary imagination. The latter is the true newcomer. Coleridge's earliest invocation of the distinction between imagination and fancy, for instance, speaks of "Fancy, or the aggregating Faculty of the mind" and of "*Imagination*, or the *modifying*, and *co-adunating* Faculty." The imagination here described seems to be the secondary imagination, and the date of the formulation, 10 September 1802, puts it interestingly close to the notebook entry of 1804 with its retrospective praise of Tetens. Furthermore, the phrase "co-adunating Faculty"—the faculty that makes many into one—could serve as a literal translation of the German *Dichtungsvermögen*, with the verb *dichten*, meaning "to join together" or "to caulk," serving as an ambivalent root along with *dichten* meaning "to compose poetry." In any event, our last question might be restated this way: What is the context in which we should consider Coleridge's use of Tetens's threefold distinction?

The answer to this question involves Coleridge's old nemesis, association psychology. The *Biographia Literaria* contains an intellectual history of Coleridge's concern to extricate himself from association psychology and at the same time attempts to elaborate a theory of imagination. Tetens, significantly, not only investigated the faculties of representation, but did so in the context of current theories of association psychology. He was, as J. H. Randall says, "in the thick of the crucial questions about knowledge raised in the 1760's." The *Philosophische Versuche*, in other words, was very much a professional piece of psychological analysis, as those terms might apply to the situation in the late eighteenth century.

This professionalism, or scientism, was extraordinarily important to Coleridge, in view both of his temperamental needs and of what he was trying to do in philosophy. The matter was, for Coleridge, not one of merely rejecting association psychology and affirming a theory of imagination against it. Blake, for instance, does that much. The attitudes of Locke and Newton were as repugnant to him as they were to Coleridge. He says, "Mans perceptions are not bounded by organs of perception, he perceives more than sense (tho' ever so acute) can discover." And he states that "to Me This World is all One continued Vision of Fancy or Imagination." Imagination for Blake asserts the mind's freedom and is opposed to the hegemony of the external. "Natural Objects always did & now do Weaken deaden & obliterate Imagination in Me." But Blake's opinions, though on these issues not very different from those of Coleridge, are formulated as insights, not as conclusions from argument or investigation. Instead of argument, Blake simply escalates, and indeed, exaggerates, his own statement:

> To cast off Bacon, Locke & Newton from Albions covering
> To take off his filthy garments, & clothe him with Imagination

As Northrop Frye notes, "Bacon, Newton and Locke do not look very convincing in the role of three-headed hellish Cerberus which Blake assigns them." Blake, for his part, says with disarming candor that men and works such as "Locke on Human Understanding" inspire his "Contempt & Abhorrence"; "they mock Inspiration & Vision Inspiration & Vision was then & now is & I hope will always Remain my Element my Eternal Dwelling place. how then can I hear it Contemnd without returning Scorn for Scorn."

Coleridge, too, looked on Locke with "Contempt & Abhorrence." For him, however, it was important not merely to abuse Newton and Locke but to argue against them on their own cognitive terms. To use his own Phraseology, it was necessary to remove "the sandy Sophisms of Locke, and the Mechanic Dogmatists" by "demonstrating that the Senses were living growths and developements of the Mind & Spirit in a much juster as well as higher sense, than the mind can be said to be formed by the Senses." The important word here is *demonstrating*. "I can assert," says De Quincey, "upon my long and intimate knowledge of Coleridge's mind, that logic the most severe was as inalienable from his modes of thinking as grammar from his language." Blake, on the other hand, dismissing both demonstration and logic, felt that

> Hes a Blockhead who wants a proof of what he Can't Percieve
> And he's a Fool who tries to make such a Blockhead believe.

But Coleridge, committed to a systematic reconciliation of all elements of experience, could not proceed in such a peremptory way. John Beer notes, in a passage that is increasingly recognized as going to the heart of Coleridge's interests, "Side by side with his visionary world of speculation, there is in his mind a positivist world of rationalist investigation, which he no doubt hoped would eventually be harmonized with it." And Coleridge himself said that the sum total of his convictions would constitute a system such "that of all Systems that have ever been presented, this has the least of *Mysticism*, the very Object throughout from the first page to the last being to reconcile the dictates of common Sense with the conclusions of scientific Reasoning." Indeed, as Richard Haven has emphasized, Coleridge

> shared the respect of his age for science and scientific theories, the confidence that human experience could be explained as physical nature could be explained, that there were laws of human nature as well as laws of motion. While he was drawn to various earlier visionaries, he was also well aware of what seemed to be their inadequacy, their inability, that is, to meet the challenge of "enlightened" analysis and criticism. What he required was a means of reconciling the experience of the oasis [i.e., of visionary insight] with acceptable conceptions of physical and psychological reality.

So Coleridge could hardly fail to be attracted by the most scientific and soberly professional psychologist of the German enlightenment. Tetens's two formidable tomes begin with a statement that seems to promise God's plenty. "The following essays concern the workings of the human understanding, its laws of thought and its basic powers; furthermore, they concern the active power of will, the fundamental character of humanity, freedom, the nature of the soul, and its development." Tetens immediately makes this comprehensiveness still more attractive by declaring himself in favor of the most respectable scientific procedures. He states (following Newton) that he has "carefully sought to avoid the admixture of hypotheses among propositions of experience"; and he says that "concerning the method which I have utilized, I consider it necessary to explain myself at the beginning. It is the method of observation that Locke has pursued with regard to the understanding, and our psychologists have followed in the doctrine of psychic experience."

Still another aspect of Tetens's procedure would doubtless have engaged Coleridge's attention. Tetens focuses not only on the tradition of Locke but specifically on Hartley and Priestley. Hartley's hypothesis, which Coleridge knew so well and from which he needed to free himself, is brought forward almost at the outset. Tetens says: "The Hartleyan hypothesis that movements of the brain. . . consist in certain vibrations of the brain fibres or even of the aether in the brain, has been set forth by Mr. Priestley in a new, somewhat altered, well executed, and most praiseworthy exposition. Since then people have accustomed themselves to regard ideas as above all vibrations in the brain." Coleridge, who was "much pleased. . . with everything that overthrows & or illustrates the overthrow of that all-annihilating system of explaining every thing wholly by association," would have been even more interested, however, in Tetens's further preliminary remarks about the "difficulties" of Hartley's view: for Tetens concludes, "It seems to me, nothing is less probable than that the whole sensible motion of the brain that constructs the material idea can consist purely and simply in vibration, as is hypothesized."

If we inquire into the intellectual origin of this discontent on the part of Tetens with Hartley's psychology of association, we are led to a single source: Leibniz. Hartley's master, Locke, had supposed "the Mind to be, as we say, white Paper, void of all Characters, without any *Ideas*," and to be furnished by "*Experience*." "SENSATION" was the "great Source, of most of the *Ideas* we have." "External, Material things, as the Objects of SENSATION; and the Operations of our own Minds within, as the Objects of REFLECTION" were to Locke "the only Originals, from whence all our *Ideas* take their beginnings."

This view of the mind's nature dominated European psychology until the second part of the eighteenth century. In 1765, however, Leibniz's answer to Locke, the *Nouveaux essais sur l'entendement*, was found and first published by Raspe. The *Nouveaux essais* immediately began to exert the strongest kind of counterinfluence on European intellectuals; indeed, the book's historical effect can hardly be overestimated. "In my opinion," said Tetens proudly in a work of 1775, "our own Leibniz has seen far more deeply, acutely and correctly into the nature of the human understanding, its modes of thought, and in particular the transcendental knowledge of reason, than the more assiduously observing Locke. He has seen further than the otherwise clear-sighted Hume, than Reid, Condillac, Beattie, Search, and Home." Such an endorsement implies an acceptance of the idea of inherent powers of mind, and thus for Coleridge's purposes a defense of the "I am" or irreducible sense of an autonomous self. For Leibniz had rejected the tabula rasa of the associationists as "a fiction," and had urged that "there are some ideas and principles that do not come to us from the senses, and that we find in ourselves without forming them, although the senses give us occasion to perceive them." Moreover, by his conception of *vis activa* (active force) or *vis insita* (inherent force) as the nature of the monad, Leibniz paved the way for a rejection of the mind's passivity. Cassirer notes, by way of inaugurating a discussion of Tetens:

"when the mind becomes a mirror of reality [as it did in Leibniz's monad doctrine] it is and remains a living mirror of the universe, and it is not simply a sum total of mere images but a whole composed of formative forces. The basic task of psychology and epistemology will henceforth be to elucidate these forces in their specific structure and to understand their reciprocal relations. . . . The psychological formulation and defense of the spontaneity of the ego now prepare the ground for a new conception of knowledge and of art." Of these late followers of Leibniz engaged in the psychological formulation and defense of the spontaneity of the ego, Tetens was, says Cassirer, "the most original and ingenious psychological analyst."

Coleridge was as much aware of Leibniz as he was of Tetens. Indeed, in the *Biographia Literaria*, the position of Locke is adduced in the language of Leibniz: "nihil in intellectu quod non prius in sensu"—"nothing in the mind that is not first in the senses." Coleridge also paraphrases Leibniz's amendment of the position: "praeter ipsum intellectum"—"except the mind itself." The amendment provides as good a programmatic statement as any of Coleridge's arguments against the associationism of his youth. And it takes on added significance in light of the fact that the two massive volumes of Tetens represent a kind of enormously expanded gloss upon the position of Locke as criticized by Leibniz's addendum.

It is in the empirical examination of two related edifices of thought, science and poetry, that Tetens looks for his evidence for active powers of mind that stand outside the law of association, and to which he gives the general name *Denkkraft*. He finds particularly vulnerable the associationist account of the mental activities revealed in poetry.

> Psychologists commonly explain poetic creation as a mere analysis and synthesis of ideas that are produced in sensation and drawn forth again. But does this really quite account for fictions? If so, then poetic creation is nothing more than a mere transposition of phantasms, from which no new simple ideas can arise in our consciousness. According to this supposition, every discrete sensuous appearance must, if analyzed into the component parts that can be differentiated by reflection, consist of nothing but pieces, which taken individually are pure imaginings or renewed ideas of sense.

But, says Tetens, such is not the case; and he proceeds to examine a certain fiction used by poets, that of Pegasus."The representation of Pegasus," he says,

> is an image of a winged horse. We have the image of a horse from sensation, and also the image of wings. Both are pure phantasms,

> sundered from other representations and bound together with one another here in the image of Pegasus. To that extent this is nothing but an effect of the fancy. But this is only an *analysis* and a *putting together again*.

After further discussion, Tetens continues:

> It seems to me that there is more in the image than a mere putting together. The wings of Pegasus might have been a pure phantasm in the head of the first poet who produced this image; likewise the representation of the horse. But there is a place in the image, at the shoulders of the horse, somewhat more obscure than the others, where the wings are joined to the body; at that point the images of the horse's shoulders and of the roots of the wings flow into one another. There is accordingly a spontaneous appearance, which disappears if the image of the horse and the image of the wings are again clearly separated from one another.

By such form of empirical observation, which seems to prefigure the phi-phenomenon that lies at the basis of twentieth-century Gestalt psychology, Tetens concludes that "*Dichtkraft* can create no elements, no fundamental materials, can make only nothing out of nothing, and to that extent is no creative power. It can only separate, dissolve, join together, blend; but precisely thereby it can produce new images, which from the standpoint of our faculty of differentiation are discrete representations. There is accordingly a "Selbstthätigkeit"—"a spontaneous activity"—in "the receptivity of the psyche," and on this "the ability to have secondary sensations depends." The "receptivity of our psyche" passes over into a "percipirende, reproducirende und dichtende Kraft"—"a perceiving, reproducing and co-adunating power."

Tetens's argument for "Selbstthätigkeit" in mental process, for "selbstbildende Dichtkraft," with such conceptions being derived in the course of an examination of association psychology, must have seemed to Coleridge like a fountain in the desert. He wrote in 1801, perhaps shortly before encountering the *Philosophische Versuche*: "Newton was a mere materialist—*Mind* in his system is always passive—a lazy Looker-on on an external World. If the mind be not *passive*, if it be indeed made in God's Image, & that too in the sublimest sense—the Image of the *Creator*—there is ground for suspicion, that any system built on the passiveness of the mind must be false, as a system." The phrase about the mind as "the Image of the *Creator*" seems to be a foreshadowing of the primary imagination as a "repetition in the finite mind" of the creative activity of "the infinite I AM." But the tone of the passage does not suggest that Coleridge at this moment had in hand the threefold elaboration of the mind's imaginative activity. The statement, however, occurred in the same month as his declaration that he had "overthrown the doctrine of Association, as taught by Hartley, and with it all the irreligious metaphysics of modern Infidels—especially, the doctrine of Necessity." Apparently, then, some sort of intellectual conversion—which for Coleridge must have seemed to be based on cognitive demonstration—took place in March 1801, against association psychology and in favor of active powers of mind. Whether we suppose the reading of Tetens to have preceded and actually to have caused this change, or to have followed and confirmed it, it seems quite unarguable that those emphases of Tetens that I have described would be of central importance to Coleridge.

They were still important when the *Biographia Literaria* came to be written, for there the problems are the same: to argue against association psychology and to affirm the spontaneous power of mind, although now in the specific form of imagination. As Coleridge says in chapter 8 of that work, association theory neither "involves the explanation, nor precludes the necessity, of a mechanism and co-adequate forces in the percipient, which at the more than magic touch of the impulse from without is to create anew for itself the correspondent object." Such an active principle was not elaborated in association psychology before Tetens. As Coleridge wryly says, "in Hartley's scheme, the soul is present only to be pinched or *stroked*, while the very squeals or purring are produced by an agency wholly independent and alien." Tetens, in insisting that a third element, *Dichtkraft*, must be added to those accounted for by the law of association, provided exactly what Coleridge required.

Therefore we must amend the theory, advanced by commentators such as D. G. James, that sees Kant as the prototype for Coleridge's discrimination of the imaginative faculties. Whatever Kant's role, the correspondences between his descriptions of imagination and those of Coleridge are by no means so close as between those of Tetens and Coleridge. There is, for instance, only a twofold, not a threefold division of imaginative activity in the first *Critique*; and Kant's "productive imagination" does not emphasize dissolving, diffusing, and blending activities as do Coleridge's secondary imagination and Tetens's *Dichtkraft*. And in any case, Kant's own theories of imagination, as De Vleeschauwer demonstrates in his magisterial work on the transcendental deduction in Kant, were themselves derived from Tetens. "As to the theme of imagination," says De Vleeschauwer, "it is evident, although Kant disguises it somewhat by its integration in the transcendental methodology, that it derives from the psychological work of the eighteenth century. The birth, in effect, of the imagination from the internal sense comes directly from the psychology contemporary to Kant, and discloses increasingly the influence of

Lockian empiricism." But, De Vleeschauwer points out, "the single memorable psychological event" that occurred in Germany at this time was the publication of Tetens's *Philosophische Versuche*, and after exhaustive discussion he concludes as follows: "We shall terminate this chapter by demonstrating that Kant studied the *Philosophische Versuche* of Tetens. Anticipating this conclusion, the legitimacy of which is guaranteed by the correspondence of Kant, we believe that it is not going beyond the bounds of prudence so necessary in this kind of discussion to say that in all probability the introduction of imagination as a factor in the critical philosophy was due to the reading of Tetens."

Coleridge's secondary imagination, therefore, looks past Kant's productive imagination to the *Dichtkraft* of Tetens. Authorized by the empirical observation of poetry rather than by a critic's notion of what poetry should be, both secondary imagination and *Dichtkraft* are themselves articulations of the metaphysical *vis activa* of Leibniz. Thus in a note of 1804 Coleridge speaks of the "*Ego*/its metaphysical Sublimity–& intimate Synthesis with the principle of Co-adunation–without *it* every where all things were a waste–nothing, &c–." Although the "principle of Co-adunation" here invoked is clearly the secondary imagination or *Dichtkraft*, the phrase about the ego's "metaphysical Sublimity" can refer neither to poetry nor to psychology, but only to metaphysics–that is, not to Tetens but to Leibniz.

Indeed, one of the epigraphs to chapter 13 of the *Biographia Literaria*–a chapter, we may recall, bearing the subtitle "On the imagination, or esemplastic power"–is a Latin quotation from Leibniz's *Specimen dynamicum*. It is, significantly, in this treatise that the conception of *vis activa* is most fully discussed. "Active force," says Leibniz there, is either "primitive or derivative"; the "primitive force" (which is what concerns us) is "nothing else than the first entelechy" or "the soul." Coleridge's epigraph comes from a passage a few pages further on, and it stresses metaphysical rather than poetical principles. "In addition to considerations purely mathematical, and subject to the fancy, I have concluded that certain metaphysical principles must be admitted. . . . A certain higher, and so to speak, formal principle must be added to that of material mass."

The epigraph, however, is not drawn wholly from *Specimen dynamicum*. Its first sentence is from the *De ipsa natura*, the treatise in which Leibniz discusses active force in the alternative phrasing of *vis insita*, or inherent force. The sentence from this treatise refers to the Platonists as recognizing the necessity of formative powers as well as matter; and elsewhere Leibniz speaks of Plato himself as supplying in his doctrine of *anamnesis* a prototype of the doctrine of inherent mental force.

So we may conclude that the lineage of the secondary imagination extends not only backward beyond Kant to Tetens but also beyond Tetens to Leibniz, and finally beyond Leibniz to Plato. With antecedents of this kind, it is inevitable that Coleridge's threefold theory of imagination actually bears less on poetry than it does on those things that always mattered most to him—as they did to Leibniz and to Kant—that is, "the freedom of the will, the immortality of the soul, and the existence of God."

And yet, even as one notes the special transmitting role of Tetens in the channeling of the current of secondary imagination back to the high reservoirs of Leibniz, Plato, and Christian concern, a corollary fact must be noted as well. Tetens was the most scientifically responsible of the eighteenth-century investigators of imagination; but there were others, even if without his demonstrative rigor, who were saying very much the same things.

Every decade, in truth, produced similar formulations. For instance, though Tetens's work appeared in 1777, a large part of what he was urging was adumbrated precisely ten years before, in 1767, and adumbrated also precisely ten years before that, in 1757. Thus in that year Edmund Burke wrote:

> Besides the ideas . . . which are presented by the sense; the mind of man possesses a sort of creative power of its own; either in representing at pleasure the images of things in the order and manner in which they were received by the senses, or in combining those images in a new manner, and according to a different order. This power is called Imagination; and to this belongs whatever is called wit, fancy, invention, and the like. But it must be observed, that this power of the imagination is incapable of producing any thing absolutely new; it can only vary the disposition of those ideas which it has received from the senses.

Except that Tetens conducts his investigation as a formal psychologist taking note of empirical data, there is little he says that is not at least in principle contained in Burke's statement. Burke understands that images derived from sensory experience are necessary to imagination; he also understands, quite in accord with Tetens's *Dichtkraft*, except that he does not elaborate the understanding, that "the mind of man possesses a sort of creative power of its own . . . in combining those images in a new manner and according to a different order."

The same factors are bubbling in William Duff's mind ten years later, in 1767. "Imagination is that faculty whereby the mind not only reflects on its own operations, but which assembles the various ideas conveyed to the understanding by the canal of sensation, and treasured up in the repository of the memory, compounding or disjoining them at pleasure; and which, by its plastic power of inventing new associations of ideas, and of combining them with infinite variety, is enabled to present a creation of its own, and to exhibit scenes and objects which never existed in nature."

Such repetitions of analysis and formulation surely testify as much to the common urgencies of the topic when confronted by individual minds as to their authors' reading of one another. Granted the dominance of a psychology based on the association of ideas, inevitably the capacity of the mind to "present a creation of its own, and to exhibit scenes and objects which never existed in nature"—a capacity that anyone can verify from his own experience—would pave the way for conceptions that strained against the hegemony of the Lockean tradition. Tetens, in line with the paradoxes insisted on throughout this volume, was at one and the same time an original investigator and one who could claim actual priority on only one small if crucial point, and even that only as a matter of specific demonstration in scientific context.

JEROME CHRISTENSEN

The Marginal Method of the Biographia Literaria

To call Coleridge's borrowing plagiarism is indeed profitless: the moral blanket smothers the unarguable vitality and complexity of the text. We must mince our words as Coleridge minced his. Yet the moral remission involved in the label "mosaic composition," the suggestion that Coleridge is simply a self-effacing, skillful craftsman, is equally misleading. Although Coleridge has appropriated passages from other writers, every word in the *Biographia* has become his. A book is not a mosaic. Words are not brightly colored stones, which the artist finds and then arranges on a background; even the crude facsimile of the most clumsy plagiarist alters its source by mediation and displacement. Moreover, Coleridge scarcely seems to have composed the *Biographia*, if by compose we mean the act of an intending consciousness bringing disparate materials into equilibrium. To recuperate Coleridge's disturbing prose by means of a metaphor from the visual arts is to suppress the crucial discursive advance he has made beyond Hartley's wishful sketching and to end inevitably by cataloging Coleridge as just another emblematic figure in philosophy's great picture book. One benefit of close attention to Hartley's metaphors for philosophical writing is the ability to see that, though Coleridge found writing as problematic as the associationist, by the time of the *Biographia* he read and wrote that problem in a way that requires us, if we intend to adhere to Coleridge's discourse rather than to transume it, to trope his writing *as* writing. The *Biographia* is not a book of philosophy. Coleridge wrote none. What Coleridge practices is not mosaic composition but marginal exegesis, not philosophy but commentary.

In his discussion of Coleridge's kinship with Friedrich Jacobi, McFarland

---

addresses the peculiar character of marginal commentary when he is faced with the problem of accounting for the fact that Coleridge hardly ever mentions Jacobi, and that when he does, it is primarily in marginal comments with a distinctly disapproving tone. To explain this McFarland seconds W. Schrickx's "plausible hypothesis about the special emphasis of marginalia": "Schrickx argues that it is 'natural for those who enrich books with their marginal comments rather to disagree with or counter views of others and to impose their own than to express enthusiasm for the author who is being annotated.'" McFarland uses that hypothesis to support his own conviction of a special sympathetic relationship between Coleridge and Jacobi. In other words, he plausibly employs Schrickx's hypothesis to justify the presumption of marginal comments as inherently equivocal. The hypothesis of equivocalness is plausible because a structural equivocation is built into the annotative situation: an apparently single voice is doubled by the addition of the note. Once added to the margins of the text the comment makes it uncertain what the text *is*. The original text may presume inalienable priority, but the marginal comment always threatens the reduction of the original text to a pretext for commentary—commentary, however, which could not be where it "is" were it not for the margins provided. The marginalium is, thus, both enrichment and deprivation of its host, just as it is, equivocally, neither inside nor outside the text. Marginalia exploit the articulations of sense and signification where respires the text's mortality.

Considered as discourse a marginal method is similarly equivocal: philosophical goods are transported by a rhetorical vehicle. The beginning of Chapter VI, where Coleridge launches his specific criticisms of Hartley's system, furnishes a good example. Coleridge has two targets: the hypothesis of vibrations and the reduction of the laws of association to the single law of contemporaneity. The only logical criticism that Coleridge applies to Hartley, one of "a hundred possible confutations," is taken from Maass's analysis of the mechanical hypothesis:

> According to this system the idea or vibration *a* from the external object A becomes associable with the idea or vibration *m* from the external object M, because the oscillation *a* propagated itself so as to re-produce the oscillation *m*. But the original impression from M was essentially different from the impression from A: unless therefore different causes may produce the same effect, the vibration *a* could never produce the vibration *m*; and this therefore could never be the means by which *a* and *m* are associated.

Coleridge employs two other deductions by Maass to answer possible objections to the first. Those deductions are refutations in kind of the scientific propositions that Hartley enumerated in the first chapter of *Observations on Man*. Coleridge does not, however, leave imagination to starve while reason luxuriates in its proper paradise: he ornaments the margins of Maass's syllogisms with his own polished enthymemes—metaphorical illustrations of the German's confutations. The method is effective: the deductions convince; illustrations such as the metaphor of the stone soup persuade.

Equally persuasive is Coleridge's summary comment on the consequences of Hartley's "material hypothesis":

> Thus the principle of *contemporaneity*, which Aristotle had made the common *condition* of all the laws of association, Hartley was constrained to represent as being itself the sole *law*. . . . Again, from this results inevitably, that the will, the reason, the judgement, and the understanding, instead of being the determining causes of association, must needs be represented as its *creatures*, and among its mechanical *effects*. Conceive, for instance, a broad stream, winding through a mountainous country with an indefinite number of currents, varying and running into each other according as the gusts chance to blow from the opening of the mountains. The temporary union of several currents in one, so as to form the main current of the moment, would present an accurate image of Hartley's theory of the will.
>
> Had this been really the case, the consequence would have been that our whole life would be divided between the despotism of outward impressions and that of senseless and passive memory.

Coleridge has responded to Hartley's attempt to give a philosophical description of things as they are with an interpretive sketch of what things *might* be like if Hartley's account were accurate. First, he compares Hartley to Aristotle; then he comments on the inevitable consequences of Hartley's theory; then he asks us to conceive an image; *then* he says, "Had this been really the case." If *what* had really been the case? If the mind had really been a stream winding through a mountainous country? For a moment the reference floats: the clear image seems to displace the priority of the difficult concept of contingency that it is meant to represent. That grammatical slippage is paralleled by the rhetorical displacement which Coleridge uses the image to effect. He employs his metaphor as a device to invert his opponent's own position and to turn his arguments against him: the stream image enables Coleridge to associate the associative model with caprice rather than necessity. By removing the metaphor from its "natural" connection, he achieves a remarkable *tour de force*. Yet the consequences of that rhetorical subversion are as ephemeral as those involved in the momentary grammatical displacement. Because of its rhetorical character Coleridge's criticism is inadequate as a refutation; instead, his removal of the image from its proper context, his "denaturalizing" of the metaphor, suggests that it can be reappropriated to serve antithetical ends: without the anchor of the autonomous will, Coleridge's turn is liable to a similar overturning.

Coleridge's rhetoric has its effect. But that effectiveness has its cost. One of the costs of a marginal method is the complication of the writer's relationship to an ambiguous text or an undisclosed truth, a relationship similar to the Hartleian dyad of decoder-code. The decoder, like the annotator, may be conceived to be in the margins of the text that he is analyzing, and that position is likewise equivocal; but he intends his situation to be only provisional: when he solves the code and establishes the true text, he will have relieved the text of its obscurity and relinquished his own ambiguous position. The marginal commentator, however, relies on the bulk of his text to relieve *him* of the responsibility for systematic discourse, as the rhetorician's persuasive aims relieve him from the need for syllogistic rigor. The shift from a deliberate, scientific argument of inductive or deductive proof to a mobile, fragmentary discourse of persuasion provides the annotator with a kind of (illegitimate) freedom that the decoder does not have: the annotator has no ground to defend because his room—margins, interlinear spaces, gaps between words and letters—is provided for him by his host. The resourcefulness of the commentator derives from a tactical freedom to exploit aggressively any source of argument, which, in turn, depends on his fundamental distance from any general premise, just as the rhetorician's persuasiveness is derived from his method's distance from any ultimate origin or end. The anxiety of the marginalist is owed to the fact that his resourcefulness is always derived, his freedom licensed, as it were, by his host—the authority on which he obsessively relies and which he compulsively disrupts. Prosperous in its poverty, sportively impertinent yet embarassingly intimate, the marginalium never quite fits; but once intricate with the text it cannot be cleanly removed. Rather like some weeds: "In the after editions, I pruned the double epithets with no sparing hand, and used my best efforts to tame the swell and glitter both of thought and diction; though in truth, these parasite plants of youthful poetry had insinuated themselves into my longer poems with such intricacy of union, that I was often obliged to omit disentangling the weed, from the fear of snapping the flower."

To adopt another metaphor (or another metaphor for metaphors), the politic aggressiveness of the marginalist may be attributed to the contingency of living in a borrowed home: the security of a sheltering text is crossed by the unsettling awareness that it is someone else's text. Inhabiting margins is "expropriation, being-away-from home, but still in a home, a place of self-recovery, self-recognition, self-mastery, self-resemblance: it is outside itself—it is itself." *Almost* itself because not quite still a home—or, rather, not quite a still home because borrowed. One must constantly maneuver to maintain one's place until one has a place of one's own. For Coleridge the possible cessation of the anxiety that shadows every turn of the pen attends the fantasy of a home he will never have:

> 'My dear young friend, . . . suppose yourself established in any honorable occupation. From the manufactory or counting-house, from the law-court, or from having visited your last patient, you return at evening,
>
> > Dear tranquil time, when the sweet sense of home
> > Is sweetest—"
>
> to your family, prepared for its social enjoyments, with the very countenances of your wife and children brightened, and their voice of welcome made doubly welcome, by the knowledge that, as far as *they* are concerned, you have satisfied the demands of the day by the labor of the day. Then, when you retire into your study, in the books on your shelves you revisit so many venerable friends with whom you can converse. Your own spirit scarcely less free from personal anxieties than the great minds, that in those books are still living for you! Even your writing desk with its blank paper and all its other implements will appear as a chain of flowers, capable of linking your feelings as well as thoughts to events and characters past or to come; not a chain of iron, which binds you down to think of the future and the remote by recalling the chains and feelings of the peremptory present.'

But the text exacts day labor, home denied. Although Coleridge wishes to write the philosophy of the owner or proprietor who capably and lawfully executes his will within his rightful domain, as unbidden guest, lacking the franchise of a home, his working prose imitates (imitates and refines) the contingency it attacks. In Chapter VI, Coleridge's remarks on the probable lawless consequences of the Hartleian hypothesis are followed by a magisterial gesture toward precision: "There is in truth but one state to which this theory applies at all, namely that of complete light-headedness; and even to this it applies but partially, because the will and reason are perhaps never wholly suspended." He begins the next paragraph in this way: "A case of this kind occurred in a Catholic town in Germany a year or two before my arrival at Göttingen, and had not then ceased to be a frequent subject of conversation." We recognize the rhetorical appeal to the example, which is intended to clarify and fortify the argument. But it is also evident that the example does not fit neatly into a formed argument: we cannot be entirely certain what "this kind" of case is, an instance of uncontrolled delirium or a case of light-headedness which shows that the reason and will are never wholly suspended. Coleridgean distinctions dance away their rigor. The equivocation in the reference here reflects the discontinuity between the sections of the refutation and highlights the jerry-built transitions between annotations, linked by neither floral nor iron chain but by their equivocal reference to the host text.

What follows is a psychological whodunit. An illiterate maidservant "was seized with a nervous fever; during which, according to the asseverations of all the priests and monks of the neighbourhood, she became *possessed*, and, as it appeared, by a very learned devil. She continued incessantly talking Latin, Greek, and Hebrew, in very pompous tones and with distinct enunciation." Fortunately the woman is visited by a young physician who is "determined to trace her past life step by step," and who eventually tracks her pedantic ravings to the nocturnal ambulatory readings of a scholarly former master—traced so satisfactorily "that no doubt could remain in any rational mind concerning the true origin of the impressions made on her nervous system." In other words, the case can be explained in strictly associationist terms: there is no mention of the will or reason. The equivocal reference of "this kind" has, in its correction, given way to an equivocalness more crucial. Why has Coleridge bothered to tell a story, which, if it performs any function, reinforces the position of his adversary, albeit in a pathological extreme? Has the impulse to give a good rhetorical example been interrupted by Coleridge's desire to tell one of *his* stories? Is the story irrelevant to the context, or is the chapter on Hartley only a pretext for the opportunity to insert this anecdote?

The combination of a grammatical slippage between one paragraph and the next with the logical slippage that the anecdote introduces into the argument opens up the text to these questions and encourages the reader to search for the relevance of the illustration elsewhere than in its simple rhetorical function. The theme of the story is possession. A maid, illiterate and "known" to be a heretic, lives in a home which is not, of course, her own. She possesses nothing. Not only is she possessed by her master, she comes to be possessed by a very learned devil. An investigator discovers, however, that she is guiltless of diabolical communion and completely the victim of her circumstances. The moral may be taken from Chapter VII of the *Biographia*: "God only can know, *who* is a heretic." Although one may be tempted to associate Coleridge, the writer, with the dogged investigator, it is actually the maidservant who in her feverish glossolalia most closely resembles the writer. We may recall the remark from Chapter IX of the *Biographia*, often quoted in defense of

Coleridge's borrowings, where he says that he regards "truth as a divine ventriloquist." This story is a case of ventriloquism in which, (truer) to experience, a person is ventriloquized not by truth but by learning, truth's simulacrum. One of the major themes of the *Biographia* is also possession: Coleridge's possession of his ideas before his contact with Schelling's works, his account at the end of Chapter IV of his being possessed by the genius of Wordsworth, his mention of how Kant "took possession of [him] as with a giant's hand," his possession by the learned devil of Schelling in Chapters XII and XIII. We may, at one level, read this anecdote as the disguised expression of an excuse and a wish. Coleridge excuses himself as being guiltlessly taken over by forces beyond his control, and he imagines the advent of a romantic physician who will exorcise his demons and thus free him from the charge of heresy by a rational explanation of their cause. Living in a borrowed home, a house of language where one is subjected early and often to a barrage of words, one becomes transformed into a vehicle for a volatile, fragmentary discourse which consists of sentences "coherent and intelligible each for itself, but with little or no connection with each other." It is notable that when Coleridge looks for an excuse he eagerly adopts the Hartleian model of mind (ideas can be tracked "step by step") and expression (either possession or ventriloquism); conversely, when he has done something good, he wants credit for it. It is apt that the maidservant is overpowered by books, and not just books but sacred books and their commentaries, which in a bizarre process of promiscuous self-reproduction seem to imprint themselves on the woman's mind, willy-nilly appropriating her to their margins. Yet in this place Coleridge provides, however underhandedly, the tools to deconstruct those ethical excuses. If we take Coleridge seriously we can take the story one step farther along. Although rational investigation shows that the girl's ravings are wholly mechanical, *we know* that the "will" and the "reason" are never entirely suspended—we know because Coleridge has told us so. Somewhere within, the woman desired to be possessed: she cannot be entirely guiltless because the activity of the learned machinery received its blessing somewhere in her mind. The converse implication is also true. The most willed, reasonable action of the woman or the physician is in some way conditioned and cannot be completely to his or her credit. Who can tell the rudder from the stream? In truth, Coleridge can be considered as both patient and physician, the demystifier of his own supposed possession whether by Hartley, Kant, Schelling, or anyone else. No one can fully possess anything—certainly not language, least of all himself. Everyone lives in a borrowed home in the economy of the Coleridgean text because no one has a home of his own. That is not the "lawless consequence" of Coleridge's writing but its characteristic equivocation, which puzzles the bond between act and consequence. The indefinite repetition of the Coleridgean "I AM" in the chamber of the text resounds our sense of voice and echo.

Coleridge deploys various topoi besides the illustration to give point to his criticism of association, such as persuasive definition: "the despotism of the eye"; the *occupatio*: "we will pass by the utter incompatibility of such a law"; *reductio ad absurdam*: "the whole universe cooperates to produce the minutest stroke of every letter"; hyperbolic pathos: "the poor worthless I." The one among them that most clearly demonstrates the equivocalness of his method appears in Chapter VI where he assists Maass's criticism of Hartley's vibrations by comparing the function of the nerve in Hartley's theory to "the flint which the wag placed in the pot as the first ingredient of his stone-broth, requiring only salt, turnips, and mutton for the remainder!" The implicit claim of this metaphor is that the material factor is deficient in explanatory power without the superaddition of active, vital ingredients to the material model. To give life to matter life must be added. That comparison is not a new one in Coleridge's writings; it was used in lecture five of Coleridge's 1795 Lectures on Revealed Religion, a defense of Priestleian unitarianism:

> Thus I have heard a very vehement Trinitarian explain himself away into a perfect Humanist! and the thrice strange Union of Father, Son and Holy Ghost in one God, each Person full and perfect God transmuted into the simple notion that God is Love, and Intelligence and Life, and that Love, Intelligence and Life are God! a Trinity in Unity equally applicable to Man or Beast! Thus you are told of the wonderous Power of the Cross, yet you find that this wonder working Sacrifice possesses no efficacy unless there be added to it everything that, if God be benevolent, must be sufficient without it. This is the mysterious cookery of the Orthodox—which promises to make Broth out of a Flint, but when you are congratulating yourself on the cheapness of your proposed Diet, requires as necessary ingredients, Beef, Salt and Turnips! But the Layman might say—I can make Broth out of Beef, Salt and Turnips myself. Most true! But the Cook would have no plea for demanding his wages were it not for his merit in dropping in the Flint.

The same comparison is used by the trinitarian Coleridge to characterize a uniformitarian concept of man that had earlier been used by a unitarian Coleridge to ridicule a trinitarian position. Whether defending Priestley or attacking him, the parable of the mysterious cookery is equally serviceable because though it appears to be the commonest of sense, it has no sense except as a rhetorical dislocation of the argument to which it is affixed. The flint metaphor works well as a criticism of Hartley's premise because it would work well as a criticism of any philosophical premise (what is the free will but the flint . . . ?) or as a criticism of metaphysics itself (what is Being but the flint . . . ?). The flint metaphor's omnipersuasiveness derives from its almost imperceptible distance from any essential truth. Indeed, Coleridge's practice indicates that the flint metaphor may be not only a metaphor for all the metaphors in the stone soup of the *Biographia*, but also for all philosophical metaphors, which are the flints to which the (metaphorical) herbs and meat of the (metaphorical) truth must be added. Is it the metaphor or the truth, then, that is additional? The sophisms that the commentator detects in the text are recapitulated on the margins in a finer tone.

The conclusion of the Hartley section exhibits Coleridge's argument and method at the breaking point. He reduces the errors of association to "one sophism as their common genus: the mistaking the *conditions* of a thing for its *causes* and *essence*; and the process by which we arrive at the knowledge of a faculty, for the faculty itself." Although Coleridge fortifies this distinction with examples, they assist him no more than to distinguish the Aristotelian species of association, which categorizes the various immediate causes of combination, from the simpler Hartleian kind, which attributes association solely to contemporaneity. One reduction, however, is to open to another. What is the cause of the Aristotelian causes? Coleridge does not phrase that question, but he elicits it when he admits that the Aristotelian categories "cannot be indeed *separated* from contemporaneity; for that would be to separate them from the mind itself." In other words, the notion of an integral consciousness (the ego, the self which is somewhere present to itself) depends on the premise of the contemporaneity of the mind – its temporal identity with itself. Hence it would appear that it is *essentially* accurate in respect to Coleridge's own ontology to hold the contemporaneity of the mind as the *condition* and final *cause* of all acts of the mind; the discrimination of final from efficient causes does not alter the necessary connection. Coleridge recognizes that to *really* progress beyond necessitarian association requires, somewhere along the line, the rejection of contemporaneity, but he also sees that that would entail an admission of a constitutive or deconstitutive difference, which would in turn jeopardize the primordial unity of being that grounds all principle and all philosophy, that keeps the arbitrary play of the will within bounds. It is only in the decomposition of a tyrannous unity of consciousness that freedom can be located, if at all, although to locate it "there" would be to reduce freedom to a deconstitutive interruption of all certainty, including the certainty of freedom itself. Too close attention to the ground of freedom would lead to questions arising in an endless series, and freedom would be submitted to that ceaseless, discontinuous change from which Coleridge recoils. Such a closure of metaphysics is the terminal hazard that Coleridge's method constantly struggles to evade. That it is foreseen and feared makes all the difference in his prose. As he has displaced the text with marginalia, philosophy with rhetoric, logic with metaphor, so here he substitutes a dispute over efficient causes for the central question. In the service of a greater certainty Coleridge swerves into equivocation. He saves the metaphysics of will by losing it in willful commentary. The chapter closes with a wish that has only marginal significance:

> Sound logic, as the habitual subordination of the individual to the species, and of the species to the genus; philosophical knowledge of facts under the relation of cause and effect; a chearful [*sic*] and communicative temper disposing us to notice the similarities and contrasts of things, that we may be able to illustrate the one by the other; a quiet conscience; a condition free from anxieties; sound health, and above all (as far as relates to passive remembrance) a healthy digestion; *these* are the best, these are the only ARTS OF MEMORY.

Coleridge acts out the dilemma that Hartley had already expressed, that "it is difficult to explain Words to the Bottom by Words; perhaps impossible." He does so by, in effect, giving up a quest that might open up an infinite and infinitely debilitating regress. For that search, however, Coleridge has simply substituted its proper metaphor, a thoroughly marginal method. Entirely rhetorical, Coleridge's own metaphors have no philosophical content. But his rhetoric has philosophical significance just because it traverses the boundaries of philosophy. Because Coleridge's rhetoric is added to a philosophical argument, because his marginalia are inserted in the text, they make the point that philosophy, susceptible to interruption, is equivocal, that it has margins. That point is, of course, without substance. Coleridge's marginal method may indeed suggest that Hartley's system (or Schelling's system) has inconsistencies, but such a criticism can be annexed to any system—to philosophy itself. All philosophical certainties have inconsistencies and interruptions; all texts have margins.

LESLIE BRISMAN

Coleridge and the Supernatural

My point of departure is Coleridge's use of the term *supernatural* in a note on Hooker's *Laws of Ecclesiastical Polity*. Hooker offers, as a reasonable ground in which to root faith, the idea that the desire for happiness is natural in man: "Now if men had not naturally this desire to be happy, how were it possible that all men should have it? All men have. Therefore this desire is natural." Unlike the desire for Christian blessedness (which some men have and most do not, at least by that name), the general desire for happiness is not determined by an exposure to a specific culture or dispensation. *Natural*, for Hooker, means "pertaining to human nature generally," whereas *supernatural* means "pertaining to God's Christian dispensation." Hooker thus happily proceeds on natural ground, in the footsteps of Aristotle rather than Aquinas, when he delineates three forms of desire:

> Man doth seek a triple perfection: first a sensual, consisting in those things which very life itself requireth either as necessary supplements, or as beauties and ornaments thereof; then an intellectual, consisting in those things which none underneath man is either capable of or acquainted with; lastly a spiritual and divine, consisting in those things whereunto we tend by supernatural means here, but cannot here attain unto them.

Introducing the term *supernatural* into his definition of this third form of desire, Hooker does not mean that it takes supernatural means to make us tend to the divine; rather, supernatural means (the Christian gospel) are vouchsafed

From *Studies in Romanticism* 21 (1982).

to us on earth to aid us in the pursuit of a natural desire that cannot be satisfied on this earth. The desire for spiritual satisfaction becomes itself religious; but the desire begins in nature, in common human nature, and Hooker ends the paragraph by returning us to the principle that the third and highest form of desire is, no less than the first two, the offspring of mother nature: "So that Nature even in this life doth plainly claim and call for a more divine perfection than either of these two [desires] that have been mentioned."

It is in response to this last sentence that Coleridge writes,

> Whenever I meet with an ambiguous or multivocal word, without the meaning being shown and fixed, I stand on my guard against a sophism. I dislike this term 'nature,' in this place. If it mean the *light that lighteth every man that cometh into the world*, it is an inapt term; for reason is supernatural.

To be sure one could say of Coleridge's *supernature* no less than Hooker's *nature* that it is an ambiguous or multivocal word. But the charge is less interesting than the accouterments, and Coleridge escalates the rhetorical arms race he instigates by putting on the armor of God, going back to Scripture for the phrase "light that lighteth every man that cometh into the world." Yet why pick this quarrel with Hooker, why deny him his desire to ground in nature the desire for something more than nature? It may be that we have here a little illustration of that cardinal principle of poetic influence that a man is known by the father he keeps, and known best by the aspect of the father against which he keeps guard. Coleridge establishes his ground over and against Hooker just where Hooker sounds most "romantic": in trying to ground the transcendent in the natural. Imagine Hooker to be repeating the nineteenth psalm: "The heavens declare the glory of God; and the firmament showeth his handywork." Nature declares the more-than-natural; that is, human nature, with its desire for the more-than-natural heaven, reveals to us a God above nature. Phrased thus, Hooker's dictum sounds as romantic as it is Biblical; but in accord with Coleridge's typological reading of the psalms, Hooker's emphasis on the natural may be said to form a model Old Testament text which the romantic interprets in the spirit of the New, Wordsworthian Testament: the Presence that is not to be put by has its dwelling in heaven (in the light of setting suns)—and in the mind of man. Though the glory and the dream fled from the earth with the death of the incarnate Son, a Presence called by the church the Holy Spirit still makes its dwelling in the mind of man. Taking this indwelling Spirit to be a fundamental faculty of mind, Coleridge binds Christian piety and natural piety, Biblical criticism and the theory of the imagination.

Coleridge borrows the term *Reason* from Kant, but all his own is its association with the Holy Spirit over and against the Understanding and the "natural" faculties of mind. Both the imaginative leap from ordinary sight to perception "into the life of things," and the leap of faith from matters of the Understanding to the sweet reasonableness of Christian doctrine are leaps energized by the Holy Spirit—leaps *of* the Spirit. He can therefore take as a cardinal imaginative and religious principle Paul's dictum, "no man can say Jesus is the Lord, but by the Holy Ghost." Coleridge uses this not only against Hooker, but against the natural theologians of his own time: "How little have our latter Divines, of the School of Paley and Watson, meditated on the last clause of [Paul's] verse. If only by the Spirit, then assuredly not by arguments of the common Understanding grounded on miracles." For Coleridge it is neither Hooker's "arguments of the common Understanding" nor the sight of miracles (and hence the agency of the senses) but the capacity of the mind to come to faith without logical proof or evidence of the senses that declares the supernatural agency of human Reason.

Calling the Reason *supernatural*, Coleridge pushes the crucial bourn between heaven and earth back to earth, to man, to a line traced (or retraced, rather, in every imaginative experience) within the mind of man. If the Understanding is the natural faculty—the faculty that, under the name *fancy* in the famous definitions, plays with fixities and counters of sense experience—then the Reason, as the supernatural faculty, is ultimately to be identified with (not just mediated by) the imagination. Unlike the image-making faculty, the Imagination is "the living Power and prime Agent of all human Perception"—the agent and power by which human perception is distinguished from mere physical, animal sight. "Human perception" is man's capacity to view the world whole, to view the world as the organic creation of the living Power, God. And the "primacy" of the primary imagination is the primacy of God. By this Coleridge understands not just the temporal priority of the Creator over his creation but the primacy of thou-consciousness over the world of things. Coleridge imagines God Himself explicating His gnomic self-definition in Exodus: "I am all that truly is, and yet 'Thou art—how?—my Son: in the eternal This day have I ever begotten thee." Interpreting "this day" as an eternal present, Coleridge lays the ground for seeing imagination as man's capacity ever to repeat (this day) the infinite *I am* in saying, with God the Father, "Thou art!" to the Son. The primary thing in a man's life is this capacity for religious vision, this supernatural faculty; secondary to that, though like it in kind, is the poetry-making faculty. The secondary imagination, which Coleridge describes as "co-existing with the conscious will," returns the poet in the act of creation to "the eternal self-affirmant, the I AM in that I AM . . . the pure idea of the will." Were the primary imagination, as so many critics have asserted, the mere image-making faculty, the secondary could in no way be described as "identical with the primary in the *kind* of its agency, and differing only in *degree*, and in the *mode* of its operation." But if we understand the "kind of its agency" as supernatural, we can understand why poetic creation differs only in degree and mode from divine creation or the perception of creation as divine, and why poetic creation is "essentially *vital*, even as all objects (*as* objects) are essentially fixed and dead."

If we assimilate the quarrel with Hooker to the theory of the imagination, we can understand Coleridge's romanticism as a form of radical Protestantism. The quest romances of Coleridgean romanticism may be mapped on a Mercator projection in which east means an epiphanic mode, and west a more "enlightened," symbolic Christianity. The subjectivism of such romanticism is that by which the kingdom of God is not "temporal, visible, objective" but here and now, "within you." Its zeal for the sublime is religious zeal, not to be reduced to phenomenology or psychology, and its semiologies—its dramatic portrayals of excesses on the planes of signifier or signified—are variations on *the* metonymy par excellence, the Son as nom-du-père, His name's sake. Coleridge's promised essay on the supernatural, in which the "powers and privileges of the imagination" are further declared, was not promised in vain after the definitions of primary and secondary imagination; the essay was written about the privileged, "reformed" meaning of *supernatural*, and it was already written *in The Rime*, in every poetic exercise of the Holy Spirit or Reason in its secondary manifestation as poetic power. Coleridge's distinction between the Reason and the Understanding, his labeling the Reason *supernatural*, lead thus not to Germany but to Jerusalem, or back through Germany to Jerusalem. The goal is not idealism but God, not Plato but Paul, not Kant but *Emmanuel*, the Lord is with us. Idealism, like John the Baptist, "was not that light, but was sent to bear witness of that Light. That was the true Light, which lighteth every man that cometh into the world" (John 1 : 8–9).

With this metaphor, we must return to Coleridge's note to Hooker and admire a very beautiful and characteristic maneuver. Hooker is talking about a desire all men know regardless of whether they are vouchsafed the Christian means to the satisfaction of this desire: "Nature even in this life doth plainly claim and call for a more divine perfection. . . ." To this Coleridge objects that the faculty that claims and calls for a more divine perfection is itself divine. But observe what happens as he pauses before denominating the desire *Reason* and calling it supernatural. At this point of uncertainty, a "top of speculation" that begins as a semantic uncertainty and becomes an either/or moment of faith, Coleridge queries: "if it mean the light that lighteth every man that cometh unto the world." Does Hooker mean that? Insofar as the phrase Coleridge quotes refers, without special dispensation, to every man, the answer is yes, that is a decent paraphrase; Hooker means by *nature* human nature at its highest, antecedent to or exclusive of the idea of Christ. But Coleridge's paraphrase is no neutral one. The light that lighteth every man that cometh unto the world *is* Christ. Like God answering Milton in the great sonnet on his blindness, Coleridge "to prevent that murmur"—the murmur of desire thwarted in a world of nature, of Understanding, of purely sensory perceptions—locates Christ *there*, already there, in the mind of man. The desire for a more divine perfection is the kingdom of God within man, whether or not man knows it through the historically vouchsafed doctrine of Christianity.

Carried to its Blakean extreme, the substitution of "the light that lighteth every man" for "nature" denies the churchly understanding of a historically vouchsafed Christian dispensation. And this far Coleridge does not go. His next sentence in the note returns us to his faith in historical Christianity, albeit in a manner I find a bit obscure: "Now that reason in man must have been first actuated by a direct revelation from God, I have myself proved. . . ." Perhaps he means by this proof the principle he articulated elsewhere that there are in nature no origins (everything in nature is traceable to something else in nature), so that the first motion of Reason, as the supernatural faculty, must have been a direct revelation; perhaps he simply "proved" revelation to himself in having decided to grant it historical authenticity in order to argue more freely for the independence of faith from miraculous intervention. Whatever the origin of the thought of this proof, I suspect that he intends this statement of self-assurance of his orthodoxy as a cover for his more general claim about the supernaturalism of Reason. In his following note on Hooker he laments the general confounding of Reason with the Understanding:

> In Hooker, and in the great divines of his age, it was merely an occasional carelessness in the use of the terms that reason is ever put where they meant the understanding; for from other parts of their writings, it is evident that they knew and asserted the distinction, nay the diversity of the things themselves; to wit, that there was in man another and higher light than that of the faculty judging according to sense.

Alas for the writers of the Reformation, they knew not Kant! But is "higher light" in this quotation an equivalent for "the true light that lighteth every man" in the preceding note? In identifying the higher light of Reason with the inner light of Christ, Coleridge does not wish to empty Christianity of its historical myth and reduce Christ to a figure for the higher light. That would be Blakean allegory, and would involve, from Coleridge's point of view, a loss not to be sustained. He writes in several places of the sadness of the dissenters' appropriation of a Christian significance without its substance, and the sadness of the Unitarian demythologizing of Christ. If Jesus simply represents Christian virtues, or if the eucharist simply re-presents to the memory Jesus' last supper, religion has turned into melancholy allegory. Coleridge's own, less radical Protestantism distinguishes symbol from allegory in that the contemporary ritual and the historical Jesus are seen to participate synecdochically in the significance for which they stand. The allegorical Jesus is the light that lighteth *every* man, Christian or non-Christian; he is a figure for the kingdom of God within—within the mind of every, fully conscious man. The symbolic Jesus is the light who once came to earth to lighten the burden of sin for every man, or every believer, or every one of the elect; a synecdoche for the kingdom of God, Jesus declared to the apostles "that he had dwelt a brief while *with* or *among* them in order to dwell *in* them permanently."

The Coleridge note on Hooker with which I began implicitly expounds this concept of the symbolic with its inclusion of the historical and the allegorical: Coleridge asserts "that faith as the means of salvation was first made known by revelation; but that reason is incapable of seeing into the fitness and superiority of these means, or that it is a mystery in any other sense than as all spiritual truths are mysterious, I do deny." The faith first made known by revelation is the faith in Jesus who dwelt a brief while with or among them; the Reason capable of seeing the fitness and superiority of Christian faith is the Christ who dwells in us permanently. As both poet and Christian Coleridge is committed to this symbolic mode, and he translates into a multiplicity of contexts a faith in the historical (or narrative) progress from a literal to an internalized spiritual truth. But before we examine some of the poetic consequences or analogues of such faith, we must pause over this dual faith as a principle for reading scripture generally.

Were it not that Coleridge preempted the term *supernatural* and revalued it (as Blake did the word *holy*) to a more general, humanistic meaning, we could describe the symbolic faith as the faith in the supernatural, the natural, and the historical progression between them. The term that Coleridge (unlike Blake) reserves for the older and more specific sense of supernatural is *miraculous*. Thus for Coleridge the Son of God was once miraculously incarnated on earth, and the principle of redemption he first made known lives on as the salvific means by which we transcend our natural selves. This same distinction between a onetime miraculous revelation and a subsequent potential spirituality Coleridge applies to the Bible at large. That is, he accepts the tenet that all the prophets of the Bible were miraculously inspired, and finds in the Bible itself the supernatural traces of a divine glory once—but antecedently—made manifest. The two tropes for God's presence (or more accurately, for the holder of the symbolic faith, the two modes of revelation) are voice and writing. Unlike Jacques Derrida, Coleridge would not dismiss as mystification the idea of Presence and its association with voice; but while granting it temporal priority, he might concur in giving priority of importance to the trope of writing and the concept of the trace. Thus, for example, when Paul says "for we say unto you by the word of the Lord . . ." (1 Thess. 4 : 15), Coleridge prefers to regard the supernatural authority of the apostle as his power of insightful interpretation of a prevenient *text*. To believe that "St. Paul declares himself to have derived this assurance by a direct revelation from Christ" is to degrade Presence into the mystique of the miracle; but to believe that Paul means "such appears to me to be inferred from Christ's own account . . . The Gospel, written or oral," is to privilege the eternal, supernatural power of interpretation over the preternatural, historical appearance of Christ. The voice of the living Jesus *was* present to the apostles, Coleridge thought, and the voice of God was once miraculously present to the prophets; but the Bible, as a written document subject to inspired interpretation, is the natural—or rather the nonmiraculously produced—record of such voice, and the God who would not show Moses His face revealed Himself to us in His going—in the traces that mark the historicizing of revelation, in the written record of interpretation and reinterpretation. One may wish to summarize Coleridge's hermeneutical principle as the principle that there is nothing supernatural about the *composition* of the Bible, but once again we find the term *supernatural* preempted, for though the Bible was not miraculously written by a divine hand or a divine voice dictating to so many automaton recorders of the Word (Coleridge's own figure), any trace of the voice of God, however blurred, can, if rightly understood, raise us above the natural curse: "Only in the apprehension of this do we live a higher life." Coleridge came to see biblical criticism as the richest field for the exercise of self-transcendence. And the Bible itself is both the record of, and our means to, the sublime. It contains, though it does not constitute, Christian religion. Coleridge catches the turn from *supernatural* in the sense of "miraculous" to *supernatural* in its more romantic sense when he says, "the faithful recording of the words of the prophets does not of itself imply, or seem to require any supernatural working, other than as all truth and goodness are such." In the phrase "any supernatural working" he is using *supernatural* in its older sense; in correcting himself, he recapitulates what he understands to be the history of Christianity.

Coleridge's view of the relation of miracles to faith may be regarded as the very center of his religious thought. In the note on Hooker he writes that he does not "deny that faith as the means of salvation was first made known by revelation." The temptation to be resisted is the temptation to read behind "I do not deny" the whispered confession "I really do deny, but that is another matter." Coleridge's faith in the authenticity of miracles could be explained as his sop to Cerberus, his concession to a conscience of religious orthodoxy that the miracles may have been authentic, in order to argue that it is no matter, that the supernatural operation of the will is free from the tyranny of the miraculous, the tyranny of the evidence of the senses over the Reason. But such an argument would palpably misrepresent both the note to Hooker and dozens of other references in the notebooks. The faith of Coleridge the symbolic thinker is that the special revelation of God to his prophets did occur, and that these oracles of God participate synecdochically in the biblical statement; the special miracles performed by Jesus did take place literally, and these events now serve allegorically as reminders of God's concern for man. A notebook entry for November 1801 records this conviction so central to both his poetic imagination and the special inspiration of his religious prose:

> Miracles must be judged by the doctrine which they confirm [,] not the doctrine by the miracle [.] The Romanists argue preposterously while they would prove the truth by miracles, whereas they should prove the miracles by the truth.

In Coleridge's day it was not just Romanists (and in our day it is no longer Romanists) who argue preposterously; but though the controversy over the evidences of Christianity was an internecine Protestant one, Coleridge uses the Catholics polemically to represent holders of a doctrine "we" communally reject. Whether or not one believes in the literal truth of a particular Bible story, Protestants ought to share the conviction that one does not reason that way, that religious argument should not proceed from miracles but up to them, symbols or literalisms as they may be. Faith must not be grounded in what Coleridge calls the Understanding: the faculty that assimilates sense impressions. If the supernatural faculty within is to respond to the supernatural without, it must do so freely, through the conscious will, unbound to one's own or other's perceptions of a suspension of the laws of nature.

Though it is easy to understand what position Coleridge rejects and why he so often repeats that rejection, it is harder to explain the phrases that so elegantly turn on its head the rejected doctrine. Granted the impossibility and the undesirability of making the doctrine depend on the miracles, what does it mean to judge the miracles by the doctrine which they confirm? Does *judge* mean "decide about authenticity" or "weigh its spiritual significance"? In the phrase "prove the miracles by the truth" does *prove* mean "test" (attest to) the historical occurrence, or "demonstrate that these mythic actions are valid symbols of moral truths"? As a religious thinker Coleridge stops short of affirming this second, more Arnoldian position. In his own terms, the miracles are not allegories of general ethical principles; they are symbols whose authenticity (and that means historicity as well as suitability for allegory) is supported by the sense we have that it is fitting that one vouchsafed divine power expend that power in charitable acts. Take, for example, the miracle of the loaves and fishes. Reading the story in Mark, Matthew, or Luke (Matt. 14 . 13–21; 15 . 32–39; Mark 6 . 32–44; Luke 9 : 10–17) the Arnoldian Protestant, unlike the Augustinian allegorizer, would see its meaning as exclusively figurative. He might see in the story a parable of the Word of God given in a frail man's still small voice but efficaciously preached to the multitudes; the sharing of the bread allegorically represents the dissemination of the Word, for man does not live by literal bread alone. Blake might have concurred: Jesus preaching forgiveness of sins—and the word catching on! Can you have greater miracles than these? But Coleridge accepts the literal miracle as such, and then questions, with Jesus, whether it is not wrong to use the miracle as a basis of faith.

My example is not arbitrarily chosen, for both Jesus and Coleridge comment specifically about the story of the loaves and fishes. Coleridge uses this miracle to exemplify the allegorical mode and his dissociation from it:

> The understanding of Metaphor for Reality (Loaves and Fishes = Apostles, Fisherman, Christ's Doctrine/&c &c) one of the Fountains of the many-headed River of Credulity which overflowing covers the world with miscreations & reptile monsters, & then gives its huge supply thro' its many mouths into the Sea of Blood.

Perhaps the most striking thing about this passage is that in saying *no* to the allegorical mode Coleridge releases a surprising rush of allegorical imagery, as though he momentarily turned the spigot to demonstrate the work that the valve of literalism must do. The opening phrase remains difficult, perhaps because Coleridge himself, eager to get to the figure he prized, rushed past the statement of principle. He may have meant to say "the understanding of reality for metaphor"—that is, the act of taking the fish and loaves, which are realities (literal fish and loaves) as metaphors (figures for the apostles or Christ's doctrine). But I think, rather, that he meant to valorize and reserve for ultimate significance the term *metaphor*. In this reading "the understanding of metaphor for reality" refers to the process of mistaking symbols (the loaves and fish were literal, but they came to be true metaphors for Christ) for "realities" (signifiers with less ultimate, more "real" signifieds like men and moral principles).

In clarifying the relation of signifier and signified, we may appeal, as Coleridge himself does elsewhere, to Jesus' own words in the Gospel of John.

Whereas the synoptic gospels give us the story of loaves and fishes by itself, John 6 : 30 ff. has Jesus return to the miracle story of the opening of the chapter in order to demonstrate, as it were, the Coleridgean maxim that "with each miracle worked there was a truth revealed, which thence forward was to act as its substitute." The miracle is worked, and its truth misprized or forgotten by verse twenty-eight. The people say to Jesus: "What sign shewest thou then, that we may see, and believe thee? what dost thou work?" Coleridge now: "And how strangely does Jesus answer them[!] Was it not natural for him to have referred to his stupendous miracles, done in their own presence, but a day or two before?" Jesus declines to answer "You have just seen a sign! Are your bellies empty and the sign forgot?" Instead, he assimilates to the recently past literalism of the miraculous feeding, the long past literalism of the Old Testament feeding. The people suggest that he match the Mosaic miracle—bread from heaven—and Jesus replies: "Verily, verily, I say unto you, Moses gave you not that bread from heaven; but my Father giveth you the true bread from heaven. For the bread of God is he which cometh down from heaven, and giveth life unto the world." The principle of exegesis Jesus proclaims is that of symbolic reading. He does not deny the historicity of the manna but asserts with Coleridge that the truth of the miracle which he now reveals "thence forward [is] to act as its substitute." He says "It was not Moses who gave you bread from heaven," rather than "Moses did not give you (literal) bread from heaven." The latter would be the allegorist's reading; the former asserts the onetime physicality of the bread and then makes the metaphoric displacement (from literal to figurative bread) coincident with the displacement of source (from Moses to God the Father). Moses' manna, and Jesus' own miracle of the loaves and fishes, are emblems of God's participation in and valorization of human history; the metaphoric displacement participates synecdochically in the great translation from the kingdoms of this world to the kingdom to come.

In turning from the past ("it was not Moses who gave you") to the present ("it is my Father who gives you") Jesus symbolically represents two principles of biblical exegesis that are also two principles of literary theory for Coleridge. The first is the principle of copresence of signifier and signified. As Coleridge says, turning to this passage in John and rejecting the allegorical reading,

> If Scripture do not mock our common sense, and the plainest words are not to be interpreted into the most outrageous metaphors for the most commonplace truisms, Mountains in labor with a Mouse, he is at once (*he*, not merely his moral precepts) he is at once the Feast and the Master of the Feast.

Blake (for those who do not joy in his plain words the way Christians do in those of Jesus) is always open to the charge of using the most outrageous metaphors for the most commonplace truisms. Such is the charge to which prophetic speakers and prophetic writers—I think the latter term legitimate—are subject in all ages. Coleridge's hermeneutic principle here could be taken as a welcome reminder that no poet is wholly allegorical, that all literary texts worth reading as literary texts are to some degree self-referential: the "meaning" of their characters and motions is not translatable into truisms, the signified is not something isolatable from the signifiers.

When the text is the Bible, Coleridge's first hermeneutic principle yields an emphasis on the symbolic, representative Christ who simultaneously "represents" us all ("the purpose of our Lord's mission and miracles was to represent the Universal in an Individual") and redeems us in that privileged representation. To be baptized into the death of Christ (Rom. 6 : 3) is "to take up the *cross* of Christ—what was effected at once in the unity of the Root must be repeated successively and individually in each twig or fibre that grows out of the Root." The same principle of symbolic participation in the reality represented pertains to biblical criticism generally. Coleridge rejects as "beautiful, but I fear, far too refined and sentimental," a reading of the biblical cosmogony as "representative" of the way "every Dawn *re*-creates the world to us . . . First all indistinction, darkness—then a Breeze—then Break of Light—then the distinction of the Sky—then of Land & Water—then of Trees & Grass—then the Sun rises. . . . " Though Coleridge toyed with such a view, he rejected it as an interpretation of Genesis and recognized that he was indulging his fancy rather than his imagination in considering it; because it mythologizes the quotidian rather than symbolically represents and participates in an overwhelmingly greater reality, such a reading trivializes rather than transcends. Making familiar things seem a bit more supernatural was Wordsworth's half of the task in *Lyrical Ballads* anyway, and the notion that Creation stands for the re-creation of each day would be—like the notion that the Eucharist represents the daily wonder of bread brought forth from the earth—a naturalization of the Spirit. Coleridge was troubled by the hexameral Creation, particularly by the creation of light the first day and the sun on the fourth. Though it would not do to note that "in fact" we see daylight before we see the sun, Coleridge found a reading much more to his supernatural taste in the idea that metaphysical light anteceded the idea of the (literal) sun. In the Genesis account of the first day, "Light and Darkness are here used as the Powers of Light & of Darkness." Coleridge never developed a theology of evil, but if by the Power of Light he meant the Son—the Light that lighteth every thing that could come into the world—then the promulgation of the Son could be represented as the work of the first "day" of creation. Alternatively, "the Powers of Light & of Darkness" could represent not the ultimate Powers in themselves but abstractions of their earthly manifestations. In this reading, the first day's work was the work of allegory, but allegory that itself participates synecdochically in the hexameral progress from Gnosticism to nature, from metaphysical to physical sun. The idea that the first day's work was allegorical—like the theological idea of a prevenient begetting of the Son—participates in a symbolic reading of Creation.

For symbolic poets like Coleridge himself, such exegeses point equally to a principle of composition. The imitation of Christ, for the poet, means the work of composing miracle stories where we feel "at once" the presence of the Signified—the Presence of God as the Master—while narrative presents signifiers, stories of feasts. Actually, though Coleridge's theory of the symbolic half licenses this interpenetration of terms, we should use the symbolic terms the other way round: Christ the feast is the ultimate signified, while the Gospel narrative gives us stories of Jesus as presider over the table, master of the feast. For the secular writer the equivalent of feast rituals and miracle stories are the fictions that require our suspension of disbelief. These may be preternatural (dealing with events impossible in the course of nature) or natural (dealing with incidents of ordinary life); but both kinds of poems strive, according to this first principle, the principle of copresence, for the sacramental consubstantiality of signified and signifier, feast and master of the feast. Each text weaves about itself a hermeneutic circle trismegistus: the poem declares the consubstantiality of signs and signifiers to be holy, holy, holy, and the critic who would violate its sanctum to be playing with a consuming fire. He may not be physically (professionally) destroyed, but like the Unitarian or Socinian casting a cold eye on Christological mythology, he will find his intellectual fire turned into the fires of hell: all light and no heat.

The poet who believes that Christ is the signified, not just the grand signifier, is committed to avoiding even the appearance of reduction to truism that talk about signifiers and signified tends to have. How much richer is the trope of feast and master of the feast! I have said that we should take Christ as master of the feast in the sense of a character, a narrative signifier pointing elsewhere. (Coleridge himself loved to play on *numen* and *nomen*, the name that is here and the numinous reality that is what Milton called "the meaning, not the name.") Yet the trope is more complex than that, and "master of the feast" both actualizes and summarizes, or synecdochically represents, Christ in his various pedagogical poses. Christ as feast means that not Christian precepts but he himself (his authority for saying "I am *he* whom the prophets foretold; I am he whom you desire") is what is taught; the "elsewhere" always implied by metaphoric language is, ironically, *here*, within you. At the same time that we feel the rich display of consubstantial signifiers to be commonplace before recoiling from it or relinquishing it to the interfeast, to be the divine Signified above and beyond all figuration. To eat this Word is to acknowledge simultaneously the presence of God and His absence—his transcendence of any figurative representation. The absent signified already points beyond the incarnate Christ to "The Evolver," the ultimate signified behind Coleridge's second principle.

The attempt to articulate a theory of poetry based solely on Coleridge's *first* principle, the principle of consubstantiality, is bound to limited success. Once one has articulated the consanguinity of signifier and signified, and the correlative fraternity of all signifiers, all things of this earth as signs pointing beyond themselves, there remains only the endless, if priest-like task, of identifying passages where we sense literary language specially heightened into expressions of copresence. Without an idea of Christian history, without a theory of how the concept of symbol is related to the idea of narrative, one is in danger of endlessly repeating the phrase "oneness of things" and reducing some of the greatest and most complex passages of poetry to the One Life idea. Here then is a second principle related to Coleridge's reading of the miracle of the fishes and loaves: Just as Jesus came not to deny history or the literal but to recapitulate and fulfill the movement from shadowy type to truth, so must the poet attempt to give us the real miracle of the commonplace before recoiling from it or relinquishing it to the interpreter who will sublime facticity into "truth." If the first principle can be represented by the faith that Christ is the bread whereof he speaks, the second principle can be represented by the prayer, Give us this day our daily bread: imaginary gardens with real loaves and fishes in them. Believe that the act of re-presenting those is divine, and the transubstantiation will be added unto you. Though "miracles must be judged by the doctrine they confirm, not the doctrine by the miracles," the *history* recounted in and by a poem must be the progress from miracle to doctrine. The literary critic is the interpreter of such progress, the cartographer of its labyrinth.

Let us test this second principle against a humble example of a text where the first principle alone would yield no raptures:

Pity

Sweet Mercy! how my very heart has bled
  To see thee, poor Old Man! and thy grey hairs
  Hoar with the snowy blast: while no one cares
To clothe thy shrivell'd limbs and palsied head.
My Father! throw away this tatter'd vest

> That mocks thy shivering! take my garment—use
> A young man's arm! I'll melt these frozen dews
> That hang from thy white beard and numb thy breast.
> My Sara too shall tend thee, like a child:
> And thou shalt talk, in our fireside's recess,
> Of purple Pride, that scowls on Wretchedness—
> He did not so, the Galilaean mild,
> Who met the Lazars turn'd from rich men's doors
> And call'd them Friends, and heal'd their noisome sores!

I would not argue either that this poem is among the handful of Coleridge's most memorable achievements or that it presents a problem of exegesis that requires abstruse research into Coleridge's religious musings. But partly because the turn to Sara or her equivalent is crucial in a number of Coleridge's greatest poems, it is worth pausing over this sonnet and inquiring whether the formal turn or turns of the poem are illuminated by Coleridge's sense of the religious turn from miracle to doctrine. On first reading one might instinctively locate *the* turn of the poem between wretchedness and Christ, between the dash at the end of the first eleven lines and the parousia of Christ, the signified, in the last three. But is Christ the signified or another signifier for the commonplace truth, the moral virtue announced in the poem's title? Presenting Coleridge himself in the role of the Good Samaritan, the poem presents the same problem as the parable in Luke 10 : 29–37. Is the Samaritan in Luke the type of the Christian or a figure for Christ? Does the parable signify charity, or does it point rather to salvation, unobtainable through priest, Levite, and the Judaism they represent? One reminder that we cannot rest with the notion of the necessary copresence of Christian virtue and Christ comes in the gospel story closely tied to the healing of lepers where Jesus sanctions the expenditure on him of oil that could have been used for "sweet mercy," for charitable purposes. Matthew (26 : 6–13), Mark (14 : 3–9), and John (12 : 1–8) all set the scene of the anointing at Bethany in the house of Simon the leper. Leaving us with Jesus the healer of leprosy, does Coleridge's poem stop short of the problem of the relationship between charity and soteriology? Or does Coleridge's choice of where his poem goes and where it stops implicitly serve as an interpretation of the gospel—a new gospel in fourteen lines, with a new version of the relation between miracle and doctrine?

One corollary of the second principle, that poetry reflects Christian history as well as the atemporal vision of the One Life, is that we must take very seriously both the history or narrative sequence within the poem and the intertextual history or the relation of the poem to its drafts, precursor texts, and references. Consider first this alternative ending of the sonnet, published by Coleridge in 1793 and 1803

> He did not scowl, the Galilean mild,
> Who met the Lazar turn'd from rich man's doors,
> And call'd him Friend, and wept upon his sores.

Coleridge may have been moved by purely aesthetic considerations (revulsion from the suggestion of weeping "on" the sores) to prefer the version that reads Christ "heal'd their noisome sores." But since weeping is a demonstration of pity, while healing is an efficacious act—more efficacious than Coleridge's hospitality—the decision to leave the poem with the work, the miracles of Christ, rather than the pity, the doctrine of Christ, is not a purely aesthetic one. The preferred version sacrifices, on the altar of faith, the pathos of "wept"; gaining decorum in the relation of Coleridge's charity to the divine mercy, the second version regains the richness of a symbolic faith, a richness otherwise sold to provide the poor fare of allegory, Christ as a figure for charity.

Far from resting with the consubstantiality of charity and Christ, the poem reminds us also of the temporality of the Logos in the gospel itself. Coleridge's reference to Christ's healing is actually a series of references remarkably condensed into the sonnet's concluding couplet, and the startling phrase, "and call'd them Friends" (stronger still in the version that has "and call'd him Friend") makes this living word, as though actually spoken by Christ, a synecdoche for the whole operation of the Logos in history. Jesus was thought of as the friend of sinners and publicans; he did address his disciples as friends (John 15 . 15); but there is no single occasion on which he heals a leper and calls him "friend." Coleridge's poem refers first and most specifically to the story of Lazarus in Luke:

> There was a certain rich man, which was clothed in purple and fine linen, and fared sumptuously every day: And there was a certain beggar named Lazarus, which laid at his gate, full of sores, And desiring to be fed with the crumbs which fell from the rich man's table: moreover the dogs came and licked his sores. And it came to pass, that the beggar died, and was carried by the angels into Abraham's bosom: the rich man also died, and was buried; And in hell he lift up his eyes, being in torments, and seeth Abraham afar off, and Lazarus in his bosom. And he cried and said, Father Abraham, have mercy on me, and send Lazarus, that he may dip the tip of his finger in water, and cool my tongue; for I am tortured with this flame. . . . Then he said, I pray thee therefore, father, that

> thou wouldest send him to my father's house: For I have five brethren; that he may testify unto them, lest they also come into this place of torment. Abraham saith unto him, They have Moses and the prophets; let them hear them. And he said, Nay, father Abraham: but if one went unto them from the dead, they will repent. And he said unto him, If they hear not Moses and the prophets, neither will they be persuaded, though one rose from the dead.

That Coleridge may have been especially drawn to this passage we can surmise from its conclusion, its authoritative word from heaven that faith cannot be based on miracles—even resurrection from the dead. If Abraham does not yet appear to be proclaiming the Coleridgean maxim that "miracles must be judged by the doctrine which they confirm, not the doctrine by the miracle," all that is needed is to have the doctrine here proclaimed in Luke confirm the miracle, the resurrection of Lazarus, effected in John. This connection, this path from Luke to John (the Gospel Coleridge most preferred), is the gospel according to Coleridge. His sonnet refers specifically to the Luke story through the figure of "purple Pride," the clothing of the rich man in Luke 16 : 19. The sonnet refers to the story in John (11 : 1–12 : 10) by reaching there for the pathos of 11 : 35: "Jesus wept." Though "heal'd their noisome sores" may refer to miraculous healing, it describes a charitable act much domesticated from the awesome resurrection of Lazarus from the dead; the phrase "wept upon their sores" marks an even more radical domestication or reduction of the preternatural element. Coleridge does not deny the literal resurrection of Lazarus, but by choosing to refer to the more frequent, more familiar action of Jesus healing the sick, he chooses with Milton "to prevent that murmur," the murmur of the sign-seekers, the seekers after preternatural manifestations of Christ. He pre-vents the miraculous, going before it with his own domesticated form of Christ's charity and arresting the sonnet just there, in the natural evermore about to be something else.

In the notebooks there are any number of occasions on which Coleridge denies the allegorical interpretation of Christ and insists on the historicity of the symbolic instance. "If Christianity be indeed a scheme of Redemption [and not, we might specify, a set of metaphors for the redemptiveness of right conduct] we may be assured that its doctrines must be such as that all must converge to one point, & with them all the essential faculties and excellencies of the human Being—so that Christ in the Man, and the Man in Christ, will be *one* in *one*." The incarnate God (man in Christ) and what Blake called the divine humanity (Christ in man) converge when and if the Good Samaritan is both Christ and a figure for Christ, when and if the Jesus who cures the leper from the ultimate disease of death is both a divinely charitable man and himself "the resurrection and the life." To go beyond "convergence" to a concept of spiritual *history* we need to think of kenosis as a repeated act, and we need to think of kenosis both as the postponement of the "doctrine" (for Coleridge the true supernatural) so the preternatural miracle can transpire first, and as the postponement of an ultimate revelation so the divine humanity can act in human time. Jesus postpones the symbolic sense in which he is the resurrection and the life in order to give local habitation and a name to an act of resurrection: the raising of Lazarus. He also postpones the sacramental for the charitable, and suffers the anointing in Bethany (in preparation for his own death) only after having raised Lazarus. He can say "the poor always ye have with you" (John 12 : 8) because he has brought Lazarus back from the dead to be with Mary and Martha his sisters. One can hear Coleridge meditating on just this sort of temporalization of the symbolic when he speculates that Christ on the cross "in repeating Eli Eli, lama sabachthani, really repeated the whole 22nd psalm." If we read Jesus' quotation out of its Old Testament context we emerge with pure humanism, the affecting idea of the man-god in agony momentarily forgetting his identity—or at this moment learning the essence of human identity—the way Cleopatra learns to renounce the moon and call herself "no more but e'en a woman." Coleridge's speculation that Jesus recited the whole psalm restores the temporality of symbolism. The psalm begins with the cry of human despair and concludes with divine triumph: "Yea, to him shall all the proud of the earth bow down; before him shall bow all who go down to the dust, and he who cannot keep himself alive. . . ." In place of the pathos of having Jesus cry out that God has left him, Coleridge restores the logos, the temporalized word retracing spiritual history through the psalm and through the path from the psalm to the crucified Christ.

Eschewing allegory, the Coleridge poem symbolically participates in a kenosis of sorts, a humbling to the conversational and domestic (the level of real loaves and fishes) that lets us see the man before he is united to the logos. Ultimately, I should like to argue that the whole project of the domestication of the sublime—that the "theology" as well as the style of the conversation poems, for example—is the expression in poetry of the imitation of Christ. In this sonnet, however, the theological overtones to the stylistic shift enter like lords unannounced, "certainly expected, and yet there is a silent joy in their arrival." In a sense the real turn of Coleridge's sonnet (the conversion it reenacts) is just where literary tradition would put it—between the octet, with its grand style, and the sestet, with its surprising discovery of "my Sara" and "fireside's recess." My belief that Coleridge's rewriting Hooker's *nature* as *supernature* represents a development in literary theory might here find microscopic emblem. Pushing back into the mind of man the bourn between the natural and supernatural, Coleridge establishes not just for the romantic period but for the ever-enduring romanticism thereafter the antithesis of natural and supernatural since mythologized by Yeats and related to literary theory by Harold Bloom, who calls his work "antithetical criticism." The antitheses in antithetical criticism are that between the present and the past and that between the natural and the supernatural—though the way these two sets of terms align is difficult and as various as is poetry. For Coleridge both antitheses are grounded in the Christian difference between New and Old Testament, new birth (into the supernatural) and first birth (from Adam, into the natural). In a usage Coleridge would have applauded, Bloom calls *logos* the mode or moments of poetic turning between tropes of ethos and those of pathos. Though this is not exactly what Bloom means by his terms, we might denominate *ethos* the doctrine or teaching of Christ (pity in Coleridge's sonnet) and *pathos* the facticity of Christ. The ultimate trope of pathos for the Christian is the passion of Christ, and it is interesting to find in the sonnet's opening line that the ethos of pity is immediately troped as the pathos of passion: the bleeding heart. It is only trope—even cliché—but for Coleridge it becomes the only thing needful. We must not allegorize this old man either as St. Paul's *vetus homo* or as an avatar of Jesus being brought home to Samuel and Sara, the nineteenth-century Mary and Martha. But we need to see in the rhetoric of the poem a symbolic participation on the part of "the Galilean mild" in the turn from purple Pride to humble "friends." I know no specific precursor text for Coleridge's sonnet, though I sense its best lines (at least its most purple figures) to be in the spirit of King Lear on the heath. In a sense one must first admire phrasing like "this tatter'd vest/That mocks thy shivering" before finding the style as well as the poverty described answered antithetically by "sweet mercy." The reversal of *s* and *m* sounds repeats on an auditory level the reversal, or turning away from the self, that Bloom has associated with another meaning of *s* and *m*; in this poem it is rhetoric—the orotund phrase—that represents selfhood (the poet vaunting in his craft), and if we feel the presence of such rhetoric in terms of an older style, we sense that the precursor, however composite, has been absorbed into the poet's *id*, his natural self. Antithetical to this is the supernatural element present first as Christian charity and ultimately as Christ, the figure of capable imagination.

TIMOTHY CORRIGAN

The Biographia Literaria *and the Language of Science*

As far as words go, I have become a formidable chemist.
COLERIDGE to Humphry Davy

When Coleridge began dictating his *Biographia Literaria* in 1815, he was at the same time becoming actively involved in a medico-philosophical controversy that was then drawing the attention of most medical men and philosophers in England. The fundamental issue behind the quarrel, a mechanistic versus a dynamic theory of nature, was one Coleridge had argued in one form or another throughout his career. Yet the challenge of modern science specifically had never been so strong nor had it so vociferously demanded his attention as it did in the years from 1814 to 1819. Coleridge's response is well documented: the revised and enlarged version of *The Friend*, his two *Lay Sermons*, the "Hints towards a More Comprehensive Theory of Life," and a series of philosophical letters written between November 1816, and January 1818 all testify to Coleridge's growing concern with the challenge of science and his need to validate his philosophical beliefs with scientific evidence.

In one of his letters to C. A. Tulk, Coleridge prefaces a long account of the forces of nature with these remarks: "In my literary Life you will find a sketch of the *subjective* Pole of the Dynamic Philosophy. . . . In the third volume of the Friend, now in the Press, you will find the great *results* of this Philosophy in its relation to Ethics and Theology—while the enclosed Scrawl contains a very, *very* rude and fragmentary delineation of the *Objective* Pole, or the Science of the Construction of *Nature*." The enclosed scrawl is in fact an abstract of Coleridge's "Theory of Life," his most detailed and comprehensive scientific treatise and a work which refers explicitly to John Abernethy and other major figures in the current medical controversy. The literary life is of course the *Biographia Literaria*, roughly contemporaneous with the "Theory of Life" and likewise in the orbit of the scientific debates. That the *Biographia Literaria* also refers to scientists involved in the medical debate is only tangentially significant; that the *Biographia Literaria* employs much of the scientific language used in the "Theory of Life" and implicitly derives many of its critical models from the scientific models sketched in that work is, however, extremely significant, for it shows Coleridge transferring the scientific discourse which suffused his intellectual life at the time to another discourse, literary criticism. Probably no other alteration in the language of literary criticism has affected practical criticism more.

Coleridge's prolific response to the medical controversy surrounding the composition of the *Biographia Literaria* was, of course, the product of many years of reading and thinking about science. Since his early years at Christ's Hospital, Coleridge flirted on and off with biology and chemistry, and his meeting in 1799 with Humphry Davy marked the beginning of a friendship that inspired Coleridge to seek metaphors for his poetry and solutions to metaphysical problems in scientific research. In one of the rare articles on Coleridge and science, Kathleen Coburn relates how, at its outset, this friendship between the father of the new chemistry and the father of the new criticism was mutually productive: Coleridge shared much of Davy's scientific reading, and as Coleridge searched for the laws within the impalpable, within poems, Davy "was searching out laws of substances hitherto unknown by revealing that beneath the static appearance of the stone, or the powder. . . there may be the flame, the loud bang, the explosive energy. They were both enraptured by the revelation of unsuspected relationships in the vast diversity of things, inanimate as well as animate." It is not surprising, then, that Coleridge's and Davy's description of the poet and the scientist respectively are strikingly similar or that "Coleridge's description in *Biographia Literaria* of the imagination derives at least some of its vitality and power from the fact that although he is talking about the nature of poetry, he might in places equally be talking about Davy's chemistry."

It is important to realize, however, that these affinities between Coleridge and Davy are based on Davy's work around 1802, ten years before the waning of their intellectual friendship. Coleridge avidly followed Davy's 1802 lectures and read his work for many years after, but the famous marginal note to Boehme's *Aurora* summarizes the vicissitudes of a relationship strained by the demands of modern science:

> O how gladly would I resign my life. to procure for mankind such health and longevity to H. Davy, as should enable him to discover the Element of metals, of Sulphur and of Carbon. Oh! he will do it! Yea and may perhaps reveal the synthetic Idea of the Antithets, Attraction and Repulsion.
>
> S.T.C.
>
> Alas! since I wrote the preceding note H. Davy is become Sir Humphry Davy and an Atomist!

As M. H. Abrams illustrates in *The Mirror and the Lamp*, the personal misunderstandings between Davy and Coleridge were in part the product of a general rift between science and poetry in the first quarter of the nineteenth century, Coleridge belonging to the poetic school of spirit and imagination and Davy often tending toward a progressive science which was becoming increasingly mechanistic and materialistic. Davy in fact never totally accepted the theories of atomists like Dalton, and he and Coleridge would always remain distant admirers. Yet the gap that atomistic science was creating between poetry and science made it increasingly difficult for them to share and discuss philosophies. Unhappily for the poets, the disparity between the two disciplines could only diminish poetry's value, as scientists claimed that the poetic vision was a fantastic way of knowing with little relevance to the scientific laws of nature. For Coleridge, this claim—that there was an inherent and inescapable conflict between science and poetry—was intolerable, for if the scientific validity of imaginative perception could not be maintained, the moral principles founded on that imaginative perception would be in danger of dissipating as ethereal musings. Thus in the "Treatise on Method" he bemoans a world suffering "from a subversion of the natural and necessary order of science: from elevating the terrestrial, as it were called, above the celestial; and from summoning Reason and Faith to the bar of that limited Physical experience." The visions of science and poetry must remain parallel and complementary ways of seeing, both supporting a dynamic and spiritual conception of life. The rise of a mechanistic science in 1812 became, consequently, a betrayal representative of a trend that had to be countered in every way possible.

Hard on the heels of the disagreements between Coleridge and Davy, the medical controversy of 1814–1819 erupted around issues closely resembling those that separated the two men. The writings of John Hunter catalyzed the debate, whose principal spokesmen were John Abernethy and Sir William Lawrence: Abernethy championed Hunter's spiritual and dynamic principles of life and Lawrence charged that Abernethy's misinterpretations of Hunter were ridiculously unscientific, that Abernethy and his followers arbitrarily and sometimes fantastically used strictly physical phenomena like magnetism or electricity to account for life itself. Abernethy's vital principle, according to Lawrence, was "like a camel, or like a whale, or like what you please." Documenting the main points of this argument in *Coleridge on Logic and Learning*, Alice Snyder notes that the "fundamental questions of the controversy seem to have been two: first, the relation of structure to function; second, the place of theory in physiological investigation—broadly speaking, the method of scientific thought and procedure."

The battle lines on the two questions were clearly drawn. Operating from an avowed theological foundation, Abernethy "could accept no physical science that did violence to his conception of spirit." The life force, he maintained, was independent of organization and structure and prior to it, for the priority of function to structure was essential to the concept of functional unity in any organism. Lawrence, on the other hand, kept his biology and his theology segregated. That an organism was the product of organization was in his view an irrefragable scientific fact, independent of religious questions. Regarding the second question, it is almost needless to point out that Lawrence, the pragmatic laboratory worker, strongly objected to theories and hypotheses and minimized the role of speculation in scientific labor as much as possible. But Abernethy made the most of theory and hypotheses, and "justified them on grounds that suggest the instrumentalist's point of view; he justified them, that is, on grounds of the concrete investigation that they provoked and controlled."

If these were the questions Hunter's work raised and the solutions each faction loudly proclaimed, it goes without saying that both Abernethy and Lawrence discovered in Hunter what they wanted to discover, a way of responding that Coleridge was equally guilty of when he entered the ring of the debate. After rehearsing the quarrel in his "Theory of Life" Coleridge hails Abernethy's role in developing "the true idea of life," a dynamic philosophy like Coleridge's own which gives priority to function over structure and emphasizes the laws of nature rather than the arrangement of particles. "In Mr. Abernethy's Lecture on the Theory of Life," Coleridge writes, "it is impossible not to see a presentiment of a great truth. . . . If the opinions here supported are the same with those of Mr. Abernethy I rejoice in his authority. If they are different, I shall wait with anxious interest for an exposition of that difference." Thoroughly idiosyncratic, "Theory of Life" is Coleridge's defense of Hunter's and Abernethy's vitalism; it attempts to prove and to illustrate that "life itself is not a *thing*—a self-subsistent *hypostasis*—but an *act* and *process*." The arrangement of separate bodies or atoms does not explain life; rather, "the most comprehensive formula to which life is reducible, would be that of the internal copula of bodies, or. . . the *power* which discloses itself from within as a principle of *unity* in the *many*." To prove these claims Coleridge presents a detailed outline of the evolution of life as it manifests itself through the conjunction of three forces: magnetism, electricity, and a "chemical affinity." Not surprisingly, each of these forces plays an important role in *Biographia Literaria*.

In its intent and language, "Theory of Life" is clearly a scientific tract, directed at a scientific audience and employing the scientific discourse that Coleridge knew from his attendance at Royal Society lectures and his indefatigable reading of such scientific journals as William Nicholson's *Journal of Natural Philosophy, Chemistry, and the Arts* and the Royal Society's *Philosophical Transactions*. There is some difficulty, of course, in isolating a "scientific discourse" in 1815, since a specialized language for science was only just emerging at this time, just as a specialized thinker called a scientist is only just beginning to be recognized. Coleridge obviously belongs to an earlier tradition that saw the scientist as first of all a natural philosopher, perhaps best described by the passage from Plato's *Republic* which Coleridge translated as his epigraph to an essay in *The Friend*: "In the following I distinguish, first, those whom indeed you may call Philotheorists, or Philotechnists, or Practicians, and secondly those whom alone you may rightly denominate *Philosophers*, as knowing what the science of all three branches of science is, which may prove something more than the mere aggregate of the knowledge of any particular science." Nineteenth-century scientists, however, could not be comfortable with this archaic, Coleridgean conception of their role. They needed the precision provided by specialization in thought and language. So while Coleridge disparaged Davy, "who seems more and more determined to mould himself upon the Age in order to make the Age mould itself upon him," Davy saw Coleridge's tragedy as a failure to adjust to the exigencies of modern science. Coleridge's philosophical language simply lacked the "order, precision, and regularity" to deal with the problems of contemporary science: "Brilliant images of greatness float upon his mind, like images of the morning clouds upon the waters. Their forms are changed by the motions of the waves, they are agitated by every breeze, and modified by every sunbeam. . . . What talent does he not waste in forming visions, sublime, but unconnected with the real world!"

Purporting to be more precise and better disciplined, Davy and his colleagues were isolating themselves in their laboratories and fashioning their own specialized vocabulary. Hence, whether Coleridge liked the situation or not, if he wished to argue his philosophy with these men, he had to learn to use their language. This does not mean that traces of other discourses, particularly of theology or of alchemy, cannot be found in the scientific vocabulary of 1815. But after 1800, even in Coleridge's writings, scientific discourse surfaces with enough autonomy to isolate it, and the "Theory of Life" is the clearest evidence of Coleridge's own use of that language to defend his beleagured vitalism.

Indeed, translating his science into a modern scientific idiom becomes a major project for Coleridge in 1815, but equally important is the extent to which this scientific model can explain other phenomena, such as art, and how far these other phenomena will corroborate his scientific findings, since implicit in Coleridge's monistic idealism is the common foundation of all areas of knowledge. Coleridge himself never doubts, of course, that there are these links between science and other disciplines. Writing to Tulk in 1817, he says that "true Philosophy. . . takes its roots in Science in order to blossom into Religion," and in a letter to Lord Liverpool the same year, he recalls his hope that Davy and chemistry will confirm his metaphysics: "If any thing could have recalled the Physics & Physiology of the Age to the Dynamic Theory of the eldest Philosophy, it must have been the late successful researches of the chemists, which almost force on the very senses the facts of mutual penetration and intussusception which have supplied a series of experimental proofs, that in all pure phaenomena we behold only the copula, the balance or indifference of opposite energies." Moreover, in the same letter, after discussing speculative science, physiology, and "Demiurgic atoms," Coleridge asks, "What is all this to the world at large?" His answer goes some way in explaining why he does not confine scientific language to a scientific treatise, but transfers it to other fields, notably the field of literature in *Biographia Literaria*. Throughout history, Coleridge argues, science or natural philosophy has maintained a direct structural correspondence with other cultural phenomena. "The Taste and Character, the whole tone of Manners and Feelings, and above all the Religious (at least the Theological) and the Political tendencies of the public mind have ever borne such a close correspondence, so distinct and evident an analogy to the predominant system of speculative Philosophy," i.e., natural philosophy or science, that this correspondence "must remain inexplicable, unless we admit not only a reaction and interdependence on both sides, but a powerful, the most indirect influence" of science on the other fields of knowledge. Using examples of art from the medieval period and the eighteenth century, he comments, in a way that might anticipate Michel Foucault, "These are all but the ribs, abutments and sea-marks of a long line of correspondencies in the arts of Taste to the opposite coast of speculative Philosophy."

In short, systems of thought and signification affect the structure of contemporaneous systems, so that an error in a system like speculative philosophy or science could be disseminated throughout other systems. Thus, the "recent relapse. . .of the Chemists to the atomistic scheme, and the almost unanimous acceptance of Dalton's Theory in England, & Le Sage's in France, determine the intellectual character of the age with the force of an *experimentum crucis*." And even poetry is in danger of being degraded by a mechanistic science whose laws and models will inevitably affect literary criticism and poetry. There is a "link or mordaunt by which philosophy becomes scientific and sciences philosophical," and likewise there is a link between science and poetry which would allow for the corruption of poetry by science and the substantiation of both through the truth they share. "If in the greatest poets we find Nature idealized through the creative power of a profound yet observant meditation, so through the meditative observation of a Davy, a Wollaston, a Hatchett, or a Murray, . . . we find poetry, as it were, substantiated and realized."

In 1815 Coleridge's task, then, was to establish the connections between his scientific models and the realm of poetry, connections which the scientific community especially were ignoring or denying. From the perspective of Coleridge's visionary philosophy, these connections were clearly present; he needed, however, to substantiate and realize them for the world at large and specifically for his scientific competitors. The solution was in language. Ease and accuracy in transferring the language of "Theory of Life"—the scientist's own inbred tongue—to *Biographia Literaria* became the most direct and effective way of illustrating the commensurability, even the authority, of both Coleridge's science and his poetics.

The way scientific language permeates literary definitions and practical criticism is my primary concern here, and these areas of *Biographia Literaria* generally relate to the issue of function versus arrangement. But the second topic of these debates, the value of theory in investigative research, also plays a large role in the *Biographia*. This second issue is naturally less directly involved with language itself, and has been discussed more frequently by Coleridge scholars than the first issue, though rarely in the context of the medical debates which greatly influenced Coleridge's thinking about theory. Snyder notes that during the medical debates Coleridge

> was forced into a fundamental consideration of the processes of thought. There resulted a vivid realization of the extent to which all thinking is determined by assumptions, ideas, images, and attitudes of even less tangible sorts. Coleridge's insistence that fertilized thinking involved more than induction, and experience more than

what is commonly meant to empiricists; that the premises are the critical part of reasoning, and that they depend on something other than the understanding—on a power that brings into play the total man,—these principles of thought and method were formulated through his contacts with many philosophical minds, but to no small extent their use in the physiological and chemical controversies in which he took part.

More specifically, Coleridge was faced with a choice between Abernethy's method based on theory and Lawrence's method of supposed objectivity based on observation exclusively. He rejected both, however, in favor of his own method based on law, a method derived at least in part from Kant. A scientific definition, Coleridge claims in "Theory of Life," should be neither a theory nor a generalization. It consists

> neither in any single property or function of the thing to be defined, nor yet in all collectively, which latter, indeed, would be a history, not a definition. It must consist, therefore, in the *law* of the thing, or in such an *idea* of it, as being admitted, all the properties and functions are admitted by implication. It must likewise be so far *causal*, that a full insight having been attained of the law, we derive from it a progressive insight into the necessity and *generation* of the phaenomena of which it is the law.

In *Method and Imagination in Coleridge's Criticism*, J. R. de J. Jackson treats fully Coleridge's preference for law over theory, his conclusions usually being correct and usually standard. According to Jackson, the pursuit determines the method; the specific ends determine the means employed. Thus a scientist like Abernethy apprehends truth, "the Communicative Intelligence," through material data, and must rely on the inexact method of theory, which is primarily an educated guess based on prior research. The poet, on the other hand, apprehends intelligence by looking through the material substance to the essence of the phenomena, discovering the law and then presenting the law in the material data of the poem. The poet does not depend on material data for his knowledge. Here Jackson follows Coleridge's thought quite accurately, but his discussion requires two important qualifications: first, in "Theory of Life" Coleridge argues, in opposition to theoretical scientists, for a scientific method based on law, suggesting therefore the same method for poetry and science; and secondly, in explaining method in Coleridge's theory, Jackson overlooks the reader-critic, whose method is different from the poet's and who is the real subject of *Biographia Literaria*. (If nothing else, the amount of time and space Coleridge uses to berate hack critics tells us that he is discussing a way of investigating poetry, not the way to make a poem, that in the terms of his own distinction he is explaining poetry, not accounting for it.) Though these distinctions may be fine ones, they are very important, for it is in them that the medical debates most obviously make their mark on the *Biographia*. In 1815 the scientific method that Coleridge urges on both Abernethy and Lawrence is one based on law, and accordingly, the critical methodology he proposes and uses in *Biographia Literaria* is the method of law. Both the scientist and the critic work with more or less refined material data, and for both only the method of law can guarantee objectivity and accuracy. In short, though the critic, the poet, and the scientist all search out law, the critic reading the poem is more like the scientist investigating a chemical reaction than like a poet writing a poem.

Investigating poetry in 1815, then, Coleridge works according to a scientific method in which laws are the lamps of good research, and, as is the case in biological research, these laws "of poetry cannot be given from without . . . [but] are the very powers of growth and reproduction," which the critic must perceive. Here, as in every science, "it is the essence of a scientific definition to be causative, not by introduction of imaginary somewhats, natural or supernatural, under the name of causes, but by announcing the law of action in the particular case, in subordination to the common law of which all phenomena are modifications or results." Scientific definitions are causative, not genitive. And in *Biographia Literaria* Coleridge's theoretical definitions do not describe how to make a good poem or propose generalized standards or theories against which to measure a poem. His definitions describe, rather, the laws of poetry as formal causes in every poem, and Coleridge's criticisms of Wordsworth, for instance, point out deviations from these laws. Appropriately, Coleridge's tone and method is that of a biologist noting freakish deviations in the laws of nature. After presenting the laws of poetry—polarity, the secondary imagination, the laws of meter—he examines his material in their light; concentrating on Wordsworth and Shakespeare he *explains* how their works function and where they fall short of the ideal laws of poetry. Thus the organic metaphor does not account for a poem, but explains the ideal laws of its formation. Coleridge is far less concerned with the personality behind the poem—William Wordsworth or William Shakespeare—than with the product those two minds generate.

The issue of theory versus law, however, is only indirectly a product of the scientific language in *Biographia Literaria*. The language itself is a much more immediate and powerful presence, and one of the more effective ways of emphasizing the ubiquitous presence of the scientific language is a simple comparison of passages from the scientific work and the literary work. Since these passages are among Coleridge's most frequently quoted, one well-known example may suffice. In the "Theory of Life" he writes:

> I have shown, moreover, that this tendency to individuate cannot be conceived without the opposite tendency to connect, even as the centrifugal power supposes the centripetal, or as the two opposite poles constitute each other, and are the constituent acts of one and the same power in the magnet.

And these terms transfer directly to *Biographia Literaria*:

> Bearing this in mind, that intelligence is a self-development, not a quality supervening to a substance, we may abstract from all *degree*, and for the purpose of philosophic construction reduce it to *kind*, under the idea of an indestructable power with two opposite and counteracting forces, which by a metaphor borrowed from astronomy, we may call the centrifugal and centripetal forces. The intelligence in one tends to *objectize* itself, and in those other to know itself in the object.

Moreover, some passages in *Biographia Literaria* seem to refer explicitly to the medical debate, using terms which ostensibly have little bearing on literature. This passage from chapter twelve of the *Biographia Literaria* could have been lifted directly from "Theory of Life," though in context it becomes relevant to Coleridge's epistemology and hence his poetics:

> The highest perfection of natural philosophy would consist in the perfect spiritualization of all laws of nature into laws of intuition and intellect. The phaenomena (*the material*) must wholly disappear, and the laws alone (*the formal*) must remain. . . . The optical phaenomena are but a geometry, the lines of which are drawn by light, and the materiality of this light itself has already become a matter of doubt. In the appearances of magnetism all trace of matter is lost, and of the phaenomena of gravitation . . . there remains nothing but its law, the execution of which on a vast scale is the mechanism of the heavenly motions.

Further, Coleridge himself suggests what the evolutionary scheme of "Theory of Life" means to the practicing artist. "Each thing that lives," Coleridge writes in his essay "On Poesy or Art," has "its moment of self-exposition, and so has each period of each thing"; "each step of nature hath its ideal, and . . . the possibility of climax up to the perfect form of a harmonized chaos." Therefore, the "artist must imitate that which is within the thing, that which is active through form and figure, and discourse to us by symbols—the *Naturgeist*, . . . for so only can he hope to produce any work truly natural in the object and truly human in the effect." Compare this description of imitation to Coleridge's earlier and vaguer distinction between imitation and copying, and it is obvious how his scientific scheme of evolution elaborates and extends that original notion of imitation. The scientific language transforms the earlier simplistic and static definition of imitation as "a combination of certain degree of dissimilitude with a certain degree of similitude" into a more dynamic, evolutionary concept that anticipates the pseudoscientific poetics of Hulme and others.

A final and more concrete example of Coleridge's transferring scientific discourse to the definitions and literary principles in *Biographia Literaria* is his description of genius, specifically of Wordsworth's genius. Out of context the statement on Wordsworth's development seems an ungainly simile; however, in the context of the medical debate whose occasion and primary issue was the nature of physiological disorders and diseases, the language reverberates with a special biological significance.

> It is remarkable how soon genius clears and purifies itself from the faults and errors of its earliest products; faults which, in its earliest compositions, are the more obtrusive and confluent, because as heterogenous elements, which had only a temporary use, they constitute the very *ferment*, by which they themselves are carried off. Or we may compare them to some diseases, which must work on humours, and be thrown out on the surface, in order to secure the patient from their future recurrence.

Here Coleridge's language makes meaning as it suggests a rather peculiar, biological understanding of how genius develops and how artistic faults correct themselves. Express this idea in different terms and a different idea takes its place. Discussing Coleridge's use of the word *polarity*, J. Isaacs makes the same point.

> First of all, by his underlining of the word, it is clear that Coleridge is either proud of his invention of it, or regards it as a significant and careful use; secondly, the word is a valuable contribution to our critical armoury, and its uses have not yet been exhausted; thirdly, the O.E.D. can find no earlier use of the term in this special shade of usage; fourthly, it is clear from his reference to "the polarity of the magnet," in the same encyclopedia article on "Method," that this is not merely a loose employment of the normal use of the

> word; and lastly, the fact that this use is a subtle and thought-out transference of a term to the great central problem of Coleridge's researches into the esemplastic power, the coadunating faculty, and the problem of multeity in unity, gives an emotional significance of the highest order to this otherwise cold technical term.

In each of these examples I am drawing attention to the scientific language itself as the formative agent in Coleridge's pronouncements on literature. Hence, my position is opposite to that of most critics who view the scientific language as a metaphor in a monistic system that merges different terminologies. Coleridge's monistic vision is undeniable, but the scientific discourse is clearly more than metaphoric—or at least metaphors and similes have a greater role and a more complicated function than most critics have observed in the past. If Coleridge's vision is monistic, his understanding is pluralistic.

In a recent article Jonathan Culler makes a similar point about the connotative power and cultural significance of two of Coleridge's most important critical terms, *allegory* and *symbol*. Along with Culler's other work, this article is particularly important because it leads the way in indicating how a linguistic focus can unveil the structural makeup of Coleridge's critical writings and delineate the historical, cultural codes that are the foundation of these writings. Culler begins his analysis of Coleridge by describing the structural differences that distinguish an allegorical sign from a symbolic sign. "The allegorical sign, we might say, is arbitrary: the connection between signifier and signified is imposed by the mind or fancy, while the eye and imagination are aware primarily of the difference. The symbol, on the other hand, is a motivated sign, a synecdoche, in which the signifier is naturally connected to the signified." The distinction relates, in turn, to the opposition between mechanical and organic form:

> Allegory for Coleridge is an instance of "mechanic form," of a deliberate yoking together of the heterogeneous, whereas the symbol is a case of "organic form" based on the intuitive grasp of natural relationship. The symbol achieves a fusion of subject and object because in the symbol the truth of the subject or perceiver is also the truth of the object, its natural significance. In allegory, on the other hand, one remains aware of the irreducible difference between the object itself as signifier and the meaning imposed by the fancy of the subject.

We have here two fundamental tropes or codes, "two ways of organizing the attribution of meaning." And according to Culler, a general doctrinal or cultural "shift in formal operations for the production of meaning" accounts for Coleridge's preference for the symbolic.

Culler, I believe, overstates this last point, for this shift in the operations for the production of meaning is less an undefined doctrinal shift than a product of contemporary scientific discourse and an organismic trope. That is, Coleridge's preference for the symbolic is, above all else, connected with scientific issues and scientific language of his day, which Culler explains in terms of the semantic shifts then taking place: "In the discourse of natural history Michel Foucault has traced the movement which leads from classical taxonomy, in which observable differences and similarities between plants and animals are reflected in a corresponding order of names, to the new botany and biology in which hidden properties become the most significant and the true defining characteristics of the organism. . . . The new organism tries, as Cuvier wrote, to establish the correspondence between exterior and interior forms which are all integral parts of the animal's essence; significance is what can be drawn from within the organism itself." Many other fields of knowledge, such as history, were undergoing similar changes in epistemology, but science was clearly providing the key terms and the structures according to which meaning was assigned. My point is this: formal operations in language do not change "generally," as Culler says, but alter because of changes in the operations of a specific discourse which, in turn, affect the formal operations in the discourses surrounding it. Such is the case here, and Culler, perhaps unwittingly, confirms this when he depends on the biological term *organism* to denote the linguistic shift in other discourses such as history.

Coleridge's 1816 distinction between allegory and symbol is one of his most famous critical definitions and tools; the extent to which its significance derives from and depends on Coleridge's scientific discourse is indicative of many of his literary maxims at this time. I have already shown how in a number of places his scientific language transfers directly to a literary context, resulting in principles for criticism that have made Coleridge famous and infamous at once. In those examples, the scientific language provides definitions or codes explicitly meant to organize the attribution of meaning in literature, so that reading a poem as either allegorical or symbolic has important repercussions regarding how and what the poem means. Far less explicitly the scientific discourse controls much of the practical criticism of *Biographia Literaria*, and though scientific language often has little bearing on Coleridge's descriptions and judgments of Wordsworth's poetry, just as often these critical interpretations are made by means of a scientific code or model which supplements the primary text and produces a kind of meaning one would be hard pressed to locate in Wordsworth's poetry. The features of the text which this scientific language selects for interpretation are naturally predetermined by the model itself, and a scientific terminology which has been arguing the priority of function over arrangement to a medical audience will accordingly be directed at the formal features of a poem.

So much has been written about Coleridge's formal criticism and his organic model that it is not necessary to rehash points that have become commonplaces. Worthy of attention, though, are the elaborations on that trope which follow from Coleridge's more subtle thinking about science in 1815, and the way these elaborations manifest themselves in the practical criticism of *Biographia Literaria*. For instance, Coleridge's grounds for differentiating poetry and prose, the first truly practical problem in the *Biographia*, immediately recalls the first issue of the medical controversy:

> A poem contains the same elements as a prose composition; the difference therefore must consist in a different combination of them, in consequence of a different object being proposed. According to the difference of the object will be the difference of the combination. It is possible, that the object may be merely to facilitate the recollection of any given facts or observations by artificial arrangement; and the composition will be a poem, merely because it is distinguished from prose by meter, or by rhyme, or by both conjointly.

In short, what differentiates poetry and prose is not mere arrangement of "elements," as the mechanistic scientists would argue, but the function of the two forms, the "object being proposed" by each.

The emphasis on function over arrangement informs the vast majority of critical judgments in *Biographia Literaria*, and as Coleridge attempts to employ this formula in different and more subtle ways when analyzing poems, scientific tropes and biological descriptions more overtly prejudice the judgments. In fact, biological descriptions and connotations are so ubiquitous that the scientific world of plants and organisms merges with the literary world. Differentiating Wordsworth's and Coleridge's natural world, Abrams notes that the nature Coleridge "ultimately appeals to in art is basically a biological nature," and it "is astonishing how much of Coleridge's critical writing is couched in terms that are metaphorical for art and literal for plants. . . . Only let the vehicle of his metaphors come alive, and you see all the objects of criticism writhe surrealistically into plants or parts of plants, growing in tropical profusion." Indeed Coleridge's prefatory statement on Wordsworth's "Descriptive Sketches" is a description of an organic jungle:

> Seldom, if ever, was the emergence of an original genius above the literary horizon more evidently announced. In the form, style, and manner of the whole poem, and in the structure of particular lines and periods, there is an *harshness* and *acerbity* connected and combined with words and images *all a-glow*, which might recall *those products of the vegetable world*, where *gorgeous blossoms* rise out of the *hard* and *thorny rind* and *shell*, within which the *rich fruit* was elaborating. The language was not only peculiar and strong, but at times *knotty* and *contorted*, as by its own *impatient strength*. (my emphasis)

Later, he lists as the third and fourth excellences of Wordsworth's poetry "the sinewy strength and originality of single lines and paragraphs. . . the perfect truth of nature in his images and descriptions, as taken immediately from nature, and proving a long and genial intimacy with the very spirit which gives the *physiognomic expression* to all works of nature." And finally, "as a sort of allegory, or connected simile and metaphor of Wordsworth's intellect and genius," Coleridge quotes *Bartram's Travels*: "The soil is a deep, rich, dark mould, on a deep stratum of tenacious clay; and that on a foundation of rocks, which often break through both strata, lifting their back above the surface. The trees which chiefly grow here are the gigantic black oak; magnolia magni-flora; fainus excelsior; platane; and a few stately tulip trees." Three years after these statements Coleridge called Shakespeare a "comparative anatomist" who "works from within by evolution and assimilation" and produces beautiful fruits. By contrast, Beaumont and Fletcher "took from the ear and eye, unchecked by any intuition of an inward possibility, just as a man might fit together a quarter of an orange, a quarter of an apple, and the like of a lemon and of a pomegranate, and make it look like one round diverse colored fruit."

Although Abrams hesitates to admit it and Coleridge himself back-pedals by asking pardon for the terms borrowed from chemistry and botany, he clearly intended Wordsworth's and Shakespeare's poetry literally to come alive and be seen as a living organism. Poetic language can never actually have a "physiognomic expression," but Coleridge's critical language can attribute it to Wordsworth's and Shakespeare's poetry, by using a biological language to connote and signify a biological signified. Abrams himself suggests this productive power when in *The Mirror and the Lamp* he explains how critical metaphors and analogies are often not simply illustrative but constitutive. This is certainly the case here, where Coleridge's scientific language reconstructs poetry as a living organism, a three-dimensional object, which functions in much the same way as his plants, animals, and men in "Theory of Life." Pater, I believe, is more correct than most critics admit when he complains of Coleridge's identifying the poem with an actual plant; in *Biographia Literaria* Coleridge certainly exaggerates the case this way. He may, as critics have traditionally observed, be concerned with the creative process, the subjective nature of poetry, but in the *Biographia* that process is objectified, presented as a product, by using a scientific language which transforms the forces of the process into forces of a product. The language is much more elusive in *Biographia Literaria* than in "Theory of Life," but it is quite clear that the forces operative in a poem correlate directly with the three forces of nature: magnetism, electricity, and chemical affinity. There is, in other words, a six-part homology established between the world of biology and the world of poetry. The great value in transferring this three-part model from science to poetry is that Coleridge could use it to distinguish different operations in a poem while implicitly suggesting their unity on the evidence that, as in the biological example in "Theory of Life," "the lower powers are assimilated, not merely employed—which presupposes homogeneity."

Of the three powers which Coleridge describes in "Theory of Life," magnetism or polarity is the most prominent. In that treatise Coleridge makes it clear that, as the most basic force in nature, magnetism is the first expression of the polarity principle, and in this state it is predominantly mechanical, "two equal forces acting in opposite directions." Barfield, without doubt the most lucid explicator of polarity, makes the crucial point that the mechanical *law* of polarity must be distinguished from the *power* of polarity, for if magnetism is an essentially mechanical law, it eventually becomes assimilated into a higher power that is essentially dynamic. Coleridge explains this relative nature of magnetism towards the conclusion of "Theory of Life": "Relatively . . . to fluidity, that is, to matter, the parts of which cannot be distinguished from each other by figure, magnetism is the power of fixity: but, relatively to itself, magnetism . . . is designated by its opposite poles, and must be represented as the magnetic axis, the northern pole of which signifies rest, attraction, fixity, coherence, or hardness; . . . while the southern pole, as its antithesis, represents mobility, repulsion, incoherence, and fusibility."

In their most primitive form, before their conversion into a vital power, the poles of a magnet provide an object with fixity: the magnetic poles are "the primary constituent *Powers*." As Seth Watson observes in his introduction to "Theory of Life," magnetism thus becomes the "first and simplest differential act of Nature . . . the first step from indifference to difference, from formless homogeneity to independent existence." In a poem this rudimentary act of fixity and differentiation is described by the famous pairs that constitute all poems and that become objectified elements in the poem—"sameness with difference; of the general, with the concrete; the idea, with the image; the individual, with the representative; the sense of novelty and freshness, with old and familiar objects; a more than usual state of emotion, with more than usual order." These poles differentiate a poem, define it, and balance it, as it were, in a fixed position. Balance, in fact, is the key to the polar arrangement in a poem, just as it is in a magnet, for "in all pure phaenomena we behold only the copula, the balance or indifference of opposite energies." Accordingly, where Wordsworth's feelings are "disproportionate to *such* knowledge and value of objects described" the stability of the poem is upset; accusing Wordsworth of mental bombast is a criticism of misbalanced energies. Likewise, Coleridge complains of metaphysical poets and some of his contemporaries who in different ways destroy the balance needed in a poem. "Our faulty elder poets sacrificed the passion and passionate flow of poetry to the subtleties of intellect, and to the starts of wit; the moderns to the glare and glitter of a perpetual, yet broken and heterogeneous imagery, or rather to an amphibious something, made up, half of image, and half of abstract meaning. The one sacrificed the heart to the head; the other both heart and head to point and drapery."

Because Coleridge himself rarely dissected his polarity principle and only in "Theory of Life" and his long letter to Tulk in 1817 made a sustained attempt to show clearly how it relates to the magnetic law as opposed to the electrical power, critics often confuse the polarity of magnetism and the polarity of electricity. But in order to fully understand the intricacies of the criticism in *Biographia Literaria*, and especially the role of imagination, one must be aware of these finer distinctions. Again, polarity is the first law of nature, and magnetism's property of attraction and repulsion is the first manifestation of that law. But the two poles of magnetism generate a second force, electricity, which simultaneously vitalizes the fixed magnetic field and stands as the polar opposite to magnetism. (Magnetism and electricity become intersecting axes, each axis having two poles.) In Coleridge's evolutionary scheme, the magnetic force manifests itself most obviously in inorganic metals, and later, when the electrical force becomes predominant, vegetable life and insects appear. Thus, from the conjunction of electricity and magnetism, in various proportions, the different forms of life are made. In the arrangement, represented by the magnetic poles, "life subsists"; in their strife, represented by electricity, "it consists."

The addition of this second power to Coleridge's scientific scheme should never be underestimated. Seth Watson went so far as to say that electricity was "the foundation of life" for Coleridge. This is of course incorrect, a point Coleridge made abundantly clear in "Theory of Life." Yet electricity did provide an illustration and scientific solution to the burden of magnetism and its association with lifeless arrangement. A "new light was struck by the discovery of electricity, and in every sense of the word, . . . it may be affirmed to have electrified the whole frame of natural philosophy." Electricity was a power that could convert the static arrangement of the magnetic field into a space of vital action and movement, and sometime around 1816 Coleridge added a long passage to the revised *Friend*, hailing contemporary research in electricity. After discussing the work of Hunter and Abernethy, Coleridge remarks that all theories of electricity have in common

> the idea of *two-opposite-forces*, tending to rest by equilibrium. These are the sole factors of the calculus, alike in all theories. These give the *law*, and in it the *method*, both of arranging the phaenomena and of substantiating appearances into facts of science. . . . For this reason, we anticipate the greatest improvements in the *method*, the nearest approaches to a *system* of electricity from these philosophers, who have presented the law most purely, and the correlative idea as an idea: those, namely, who, since the year 1798, in the true spirit of experimental dynamic, rejecting the imagination of any material substrate, simple or compound, contemplate in the phaenomena of electricity the operation of a law which reigns through all nature, the law of POLARITY, or the manifestation of one power by opposite forces: who trace in these appearances, as the most obvious and striking of its innumerable forms, the agency of the positive and negative poles of a power essential to all material construction; the second, namely, of the three primary principles, for which the beautiful and most appropriate symbols are given by the mind in the three ideal dimensions of space.

Method, for Coleridge, is invariably equated with a unifying process and here it is associated with "a system of electricity" which illustrates the one power operating according to the law of polarity. Magnetism, that is, can represent the law of polarity; electricity the vitalization or operation of that law. If magnetism demonstrated the law of polarity in inorganic matter, electricity assimilated magnetism to reveal the one power that brings polarity to life in organic matter. The principle of fixity fuses with the principle of dynamic motion; or, as he phrases it in a description of artistic beauty, "confining form" unites with the "electrical flashes" of "free life."

In the *Biographia Literaria* the imagination is an objectified power within the poem, and as such, it is the counterpart to the electrical power in nature described in "Theory of Life." The scientific language with which it is described is indicative of this correspondence: "The primary imagination I hold to be the *living Power* and *prime Agent* of all human Perception. . . . The secondary

Imagination I consider as an echo of the former, co-existing with the conscious will, yet still as identical with the primary in *the kind of its agency*, and differing only in degree, and in *the mode of its operation*. It *dissolves, diffuses*, and dissipates, in order to recreate. . . . It is essentially *vital*, even as objects (*as* objects) are essentially fixed and dead." (my emphasis) "This power, first put in action by the will and understanding, and retained under their irremissive, though gentle and unnoticed control . . . reveals itself in the balance or reconciliation of opposite or discordant qualities." Here the language is that of a scientific experiment in which an electrical force, the imagination, galvanizes different elements that are brought under its power: working together, the will and understanding act as a conductor that organizes a field of "opposite and discordant qualities" which the fusing power of the imagination vitalizes in a manner strikingly similar to the operation of the electrical force found in nature. Shakespeare's work is thus a "growth, evolution" whereby "each line, each word almost, begets the following—and the will of the writer is in interfusion, a continuous agency, no series of separate acts." The conducting will unites with the fusing imagination to become "an interfusion, a continuous agency" of power and control that at once organizes and activates the multiple elements of a wide and varied experience.

The clearest use of electricity in practical criticism, however, is found in Coleridge's analysis of meter. He begins by describing the origins of meter, tracing it "to the balance of the mind effected by the spontaneous effort which strives to hold in check the workings of passion. It might be easily explained likewise in what manner this salutary antagonism is assisted by the very state which it counteracts; and how this balance of antagonists becomes organized into *meter* . . . by a supervening act of the will and judgment." Meter, that is, generated out of a polarity of passion and the controlling effort of the mind that, like the magnetic field, together form a balance of antagonists between which the will intervenes like a conductor. Metrical restraint is then balanced with a language of passion: "As every passion has its proper pulse, so it will likewise have its characteristic mode of expression." In short, mental restraint and passion balance in an original act of the mind that results in meter; to create poetry, this metrical framework is in turn bound and balanced with a special, emotional language: "Meter therefore having been connected with *poetry* most often and by a peculiar fitness, whatever else is combined with *meter* must, though it not be *essentially* poetic, have nevertheless some property in common with poetry, as an intermedium of affinity, a sort (if I may dare borrow a well-known phrase from technical chemistry) of *mordaunt* between it and the super-added meter." The suggestion here, which could be made only through the scientific language in which it is couched, is that meter can be either an artificial or natural part of a poem in that "an intermedium of affinity" should *naturally* bind meter to the language of a poem. And although Coleridge never explicitly explains it in terms of the imagination, it seems clear that what activates this affinity is the imagination that he consistently describes, with similar scientific language, as the power that vitalizes and unites contrary elements. Where Coleridge fails to discover this balance and conjunction between the language of the poetry and the meter, in Wordsworth's "Anecdote for Fathers," "Simon Lee," "Alice Fell," "The Beggars," and "The Sailor's Mother," he rightly claims that these poems "would have been delightful . . . in prose, told and managed, as by Mr. Wordsworth they would have been, in a moral essay, or pedestrian tour." About "The Sailor's Mother" specifically, he quotes three stanzas and queries "whether in the *metre* itself he found a sufficient reason for *their* being written metrically?," tacitly referring here, I believe, to the model he has established whereby there must be a vitalized affinity between the meter and the language of the poem. As the two are joined but not imaginatively united in the Wordsworth poem, the meter sits oddly on the language of the poem, just as the leaves of one flower would look strange if unnaturally grafted on the stem of another species.

In "Theory of Life" Coleridge also discusses magnetism and electricity in terms of "progressive individuation," and this concept, too, bears on evaluations and judgments in *Biographia Literaria*. In nature, "the unceasing polarity of life" represented by magnetism, Coleridge writes, is "the form of its progress, and its tendency to progressive individuation" is "the law of its direction." Here magnetic polarity describes the form, and what I have associated with the imagination (in art) and the electrical force (in nature), namely, the process within the form, now becomes "the tendency to progressive individuation." One of the two principal ideas in "Theory of Life," progressive individuation implies two movements which are represented by the poles of the electrical axis, the centripetal and centrifugal powers: "This tendency to individuate cannot be conceived without the opposite tendency to connect, even as the centrifugal power supposes the centripetal. . . . Again, if the tendency be at once to individuate and to connect, to detach, but so as either to retain or to reproduce attachment, the individuation itself must be a tendency to the ultimate production of the highest and most comprehensive individuality." Progressive individuation embraces two counteracting tendencies in nature, "that of *detachment* from the universal life . . . and that of attachment or reduction into it," both of which reappear in the *Biographia* and the related essays in the term "multeity in unity," a term whose definition almost always approximates the definition of progressive individuation. In his essay "On Poesy or Art," Coleridge comments that the pleasure of art "consists in the identity of two opposite elements, that is to say—sameness and variety. . . . In order to derive pleasure from the occupation of the mind, the principle of unity must always be present, so that in the midst of the multeity the centripetal force be never suspended, nor the sense be fatigued by the predominance of the centrifugal force. This unity in multeity I have elsewhere stated as the principle of beauty." And, early in *Biographia Literaria*, Coleridge lays the groundwork for differentiating kinds of creative minds by distinguishing the centrifugal and centripetal forces in the mind: "The intelligence in the one tends to *objectize* itself, and in the other to know itself in the object."

Whether Coleridge is talking about the creative process of art or the forces of nature, the significance of the language remains the same in each of these passages. As the progressive individuation manifested in the electrical force unites and vitalizes two opposite movements in the life process, in poetry the imagination performs the same task. Though Coleridge never bluntly states this, he values a work of art most when its centrifugal-centripetal make-up resembles man, the organism in whom the two forces reach their maximum strength and scope. In nature, Coleridge says, "the tendency to individuation . . . constitutes the common character of all classes," and "the degrees both of intensity and extension, to which this tendency is realized, form the species, and their ranks, in the great scale of ascent and expansion." On this scale, the higher, more complex organisms are the ones in which more individuality unites with more universality or variety of parts, and "the individuality is most intense where the greatest dependence of the parts or the whole is combined with the greatest dependence of the whole on the parts." The pinnacle of this scale is man, for man is the "highest realization and reconciliation of both . . . tendencies, that of most perfect detachment and the greatest possible union." In man the "whole force of organic power has attained an inward and centripetal direction. He has the whole world in counterpoint to him, but he contains an entire world within himself."

Accordingly, if the paramount, most admirable organism is the one that manifests the most detachment with the greatest attachment, in literature most value will be awarded to the work that manifests the greatest individuality with the greatest universality. The works of Shakespeare and Milton are Coleridge's examples here. Shakespeare's plays not only have a universal scope and variety but also contain a proportionate degree of judgment and unity. "In Shakespeare the play is *syngenesia* a flower species—each indeed has a life of its own and is an individuum of itself, but yet an organ to the whole." Conversely, while always retaining the stamp of the individual man, the poems of Milton contain the greatest of eternal truths. Wordsworth, too, is praised as "individualized," but his characters, unlike Shakespeare's, are faulted as overly peculiar and "incongruous," "for amid the strongest individuation, the character must still remain representative." Finally, the great philosophical poem that Coleridge expected from Wordsworth would doubtless have been great because, like man, the scope of its vision would have been matched by the strength of its individuality.

I have discussed progressive individuation in its relation to the second power in Coleridge's biological scheme—electricity in nature and the imagination in poetry—since Coleridge most usually associates it with these two phenomena. Yet, as all three powers are bound together in a single organism, so the tendency to individuate cannot be separated from the third power, chemical affinity, which corresponds to the intellectual energy and reason behind a poem. Chemical affinity adds the dimension of depth to an organism when it unites with length and breadth, magnetism and electricity, and in "Theory of Life" Coleridge equates chemical affinity with sensibility. He describes this third dimension best in a manuscript note:

> All that is *outside* is comprized in length and surface—what remains must therefore be *inside*—but again, the sole definition of matter is that which fills space—now it is with length, breadth, and length relative to Breadth that space is filled. In other words, Space has relation only to the outside. Depth must therefore be that *by* not *with* which space is filled. . . it must be that which causes it to be filled, and is therefore the true substance. Depth therefore cannot be an attribute of matter, which (i.e. Length + Breadth or Extension) is itself a mere abstraction, an ens rationis; but it must be a Power, the essence of which is *inwardness*, outwardness being its effect and mode of manifesting itself.

Illustrating inwardness, "the true substance," in a poem will always be a perilous task for a critic, but nonetheless Coleridge attempts it, if somewhat coyly, by locating a particular kind of sensibility in a poem. He praises the "atmosphere and depth and height" of Wordsworth's poetic world, and he characterizes the fifth of Wordsworth's excellences, a meditative pathos, as "a union of deep and subtle thought with sensibility." For Coleridge this is an important and positive criticism of Wordsworth, and it correlates neatly with the third dimension of an organism—depth, sensibility, and inwardness of thought. An elusive and protean presence but one which most readers are aware of and recognize in a poem, "thought" is perhaps as specific as Coleridge can be about a third-dimensional property in a poem. But how to show it working in a poem is extremely difficult, which accounts for how comparatively little Coleridge says about depth in a poem. As a power in the poem it dwells in the realm of Coleridge's reason and philosophical Ideas, clearly distinguished from the imaginative power, so that, besides imagination, Shakespeare possesses another poetic power "without which the former could scarce exist in a high degree," namely, "Depth and Energy of Thought." In an 1818 lecture, Coleridge describes the conjunction of these two powers, imaginative force and depth, this way: Shakespeare "worked in the spirit of nature, by evolving the germ within the imaginative power according to an idea." For "no man was ever yet a great poet, without being at the same time a profound philosopher. . In Shakespeare's poems the creative power and the intellectual energy wrestle as in a war embrace." The thinker, as well as the imaginative artist, adds a dimension to the poem, so that balance, imagination, and energy of thought unite in a poem, like electricity, magnetism, and chemical affinity in the life process, to create an object that is as complicated and mysterious as the highest organism in nature.

Just as Coleridge never forgets this ultimately mysterious nature of art and life no matter how analytical he becomes, so his three-dimensional model should never be confused with poetic truth and life itself. If the constituent forces of life are the power of length (magnetism), the power of surface (electricity), and the power of depth (chemical affinity), "life itself is neither of these separately, but the copula of all three." Indeed the powers of life may manifest themselves in concrete comprehensible forms, yet "visible surface and *power* of any kind, much more the *power* of life, are ideas which the forms of human understanding make it impossible to identify " Likewise, the living truth of a poem exists beyond the components Coleridge chooses to isolate for criticism, and a critic's most egregious mistake would be to imagine Wordsworth's or any author's poetry simple and containable.

What Coleridge and other literary critics can do is to understand and explain life and poetry with language. Precisely because of its linguistic nature, this act of understanding will always be an act of commitment and choice—a choice of how they will understand and, subsequently, what they will understand. Scientific language does not appear accidentally or inadvertently in *Biographia Literaria*; it is the controlling discourse that Coleridge chooses for good reasons and with full knowledge of its implications. He recognizes the power of connotations; he recognizes the way different tropes and metaphors could not only organize but produce meanings. He writes about a "fusing power" in a poem, entirely conscious of its commensurability with the "fusing power" of electricity And, describing "depth" in a poem or its centripetal-centrifugal balance, Coleridge consciously creates a meaning, a biological meaning, rather than extracting that meaning from a poem. In 1815 the language of science was gaining an authority that could only diminish the authority of other languages: due to the purported objectivity of scientific practice and discourse, scientific statements simply had more validity than poetic or theological statements. For Coleridge, the way to counter this trend was to make a poem *mean* scientifically, to show that scientific truths are not confined to science any more than scientific discourse is the sole property of the theoretical physicist. If poetry should never pretend to be science, it should also never cower before the language of science. Coleridge's scientific poetics and biological tropes are an important attempt to show that poetry is at least as challenging, mysterious, and intellectually rigorous as the best of modern science.

ARDEN REED

"Frost at Midnight"

"Frost at Midnight" appears to be a very different poem from "Dejection," in that "Dejection" laments the loss of poetic power that could produce poems like "Frost at Midnight." Recent criticism has generally presented the poem as one of Coleridge's rare imaginative successes, pointing out the speaker's increasing awareness and the poem's growth in "organic unity" as it rounds back upon itself to form a perfect circle. But circles are highly problematic figures in Coleridge, and the fact that the end curves back to the beginning may signify other things besides a happy and simple resolution. In fact, I will argue that "Frost at Midnight" takes as complex and ambiguous an attitude toward imagination and writing as does "Dejection." We may begin by simply noticing that there are verbal parallels between "Dejection" and "Frost at Midnight." "Frost at Midnight" already refers to "abstruser musings" (l. 6), while the ur-version of "Dejection" looks back to the passage in "Frost" on the speaker's childhood: "(Alas! for cloister'd in a city School/The Sky was all, I knew, of Beautiful)." And in the 1809 revision of "Frost at Midnight" Coleridge added the line "Ah there was a time," revising the poem as Magnuson says, "to approximate the phraseology from 'Dejection.'" These cross-references are not sufficient evidence to conclude that "Frost at Midnight" is an early version of "Dejection," of course, only that the poems are related in some way. The opening of "Frost at Midnight" also resembles that of the contemporary "Christabel": "Frost at *Midnight*" and "the *mid*dle of the *night*," (l. 1), the owl's cry in both poems, and especially the shared phrase "and hark, again!" ("Christabel" l. 4,

From *Romantic Weather: The Climates of Coleridge and Baudelaire*. Originally entitled "The Wedding Garment and the Shroud."

"Frost at Midnight" l. 3)—the line harkens to itself "again." "Christabel" evokes a mysterious sense of unease, and in a similar way "Frost at Midnight" unsettles its calm, domestic setting by the strange and even slightly alien personification. Coleridge here modulates the "meteor" of frost into mystery.

But a more suggestive reference is the comparison "Constancy" draws between its own setting and that of "Frost at Midnight"—"the peacefull'st cot, the moon shall shine upon" (l. 20). One reason for the reference is of course that "Frost at Midnight" offers a graphic image of what it means "to have a home, an English home" (l. 8). More importantly, though, it describes the same scene of "writing" as in "Constancy": the "*stranger*" on the grate is a kind of ideal object.

> Methinks, its motion in this hush of nature
> Gives it dim sympathies with me who live,
> Making it a companionable form,
> Whose puny flaps and freaks the idling Spirit
> By its own moods interprets, every where
> Echo or mirror seeking of itself,
> And makes a toy of Thought.
>
> (ll. 17–23)

The speaker "interprets" the stranger in the same way that the woodman does his shadow: (1) by doubling himself and (2) by projecting that self onto an object made to take the form of the absent beloved. On the white film he inscribes the image of his own desire. Like the narrator of "Constancy," he knows this to be an "idle thought," but as in *The Friend*, his knowledge makes no difference: "Idle thought!/But still" one he cannot keep himself from thinking. Like the Brocken Specter to which "Constancy" refers, the portent of the "*stranger*" is a matter of popular belief rather than a private association. Nonetheless, this communal topos only serves to further his alienation.

Long before his reappearance in "Constancy" the "*stranger*" from "Frost at Midnight" is cast in the form of the Ancient Mariner's albatross. (That Coleridge would have had the albatross in mind when he described the stranger is not surprising, given the concurrent composition of the poems.) Both texts depict an absence of life and activity, the hibernal "hush of nature" (l. 17) corresponding to the bleak polar region in the "Ancient Mariner"; and "Constancy" of course spells out the connection between the ship at sea and the isolated cottage. Then, in each poem, the dead calm is broken by the motion of a single object—the bird in one case and the film in the other. This movement immediately encourages the speakers to personify both as the "companionable forms" of a "Christian soul" and "a townsman" (l. 42) The "*stranger*" even moves like an albatross, "flap[ping]" as if it had wings.

The lines on the "*stranger*" are the most heavily revised part of the poem, indicating Coleridge's own perplexity over how to interpret that figure. In all versions from 1798 to 1828 the speaker begins by characterizing the film on the grate in positive terms. Indeed, his imagination works in the way prescribed by the middle stanzas of "Dejection":

> the living spirit in our frame,
> That loves not to behold a lifeless thing,
> Transfuses into all its own delights,
> Its own volition
>
> (original version)

This interpretation of the speaker's interpretation differs markedly from its poetic antecedent, a passage in *The Task*, in which Cowper describes the "*stranger*" as an insignificant and indolent superstition. For Coleridge the "*stranger*" is never insignificant, but Cowper's association with superstition carries over into "Frost at Midnight." Thus the speaker goes on to disparage his activity as a "most believing superstitious wish." Just as in "Dejection," the imaginative act in "Frost at Midnight" has two sides: the speaker interprets the flame "sometimes with deep faith/And sometimes with fantastic playfulness" (ll. 24–25, original version). In the 1808–09 revision Coleridge tries to limit this play by suggesting, rather charmingly, that it is aware of its own erratic tendencies, not unlike the precocious child who charms his parents into overlooking what he himself recognizes to be inappropriate behavior: "wilful playfulness/That stealing pardon from our common sense/Smiles, as self-scornful, to disarm the scorn/For these wild reliques of our childish Thought" (ll. 25–28). But in subsequent editions Coleridge deletes this portrayal because it failed to resolve a characteristic embarrassment. He could not renounce the poet's power to "transfuse" life into objects—it is a habit, as "Dejection" confirms, that even the idle mind cannot shake off—any more than he could fail to acknowledge the "wild" caprice of such activity. In the final version he simply gives up trying to excuse the speaker's imaginative inscriptions by substituting for "living spirit" its contrary—"idling Spirit" (l. 20). However, he does not follow through on the implications of this volte-face. It is hard to see how what is here condemned in this line as idle dalliance differs from the speaker's subsequent imaginings, for as will become clear, he interprets the infant cradled at his side in much the same way that he interprets the "*stranger*."

What first prompted the speaker as a schoolboy to personify the film on the grate was his sense of loneliness. His imagination mitigated the foreignness of his surroundings by supplementing his companions with the familiar face of one who in that setting would appear to be a "stranger" (though the epithet also implies that there may be something strange at the heart of the familiar). But even in childhood, imagination was problematic for him, for it led him to dream, and his dreaming flowed over the margins of sleep on either side, and flooded his waking hours:

> So gazed I, till the soothing things, I dreamt,
> Lulled me to sleep, and sleep prolonged my dreams!
> And so I brooded all the following morn,
> Awed by the stern preceptor's face, mine eye
> Fixed with mock study on my swimming book
> (ll. 34–38)

The movement of his imagination forms a vicious circle. The speaker peoples the solitude of his school days with memories of his "birthplace," and we would expect these memories to give him access to a lost plenitude. But the past as he recalls it is as hollow as his present life at school. What he remembers is being, as he puts it, "haunted" by the church bells because their peals seemed to be "articulate sounds of things to come!" (l. 33). Thus, if the present provokes memories of the past, that past was the time of longing for the future. At any given point he senses his existence to be a void, which he fills with an image of its other—whether past or future being functionally unimportant. But because the other is never substantial but only something different, his imagination can never come to rest, and its quest for presence perpetuates itself endlessly. As Coleridge puts it in *Anima Poetae*, "In youth our happiness is hope; in age the recollection of the hopes of youth. What else can there be?—for the substantial mind, for the *I*, what else can there be?"

By the time he composes the poem, however, the speaker's situation seems very different. If as a child he felt homesick, now he is seated by the hearth of his own home, and surrounded by the stable presence of his sleeping family. And yet, strangely, he persists in watching the "*stranger*"; even now he is sunk in memories not of home but of homesickness. Rather than replacing or supplementing what life has taken away, his imagination invades the present and robs it of its presence by distancing the speaker from his family. As he had imaginatively transformed the film into the "*stranger*," so his imagination now turns him into a stranger, or his family into strangers in his eyes. Hence he speaks of them as the "inmates" of the cottage (l. 4)—"a word," Magnuson notes, "that at the end of the eighteenth century referred to strangers dwelling in one's house." The speaker's alienation is finally acknowledged in "Constancy," in the insight that the peaceful, moonlit cottage may well be as lonely and desolate as a ship becalmed on a distant ocean.

It is noteworthy that Coleridge mirrors the absence of the beloved in a climate of light-without-heat. the sun rendered moonlike in "Constancy," the moonlight and the "inanimate cold world" in "Dejection," and in "Frost at Midnight" the frost, the moonlight, and the fire burnt so low that it gives off no more heat. If the present of "Frost at Midnight" is winter, its past is summer, for the speaker's "sweet birth-place" was home for "the *hot* Fair-day" (l. 30, my italics). Correspondingly, he forecasts a warming trend in the future, when "the nigh thatch/Smokes in the sun-thaw" (ll. 69–70). The poem significantly associates both of these climates with sound (as opposed to the "extreme silentness" of the present hibernal setting), and more particularly with voice. Yesterday's bells rang "like articulate sounds" (l. 33) and tomorrow's redbreast will "sing" (l. 67) in the sun-thaw. In turn, the "music" (l. 29) they make introduces a note of harmony into the poem and, it is not too much to say, a muted echo of *concordia discors* (not unlike the "tempered" lay sung by the lutanist in "Dejection"). The metaphors of music and singing suggest an attempt to harmonize and integrate the temperaments or humors of the self and the weather. In an attenuated form, the power of voice can still be felt in the rhythmic breathing sounds of the infant that "Fill up the interspersèd vacancies/And momentary pauses of the thought!" (ll. 46–47). But the poem clearly reminds us that this temperate, harmonious past is a fiction: the "hot Fair-day" is a day the speaker only "dreamt/Of" (ll. 27–28), and its music, as I have remarked, makes hollow, "haunting" sounds. As a fiction, the image of the past in this poem recalls the role of *concordia discors* as a past or preromantic principle of ordering "meteors." This means that "Frost at Midnight" is also a poem about the distance or collapse of *concordia discors* in the present, or the inability of voice any longer to effect resolution. In place of the audible and reconciling language of the past, "Frost at Midnight" attempts to dramatize a cold and silent language—"silent icicles,/Quietly shining to the quiet Moon" (ll. 73–74).

Thus far I have been tracing the vicious circle the speaker inscribes in his perpetual quest for presence, and I have said that the sounds of the infant seem to break that circle by bringing the speaker home to a conscious realization of present good: "My babe so beautiful! it thrills my heart/With tender gladness, thus to look at thee" (ll. 48–49). But these gentle breathings are not weighty enough to anchor the speaker to home, and almost at once he reinterprets them as a second "unquiet thing" (l. 16)—a phrase applied to the film on the grate but also applicable to the child. That is, he turns his child into a second "*stranger*," supplementing the original supplement. As with the film (and the friend in "Dejection"), the speaker transfers his longings to the child so that the infant also becomes a sign of the times to come. Some day the baby will "wander like a breeze" through Wordsworthian natural settings, and so educated he will be able, unlike his father, to perceive life even in the dead of winter. Once again, the parallel to "Constancy" is striking. As the woodman moves endlessly through space, so the speaker of "Frost at Midnight" moves through time, both personae grasping for something evermore about to be.

Even while proposing a natural education for the sleeping infant, the poem raises questions about the efficacy of that education. The speaker himself was cut off from nature or presence as a child, and since then he has tried unsuccessfully and sometimes even against his will to fill the void by a process of self-mirrorings. Nature should offer his child a life outside himself so that he need never wander into his father's labyrinth. But nature itself is prone to the same doubling process, and like the speaker, everywhere seeks to "mirror . . . itself" (l. 22), until it too becomes a maze. The clouds "image in their bulk both lakes and shores/And mountain crags" (ll. 57–58). And just as clouds mirror lakes and mountains, so we may infer the lakes reflect the clouds, mirroring them. It might be objected that the "*stranger*" figures something absent while the clouds image the presence of mountains. But the speaker reduces nature to the same status as the "*stranger*" by similarly turning nature into the sign of something yet to appear, in this case God:

> the clouds,
> Which image in their bulk both lakes and shores
> And mountain crags: so shalt thou see and hear
> The lovely shapes and sounds intelligible
> Of that eternal language, which thy God
> Utters
>
> (ll. 56–61)

And this diminution is parallelled by reducing the substantiality of mountains to the phantom bulk of clouds. Once again, what is proposed to supplement an absence, in this case nature replacing the lonely city, itself turns out to be somehow lacking and to necessitate its own supplement. God, then, could be defined as the final supplement, the ultimate other.

Whatever the final outcome of this education may be, the invocation of God's vocal and "eternal language" is more immediately important because it points to a linguistic dimension in "Frost at Midnight" and implies by contrast a temporal, human, and written language. The best figure of this language is the "*stranger*" which, although it is traditionally read as an emblem of imagination or fancy, functions equally well—inseparably we could say—as a linguistic signifier. But instead of referring to anything in the empirical world, the "*stranger*" points only to another signifier, initiating a circle of substitution that perpetually defers its meaning. In the "present" of the poem the image of the "*stranger*" refers the speaker back to the "*stranger*" he had seen (or read, or written) at school. That earlier "*stranger*" in turn points back further to his birthplace, where, able to recede no more, the process reverses itself and directs the speaker by the sounds of the bells to the future—a time that must include the moment at which the poem begins, when he once again fixes his gaze on the "*stranger*." In its circularity this language reveals itself to be as "eternal" as God's, but the attribute is anything but cause for celebration. Rather, the poem approximates a Saussurean circulation of difference.

As long as the speaker remains trapped in his own system of signs, he clearly can never finish the poem, and one reason for his invoking the supernatural language of nature signs is, I think, to achieve closure. With divine support he can do so in a dramatic way by demonstrating how the reconciliation of opposites that had earlier occurred on a "vernal morn" can likewise happen in the dead of winter, and at midnight. That is, he attempts to make writing function in the same harmonizing way as speech. Like mist and sunlight in "Religious Musings," frost and moonlight here synthesize:

> Or if the secret ministry of frost
> Shall hang them up in silent icicles,
> Quietly shining to the quiet Moon.
> (ll. 72–74)

The rare beauty of this Coleridgean ending should not, however, make us forget that in its original version "Frost at Midnight" continued on for another six lines. Perfectly in keeping with the rest of the poem, the original ending once again departs from the present to imagine the same setting the next morning:

> Or whether the secret ministry of cold
> Shall hang them up in silent icicles,
> Quietly shining to the quiet moon,
> Like those, my babe! which ere tomorrow's warmth
> Have capp'd their sharp keen points with pendulous drops,
> Will catch thine eye, and with their novelty
> Suspend thy little soul; then make thee shout,
> And stretch and flutter from thy mother's arms
> As thou wouldst fly for very eagerness.

The effect is once again to figure the child as the "*stranger*"—he even "flutters"—and furthermore, to undo the reconciliation of opposites. In order to create that synthesis, the frost had to hang the icicles "*up*," but "tomorrow's warmth" will cap "their sharp keen points with pendulous *drops*" (my italics) that can "suspend thy little soul" only in a precarious and temporary way. In ironic contrast to "Religious Musings," the sunrise here initiates a literal fall that may adumbrate the child's fall into the labyrinth of nature.

Perhaps because he recognized that the effect of this ending was unsettling, Coleridge cut it, although not until ten years after it was written. From a formal point of view, Humphry House is surely right to call this "one of the best artistic decisions Coleridge ever made." But the fact of cancellation is significant in itself because it exemplifies the typically Coleridgean gesture of extending a line of argument or narration until it gets him into trouble. In order to salvage a synthesis here, he must resist his own tendency to excess by censoring himself. However, unlike his practice in "Religious Musings," he retards the censor in "Frost at Midnight" long enough for us to read what elsewhere we had to infer: the reconciliation of opposites in whatever form it takes (the conjunction of subject and object or mind and nature, the redemption of man in God, the fusing or "coadunating" power of imagination, the symbol, organic unity, etc.) conceals the inevitability of its own unravelling.

It remains to ask a question about the ending of "Frost at Midnight" that is so apparently simple critics have not thought it worth the posing. Assuming that the speaker watches the frost perform its ministry and looks at the icicles shining in the moonlight, as he hears the owlet's cry, what exactly does he see as he looks out his window? (The poem never explicitly represents a window in the cottage and so we must "hypopoeticize" it, but in any case the key "window" is the metaphorical one of his consciousness.) Through his window the speaker must see the moonlight filtered through the frost; however, in view of the mirrorings and projections that pervade the whole poem up to this point, is it not possible that he sees as well an image of himself and his room reflected on the frosted glass, one superimposed over the other? The poem, of course, remains true to its "secret ministry" and never tells, but Coleridge did record a like scene three winters after writing "Frost at Midnight." Because his notebook entry is cryptic, we do better to turn to the full account he published in an essay on ghosts and apparitions:

> The window of my library at Keswick is opposite to the fire-place, and looks out on the very large garden that occupies the whole slope of the hill on which the house stands. Consequently, the rays of light transmitted *through* the glass, (i.e. the rays from the garden, the opposite mountains, and the bridge, river, lake, and vale interjacent) and the rays reflected *from* it, (of the fire-place, &c.) enter

> the eye at the same moment. At the coming on of evening, it was my frequent amusement to watch the image or reflection of the fire, that seemed burning in the bushes. . . . as the darkness encreased, the image of the fire lessened and grew nearer and more distinct, till the twilight had deepened into perfect night, when all outward objects being excluded, the window became a perfect looking-glass: save only that my books on the side shelves of the room were lettered, as it were, on their backs with stars

—the heavens become a text. And in a notebook entry of 14 April 1805, Coleridge generalized this phenomenon:

> In looking at objects of Nature while I am thinking, as at yonder moon dim-glittering thro' the dewy window-pane, I seem rather to be seeking, as it were *asking*, a symbolic language for something within me that already and forever exists, than observing any thing new. Even when that latter is the case, yet still I have always an obscure feeling as if that new phaenomenon were the dim Awakening of a forgotten or hidden Truth of my inner nature.

Could the darkness in "Frost at Midnight" likewise have turned the window into a looking-glass? As the speaker sees his own image on the grate and in the cradle, might he once again see himself on the frost (which in any case he anthropomorphizes as a minister) in an ironic conjunction of subject and object? Or would the image of the "*stranger*" interpose itself to deface and disfigure his own image on the frosted glass? What figures inscribe themselves on the windowpane of his consciousness?

The one figure I have failed to discuss in "Frost at Midnight" is the frost itself. But my omission is not quite unfaithful to the text, since despite its title, the poem itself rather strangely tells us next to nothing about its key image. Or perhaps not so strangely—the profession of frost is, after all, a "secret." The only real clue we have is the alteration Coleridge made in the ending, when he changed "secret ministry of cold" to "secret ministry of frost." The evident motive was that he simultaneously excised the original ending to make the poem reiterate its beginning, and "secret ministry of frost" more precisely echoes the opening. "And hark, again!" notes the reader. But given what we know about the linguistic association Coleridge regularly made with mist, it is hard to imagine that the shift from "cold" to "frost" does not also introduce a figure for frozen language, or writing. Having stilled the speaker's voice, the ministry of cold leaves him no option but to inscribe "Frost at Midnight." This is a "conversation poem" that could only be written. But there is a further reason for Coleridge's silence on this point, namely that, at the same time that he wrote "Frost at Midnight," he was just completing another poem about frost begun several months earlier, the "Rime of the Ancient Mariner." We may learn more about the midnight frost by turning to the rimed Mariner.

SUSAN J. WOLFSON

The Language of Interpretation

In 1799 William Blake reminded the Reverend Dr. Trusler, "The wisest of the Ancients considerd what is not too Explicit as the fittest for Instruction, because it rouzes the faculties to act." This comment may be applied to the rhetorical activity of much Romantic poetry as well, especially in poems in which logical structures—the plots of an argument, a tale, or an informing legend—are the expected means of instruction. "The Rime of the Ancient Mariner," *The Thorn*, "La Belle Dame sans Merci," and "Ode on a Grecian Urn" all unfold mysteries against potential sources of interpretation: moral lessons, arguments, glosses, village testimony, portentous encounters, spectral legends. Yet however much such sources may "rouze" the mind to render intelligible "what is not too Explicit," in these poems, the materials invoked for that purpose themselves become invaded by what Keats calls "uncertainties, Mysteries, doubts." If these poems arouse expectation that there is a secure logic to be discovered for their perplexing circumstances, they tend to dramatize the difficulties of such discovery more than its success.

These are poems, in other words, about problems in interpretation, involving questions that go to the heart of the Romantic concern with language itself: What is the status of explication or logical argument in poems that appear to frustrate such modes of discourse even as they put them forth? What kind of poem, or poetry, does this activity produce? One effect, certainly, is to cast into doubt the principles of coherence (the causal sequences) on which plots and arguments alike rely and to foreground the less certain, uneasy motions

---

 Originally entitled "The Language of Interpretation in Romantic Poetry: 'A Strange Working of the Mind.'"

of mind attempting to describe such principles in the circumstances that have compelled its attention. Such stress yields a poetic syntax more psychological than logical in organization, more affective than narrative in its procedures. These poems all show the degree to which interpretation cannot consist simply of deciphering hidden patterns of meaning or discovering causal sequences, but must become an active seeking and generating of meaning.

"The Rime of the Ancient Mariner" and *The Thorn* dramatize the efforts of their speakers to elucidate mystery through recourse to the logic of moral argument and the logic of narrative, respectively. The Mariner's "Rime" itself involves several kinds of interpretation, but the most blatant sense-making scheme in Coleridge's text—the Marginal Gloss—is amassed against the Mariner's "Rime" as a parallel commentary, making the poem as a whole bear the signature of two distinct intelligences: that of the riming Mariner and that of the Marginal Editor. In *The Thorn*, Wordsworth entertains dilemmas of interpretation in the body of the poem itself; moreover, he diminishes the locutional differences between the narrator of the tale and the voice of his logic-seeking questioner—as if to suggest a unity of enterprise. In both these lyrical ballads, the sources of interpretive authority and the logical patterns they promote or delineate never quite emerge as "points and resting places in reasoning" independent of "the fluxes and refluxes of the mind" trying to interpret.

So psychological an emphasis (and the poetic texture it effects) must have impressed Wordsworth and Coleridge alike as a revolutionary enough experiment in the language of poetry. Yet Coleridge's belief that "the best part of human language . . . is derived from reflection on the acts of the mind itself" was not to be given its most radical poetic treatment until a generation later. Keats explicitly features the questions of interpretation that haunt "The Rime of the Ancient Mariner" and *The Thorn* in his own lyrical ballad "La Belle Dame sans Merci"—a poem that bears a structural resemblance to *The Thorn*. Not long after, he was at work on a series of odes (of which "Ode on a Grecian Urn" is the most striking example) in which he not only makes a premise of the problems of interpretation all these lyrical ballads trace with increasing intensity, but extends that negotiation with uncertainty to the reader's engagement with the play of his rhyme.

II

Today, most readers of "The Rime of the Ancient Mariner" are probably not as bothered as was Coleridge's acquaintance, the poet and essayist Mrs. Barbauld, about the "improbable" nature of his story. The second "fault" of which she complained to the author, however, remains something of a notorious vexation for many modern readers—namely, that the poem "had no moral." Coleridge is willing to cede the point on "probability"; but "as to the want of a moral," he counters, the poem's "chief fault, if I might say so, was the obtrusion of the moral sentiment so openly on the reader as a principle of cause of action in a work of pure imagination." Yet in "The Rime of the Ancient Mariner" Coleridge not only seems to deplore "moral sentiment"; in this work of pure imagination, he seems to want to baffle the effort to discover any principle of action. Indeed, he continues his remarks by declaring that his poem "ought to have no more moral than the *Arabian Nights'* tale of the merchant's sitting down to eat dates by the side of a well and throwing the shells aside, and lo! a genie starts up and says he *must* kill the aforesaid merchant *because* one of the date shells had, it seems, put out the eye of the genie's son." Coleridge emphasizes the causal vocabulary with knowing irony, for to the mind of the date-eater, the genie has produced moral necessity from a chance event and consequence.

But before considering what kind of moral paradigm that tale offers to the reader of Coleridge's poem, we need to turn to the Mariner himself, who finds moral uncertainties in the central circumstance of his "Rime." The world he describes, as readers from Wordsworth to the present have noted, is one informed by inscrutable forces: nature is unpredictably solicitous or persecutory, benevolent or tyrannous. As in "Dejection," the language that can be read from nature's appearances often seems barely more than the fiction of a desperate imagination. Indeed, the foggy atmosphere from which the Albatross emerges, and which always surrounds its presence, suggests both inner and outer weather:

> At length did cross an Albatross,
> Thorough the fog it came;
> As if it had been a Christian soul,
> We hailed it in God's name.

Despite the appealing rhyme of "Albatross" with "cross" (here and subsequently), the Mariner's "As if" has the effect of raising a question about what "principle or cause of action" (if any) is actually involved. For the conjecture, uttered in fogbound misery, seems to describe primarily the hopes of an anxious crew, rather than anything positive about the bird itself. The Mariner and crew attempt repeatedly to convert conjecture into a syntax of event and consequence that can join the Albatross to the fate of their ship: when the splitting of the ice and the rising of a good south wind follow the advent of the bird, they hail it as the agent of their release; when the fog disperses (along with the ice and snow) after the Mariner kills the bird, the crewmen reinterpret the Albatross as the cause of the fog, and their release into sunshine and fair breezes as a consequence of its death; and when the same breezes fail and the "glorious" sun becomes "bloody," the crewmen imagine themselves plagued by the Mariner's killing of the Albatross and rue that act. What are we to make of this continual shuffling of logic? Even Wordsworth, usually not averse to making the reader "struggle," sides with Coleridge's perplexed readers and against his "Friend" in the "Note to the Ancient Mariner" he wrote for the second edition of *Lyrical Ballads*. He cites, among other difficulties, the "defect" "that the events having no necessary connection do not produce each other." The arbitrary interpretations that gather around the Albatross are a case in point. Each new scheme of causality does not clarify any "necessary connection" between the bird and the state of the weather, as much as all together expose the fiction of interpretive acts: ascertainment of the bird's value emerges after the fact, as a logic of cause and effect is imposed on a mere sequence of events. As in the tale of the genie and the date-eater, cause and effect are matters of convenient collation rather than of inevitable connection. We begin to sense that if the Albatross signifies anything, it is the very ambiguity of signs—that is, the ambiguity with which the external world vexes a desire for interpretive certainty.

The language of cause and consequence not only surrounds the Albatross but is the very principle upon which a narrative must proceed, and so the problem of collation and connection extends to the listener of the Mariner's tale. How is one supposed to coordinate the two key events upon which his story depends: the killing of the Albatross and the blessing of the snakes? The way the Mariner himself represents these acts makes more of their irrationality than of their moral dimensions: "I shot the ALBATROSS" merely joins subject and predicate, rather than explains the act; and even when that act is apparently redeemed by the blessing of the water snakes, this, too, is given without reference to a conscious motivation: "I blessed them unaware." The parallel syntax of "I shot" and "I blessed" does make a neat pattern for the sampler homily with which the Mariner caps his tale: "He prayeth best, who loveth best/All things both great and small;/For the dear God who loveth us,/He made and loveth all." Nonetheless, a listener cannot escape awareness that this moral is for its bearer embedded in a self-denying context: the Mariner is doomed to eternal exclusion from the love and prayer he preaches. Ironically, he isolates and terrifies his auditors more than he consoles them with any sense of God's inclusive love. The would-be Wedding Guest's "wiser" state notwithstanding, that listener at least is also left "sadder" for having heard the "Rime"—perhaps more "stunned" than instructed by the Mariner's will over him. Denied the "goodly company" of the marriage feast, the Wedding Guest's very name is rendered meaningless. Left "of sense forlorn," this student of the Mariner's lesson finds himself, instead, a participant in the Mariner's alienation: listener and tale-teller alike seem at the end of their encounter "forlorn" of common "sense"—the comfort of living in a world of rational cause and consequence. As Coleridge remarks in the "Conclusion" of his own biography, "there is always a consolatory feeling that accompanies the sense of a proportion between antecedents and consequents giv[ing], as it were, a substratum of permanence, of identity, and therefore of reality, to the shadowy flux of Time."

What denies the Mariner and all his listeners this sense of proportion is that the question that is the efficient cause of his narration—"What manner of man art thou?"—eludes certain answering. What is his "substratum" of identity? Is he a killer of an Albatross, a blesser of water snakes, a preacher of God's love, or an agent of contamination? The question is voiced originally by the Mariner's first auditor, the Hermit, and as we learn, it wrenches the Mariner "With a woful agony" that requires nothing less than a retelling of all the events of his ordeal. Yet as tortured and elaborate as the Mariner's response is, it remains indeterminate: the question generates his "Rime," and his "Rime" regenerates the question. Its conclusion, in fact, gestures toward its perpetual rehearsal in the shadowy flux of time:

> Since then, at an uncertain hour,
> That agony returns:
> And till my ghastly tale is told,
> This heart within me burns.

Endlessly navigating about a core of mysterious events, the Mariner can never capture their informing logic: his text circles about this absent center but always begins and concludes in agonizing uncertainty. Nor does Coleridge's ballad itself secure the tidy closure of "moral sentiment," ending instead with a register of the aftereffect of the Mariner's tale in the mind of his stunned, forlorn auditor. If the Mariner himself "Is gone," he leaves the trace of his mystery in that interior realm, making the truest issue of his "ghastly tale" the way it haunts a listener's imagination. "I was never so affected with any human Tale," Charles Lamb wrote to Wordsworth; "After first reading it, I was totally possessed with it for many days. . . . the feelings of the man under the operation of such scenery dragged me along like Tom Piper's magic Whistle.—" Another listener confessed to feeling "insulated" in the wake of hearing the poem recited by its author. "a sea of wonder and mystery flows round [me] as round the spell-stricken ship itself."

The effect of the Mariner's "Rime" in leaving its readers thus "possessed," despite the patent moral at its close, is amplified by the interpretive apparatus with which Coleridge surrounds the text of the "Rime." The "Argument" at the head of the 1798 poem is primarily descriptive, concerned mainly with the course of the Mariner's ship and alluding only briefly to "the strange things that befell" as if by chance, accident, or inscrutable agency. With the "Argument" of 1800, however, Coleridge introduces terms of moral logic and potential instruction: "the Ancient Mariner cruelly and in contempt of the laws of hospitality killed a Sea-bird and . . . was followed by many and strange Judgements." Yet in the 1802 and 1805 editions of *Lyrical Ballads* Coleridge dropped the "Argument" altogether, as if he had decided not to prejudice his reader with authorial signals but to let his poem work its own effect. The next publication of the poem in *Sibylline Leaves* (1817) strikes a compromise, supplying a marginal gloss instead of an argument. Like the "Argument" of 1800, the Gloss often brings a moral interpretation to bear on the Mariner's story. Unlike the "Argument," however, the Gloss is a parallel text, in effect competing with the "Rime" for the reader's attention, rather than supervising it. It presumes to order the Mariner's ordeal with a logic that his own "Rime" does not disclose—as if supplying the "necessary connection[s]" whose absence Wordsworth, among others, regretted. "And lo! the Albatross proveth a bird of good omen," it declares with the authority of biblical exegesis. "The ancient Mariner inhospitably killeth the pious bird of good omen," it avers, judgment in its every other word. Or taking as a cue the Mariner's fervent hope that "Sure my kind saint took pity on me," the Gloss confidently interprets a necessary connection: "By grace of the holy Mother, the ancient Mariner is refreshed with rain." The voice of the Gloss confronts the reader as the genie does the date-eater, starting up to declare moral necessity at every turn. Yet far from clarifying whatever connections between events the "Rime" may have left obscure, the very presence of a Gloss emphasizes their absence and points to the need for explicit terms of instruction in a circumstance where all is interrogative ("Why look'st thou so?" "wherefore stopp'st thou me?" "What manner of man art thou?"). Indeed the final marginal comment, "an agony constraineth . . . [the Mariner] to teach, by his own example, love and reverence to all things that God made and loveth," gives the rehearsal of that lesson a psychological urgency ("agony") even as it declares a moral principle. Despite the faith readers such as Robert Penn Warren have placed in the authority of the Gloss, it persists as another fiction—a parallel account of the ordeal recounted by the Mariner's "Rime," or an account of another ordeal: the attempt to make sense of the Mariner's language.

There is one frame, however, that Coleridge retains in every edition, namely, the voice of the anonymous balladeer with which the poem begins and ends. Readers tend, as Lionel Stevenson does, to treat this frame voice as no more than a "perfunctory" device. Yet in a poem so fundamentally involved with issues of tale-telling and tale-listening, this view deserves reconsideration. The relative situation of the Mariner's "Rime" is what lyricizes the ballad, making it as much about the feelings the "Rime" develops in its tellers and listeners as about the supernatural character of its events or the moral wisdom of its instruction. Its concluding focus on the Wedding Guest suggests, furthermore, the frame narrator's muted but overall interest in the relation between "forced" tale-telling and "forced" tale-listening. The Wedding Guest, now possessed with the "Rime," may have found a motive for narrative similar in power to that which possesses the Mariner with his ordeal. The poem leaves open to question whether this newly haunted listener might himself become a haunted purveyor of the Rime's repetitive life: Will the Wedding Guest rise the morrow morn, compelled to reach toward an audience of his own, to say in the manner of the ballad's frame narrator, "It is an ancient Mariner,/And he stoppeth one of three"? The ballad's opening word, "It," bears the same sense of perplexed indeterminacy with which the Mariner has left the Wedding Guest, while the present tense of narration, both here and in the ballad's penultimate stanza ("The Mariner, whose eye is bright,/Whose beard with age is hoar,/Is gone"), suggests the perpetual presence of that figure in the mind that contains his "Rime." The affinity the balladeer's language bears to the psychology of the Mariner's haunted listener is further enhanced by the copresence of their voices in the poem's inaugural stanza, before the actual character of the Wedding Guest is introduced. The opening two lines flow immediately into a question—"By thy long grey beard and glittering eye,/Now wherefore stopp'st thou me?"—in which the pattern of meter and rhyme and the as-yet-unspecified identity of the questioner momentarily create the sense of a single mind moving from observation to speech.

The self-circling energies of this narrative frame and the would be containment offered by the poem's interpretive frame (the early Argument or later Gloss) suggest an extended rhetorical figure for the motions of a mind left stunned by the Mariner's "Rime" and attempting to sort out its mystery. Could the interpretive apparatus surrounding what Coleridge thought of as "A Poet's Reverie" be the textual signatures of a previously sense-forlorn auditor trying to make sense by obtruding (for himself and for his own audience) a "principle of action" on the intolerably inconclusive tale that has possessed his imagination? The Latin epigraph that in 1817 takes the place of earlier Arguments and subtitles indeed brings a problematic perspective to bear on the Mariner's mysterious experience. An excerpt from *Archaelogiae Philosophicae* by the Anglican divine, Thomas Burnet, it offers scholarly speculation on the existence of the invisible and the supernatural in the things of the universe. Yet Burnet cautions that in circling about but never attaining knowledge of the unknown, the mind must be vigilant for truth, careful to distinguish the certain from the uncertain. The action of circling about a center that defies final understanding describes the relation of the Mariner's "Rime" to its enigmatic core of events; it also figures the relation of the Gloss to that "Rime": each text surrounds a mystery, attempting to negotiate moral certainty in the face of what haunts and rouses the imagination. And the comprehensive text of Coleridge's 1817 ballad, equivocating between Marginal Gloss and Mariner's "Rime," now poses that problem to the reader. For the *apparatus criticus* and the "Rime" together shape a fuller text that, while denying unambiguous principles of instruction, offers an explicit figure for the ultimate uncertainty of interpretation.

KEN FRIEDEN

Conversational Pretense in "Kubla Khan"

Coleridge's conversation poems extend the conventions of dramatic soliloquy to an apparently autonomous lyrical form. Dramatic soliloquy and poetic monologue both generate illusions of individual speech, yet the difference in genre has decisive implications. In the dramatic context, soliloquy retains mimetic pretensions as part of a represented world, while the written conversation poem tends to draw attention to its own representational illusion. The poetic monologist is typically less concerned to describe the world than to reflect on the experiences that constitute it.

Coleridge, whose finest lyrics are representative of the Romantic monologue, writes most enthusiastically of Shakespeare's genius in connection with the great soliloquist, Hamlet. Perhaps because Coleridge identifies with Hamlet, monological forms characterize his strongest poems. Although the conversation poem does not inherently carry abnormal associations, the solitude it implies creates an opening for the aberrations of "phantom magic." Coleridge further develops the conversational mode suggested by Shakespearean soliloquy and Augustan poetry and clusters a set of related poems around supernatural phenomena.

The rise and fall of Coleridge's conversational pretense may be traced as a fictional biography, from his identification with Hamlet, through "The Eolian Harp" and "Frost at Midnight," until the subversion of the conversational mode by "Kubla Khan." The multiple voices of "Kubla Khan" disrupt the scene of vision, revealing a potential threat to composition. If Coleridge's early poetry

From *Genius and Monologue.* © 1985 by Cornell University. Cornell University Press, 1985. Originally entitled "Coleridge's Conversational Pretense in 'Kubla Khan.' "

succeeds by virtue of its firm control of the conversational tone, his more radical lyrics disturb the poetic voice that had been established.

VOICES OF DECAY

"Kubla Khan," the culmination of Coleridge's conversation poems, both employs and destroys the conversational mode. Replete with exclamations that indicate a presumed immediacy of feeling, Coleridge's strongest short poem no longer begins with a corresponding, intimate scene. Rather than present a scene of intimacy as the point of departure for imaginative wanderings, "Kubla Khan" opens with a fantastic landscape of Xanadu. The speaker's present is initially an absence from the poem, a lack that Coleridge's preface counters by describing the conditions of composition. But Coleridge presents a most peculiar scene of composition, in which the words of the poem purportedly accompany private imagery of a dream. On one level, the conversation poems strive to represent commonplace domestic situations, while "Kubla Khan" breaks off its elaborate fantasy in conjunction with a threat of madness.

The prose preface operates as do the opening lines of "The Eolian Harp" and "Frost at Midnight," delineating a place and time of creative activity. Whereas the conversation poems only implicitly represent the moment of writing in their scenes of monologue, the preface explicitly discusses the genealogy of "Kubla Khan." Narrating a scene of interruption, the preface fosters the conception of "Kubla Khan" as "a vision in a dream" that has been only partially recovered by waking memory.

Although prefaces are conventionally more literal than poems, critics have doubted the accuracy of Coleridge's autobiographical data. A naïve reading wishes to accept the preface as an accurate description of the scene of composition, while a more sober reading concludes that it is unreliable. If we recognize preface and poem as equal literary fictions, however, neither half of Coleridge's double text merits special status. Both preface and poem voice a pseudoautobiographical "I," a parallel that unsettles the facile dichotomy between prose and verse as literal (or referential) and figurative (or fictional). Preface and poem unsettle the conventional notions of representational correspondence in different genres. Too marvelous for strict autobiography, but not too literal for fiction, the preface need not depend on a pretension to autobiographical truth.

The preface, "Of the Fragment of Kubla Khan," insistently refers to "the following fragment," emphasizing a part-whole relationship between present words and some unspecified totality. Coleridge denies independent status to the poem "Kubla Khan," perhaps because it breaks the familiar pattern of the conversation poems. The synecdoche is accompanied by a perspectivizing allusion to "a poet of great and deserved celebrity," whose estimation of the poem contrasts the author's. Is the fragment great or small, heavy or light? "Fragments" also "vaulted like rebounding hail" in line 21 of the poem, before compared with "chaffy grain beneath the thresher's flail." The *ground* of this literary fragment shows itself to be as unsteady as are the fragments in "that deep romantic chasm" and will not support weightier pretensions. The fragment is published, "as far as the Author's own opinions are concerned, rather as a psychological curiosity, than on the ground of any supposed *poetic* merits" (Pr. 1) [The preface ("Pr.") is cited by sentence number and the poem ("KK") by line number as they appear in Coleridge's *Poetical Works*, ed. Ernest Hartley Coleridge.] The request of Lord Byron, whose fame appears secure, provides ground for publication, even if not on the basis of "*poetic* merits."

If "Kubla Khan" is a "psychological curiosity," the preface further insists on the authenticity of its narrative by citing purportedly real chronology and geography (Pr. 2). Yet Coleridge discusses the poem's "Author" at a distance suggested by the third-person form. The language of cause and effect, illness and cure, add to an impression of necessity in the narrated events: "In consequence of a slight indisposition, an anodyne had been prescribed, from the effects of which he fell asleep in his chair at the moment that he was reading the following sentence, or words of the same substance, in 'Purchas's Pilgrimage': 'Here the Khan Kubla commanded a palace to be built, and a stately garden thereunto. And thus ten miles of fertile ground were inclosed with a wall' " (Pr. 3–4). The author reads Kubla's command at the moment when a drug induces sleep, allowing him to evade the problems of conscious borrowing. The poem's allusions are thus casually ascribed to the influence of a virtually unconscious reading rather than to a controlled act of writing. Purchas' words appear to ground Coleridge's fragment more firmly than do "*poetic* merits." Sleep further frees the author from responsibilities associated with deliberate action: "The Author continued for about three hours in a profound sleep, at least of the external senses" (Pr. 5). If Coleridge as dreamer does not consciously control the act of composition, an external-internal opposition gives his creativity the appearance of self-generation.

By describing a three-stage procedure, Coleridge effectively traces "Kubla Khan" to a creative act based on unconscious processes.

Step 1, *dream composition*, is also not composition, because the author "could not have composed less than from two to three hundred lines; if that indeed can be called composition in which all the images rose up before him as *things*, with a parallel production of the correspondent expressions, without any sensation or consciousness of effort" (Pr. 5). Can that be called composition "in which all the images rose up before him as *things*"? The previous images of "substance," "ground," and "fragment" suggest an affinity between physical and textual realities; here the extraordinarily substantial images may be either visual or poetic. The visionary moment is itself presumably extralinguistic, because Coleridge writes of a "parallel production of the correspondent expressions." Simultaneous with but not equivalent to the images, the correspondent expressions appear as if naturally or necessarily linked to what they express. Although words suggest themselves in parallel, the narrator indicates that the unusually concrete images are his primary impression. In contrast to this claim, the underlying *poetic* meaning of "images" keeps his "vision" in literary bounds from the start. The ambiguous "image" begins to undo the primary claim of an effortless vision that naturally gives rise to correspondent expressions.

Step 2, *transcription* of the dream composition, follows immediately, when the author "appeared to himself to have a distinct recollection of the whole, and taking his pen, ink and paper, instantly and eagerly wrote down the lines that are here preserved" (Pr. 6). The instantaneous impulse to write implies that the poetic lines precisely reproduce the dreamed expressions. Unlike the prolonged dream period of "about three hours," the secondary scene of writing condenses into an instant. There is no need to judge whether the fifty-four crafted lines of "Kubla Khan" could actually be instantly or automatically composed: Coleridge's claim to a later, synchronic "recollection of the whole" is an aspect of his double text. The alleged instantaneous scene of writing strives to unify the diachronic process during which "all the images rose up before him as *things*." This moment captures the dream sequence as a simultaneous order, admitting no break until the author completes "the lines that are here preserved."

Step 3, *interruption*, occurs as suddenly as does the transcription. The "moment" of reading already appears in sentence 3 when the author "fell asleep in his chair at the moment that he was reading the following sentence." The necessity of a secondary act of reading, or dream interpretation, shows itself with the event of interruption. The published preface eludes any intimation of deliberate craft, however, by reducing the time interval to a moment: "At this moment he was unfortunately called out by a person on business from Porlock, and detained by him above an hour" (Pr. 7). The dream and period of detainment both have measurable durations, but the transcription seems to break off in the midst of its lightning-fast burst. The preface subsequently refers to "the vision" retrospectively; on returning to his room, the author "found, to his no small surprise and mortification, that though he still retained some vague and dim recollection of the general purport of the vision, yet, with the exception of some eight or ten scattered lines and images, all the rest had passed away like images on the surface of a stream into which a stone has been cast, but, alas! without the after restoration of the latter!" (Pr. 7). The mention of dissolving images affirms the independent, picturelike quality of an initial vision. But the speaker's subsequent "mortification" establishes a gloomier connection between the fading vision and loss of life: *mortificare* is to cause to die. The interruption of the processes of writing is a symbolic death, especially for the older Coleridge, who knows that he has lost his poetic genius.

As if to revise the preceding simile and derive new assurance, the preface cites ten lines from Coleridge's poem "The Picture." This allusion is part of the effort to ground "Kubla Khan" visually. A "poor youth" suffers a loss like that of the narrator, and "then all the charm/Is broken—all that phantom-world so fair/Vanishes" (Pr. 8). But for the youth of "The Picture," in a narcissistic fantasy, natural events restitute what has been lost:

> The stream will soon renew its smoothness, soon
> The visions will return!
> And soon the fragments dim of lovely forms
> Come trembling back, unite, and now once more
> The pool becomes a mirror.
>
> [Pr. 9–10]

Coleridge's conversation poems and reading of Hamlet similarly revolve around this quest after a mirror of the self. For the preface narrator, however, the metaphor fails: although he retains "some vague and dim recollection" of the vision, his fragments do not unite. In the narrative that describes the author's dream and transcription, the disruption is nonreversible and does not end in restoration. Falling short of the author's "phantom-world," the preface only mirrors another text.

The final paragraph of the preface contrasts the author's deliberate intentions and his spontaneous creation: "from the still surviving recollections in his mind, the Author has frequently purposed to finish for himself what had been originally, as it were, given to him" (Pr. 11). The author's sleep writing takes on the aura of an inspired moment, "given" by unexplainable forces and inaccessible to conscious intentions. The preface thus claims that "Kubla Khan" is an inspired fragment never resumed after its abrupt interruption. The closing sentence projects a hypothetical future and readership by citing Theocritus' words, "I'll sing to you a sweeter song another day" (later emended to "I'll sing to you a sweeter song tomorrow"). Like the final lines of the poem, this final proleptic awareness combines positive anticipation with a negative moment. "but the to-morrow is yet to come."

The last stanza of "Kubla Khan" does not appear to derive from the same effortless, unreflective impulse that allegedly produces "the lines that are here preserved." Thus critics have been as skeptical of the poem's formal unity as doubtful of its genetic unity. Several interpreters consider the poem to be divided into two disparate parts, before and after the shift to first person in the third stanza. According to the critical cliché, an impersonal voice describes Kubla's pleasure dome and grounds, after which a first-person speaker recalls a past vision, loosely associated with Xanadu. Based on the shift in "vision" that occurs in the last stanza, this received idea ignores the complications of the middle stanza, yet a two-part structure of the poem is commonly admitted.

In the closing lines of the poem, a first-person voice presents an alternative version of origins. Like the preface, these lines interpret the mysteries of vision: "A damsel with a dulcimer/In a vision once I saw" (KK 37–38). Discontinuous with previous descriptions by the first stanza, these words implicate the speaker in his visionary experience and locate the vision at a distinct, past time. The dream is over. No longer speaking as if the forests were "here" and the gardens "there," the nostalgic voice recollects something that is no longer immediately present, even to imagination. The first appearance of Kubla's world emphasizes the visual, but the damsel vision attends to sound:

> It was an Abyssinian maid,
> And on her dulcimer she played,
> Singing of Mount Abora.
> [KK 39–41]

A new set of proper names displaces Xanadu, Kubla, and Alph. The modified proper names, like the damsel's song, introduce additional words into the vision. As his earlier imaginative scene is superseded, the speaker loses his referential assurance, breaks off his representational pretense, and tries to recall the song of his imaginary figure: the Abyssinian Maid sings of a place, in a referential mode. Rather than strive to regain his attempted correspondence to immediate vision, the speaker gives up his own song in order to seek hers:

> Could I revive within me
> Her symphony and song,
> To such a deep delight 'twould win me,
> That with music loud and long,
> I would build that dome in air,
> That sunny dome! those caves of ice!
> [KK 42–47]

An imagined recollection of the damsel's music replaces the visions of Xanadu. But the relationship between damsel and dome is mysterious: what does the new vision have in common with the old? If the visions are linked, why is the damsel absent from Kubla's domain? The speaker's imagined damsel, playing her "sweet" instrument, contrasts the "woman wailing" he projects into Kubla's turbulent pleasure grounds. The speaker implicitly acknowledges the instability of poetic constructs when he anticipates building "that dome in air."

As he longs to regain his lost vision, the speaker echoes intentions stated by the preface: "from the still surviving recollections in his mind, the Author has frequently purposed to finish for himself what had been originally, as it were, given to him." As in the citation from Theocritus (Pr. 12), completion depends on the existence of an imagined audience: "And all who heard should see them there." The audience retraces the sequence of the author's creative process: his vision gives him a voice, and their hearing produces a visionary sight. *Could* the author speak his vision, the private would become public, establishing a previously isolated vision as a common referent. At the same time, the speaker would be perceived as mad and banished to a circle for the purposes of exorcism.

This hypothetical communication would be incomprehensible, and provoke excommunication, because the audience could only respond with fear: "all should cry, Beware! Beware!/His flashing eyes, his floating hair!" (KK 48–49). The speaker is inscribed in the prosopopoeia that presents others' imaginary discourse, and hearers try to remedy the inspired state he now has them represent and invoke. The previous occurrence of things visionary makes relevant a warning to "weave a circle round him thrice,/And close your eyes with holy dread." Suddenly the auditor-speakers are like Kubla: they seek to enclose the threatening poet, as Kubla's decrees try to secure his pleasure grounds. A reversal takes place: whereas the speaker earlier identifies with Kubla and the poetic effort to stabilize a dome of pleasure, now he and his vision specifically endanger customary boundaries. Once the speaker renounces efforts to build on ground, instead seeking to "build that dome in air," he is associated with the destabilizing forces that undo Kubla's pleasure. Deviation from the conversational mode unleashes dangerous forces. The radicalized mode of monologue, a self-referential innovation that pretends to present the language of a dream, threatens to overturn the entire monological reference.

Similar to the second half of the preface, the final stanza of "Kubla Khan" recognizes that the vision has faded. The preface explicitly narrates the scene of interruption and accepts the poem as a fragment. The poem, however, only implies and does not directly acknowledge the disappearance of vision. Without thematizing this loss, the speaker attempts to recuperate what has gone or rather considers the possible consequences of such a recuperation. The imagined speech of auditors at first affirms the preceding visionary stanzas, yet their response also works against affirmation. Because "I cannot" is implied by the conditional statement that begins, "Could I," the first two stanzas are undermined. If the poet cannot "build that dome in air," then the speaker himself judges his rendering of Xanadu unsuccessful. At the moment the voice reads and speaks its own failure to represent, the fictional pretense is undone and the poem ends. Though the poem ultimately strives for assurance, its final prosopopoeia narrates as complete a deterioration as the preface, only figuratively. While the preface unifies the poem by linking it to a single scene of writing, the final stanza of the poem shifts scenes as it projects voices and intensifies the speaker's retrospective confession of dissolution. The preface recalls a visionary writing that is abruptly disrupted; the poem (p)refigures this external interruption as an internalized self-undoing.

Coleridge's conversational poems and "Kubla Khan" exemplify one stage in the shifting traditions of literary monologue. Expressing a particular moment in time and treating "Kubla Khan" as a psychological curiosity, Coleridge presents a text that purports to transcribe mental processes. Romantic and postromantic monologues combine lyrical voice and dramatic scene to create a moment of feigned discourse, on the boundary between writing and representation.

Coleridge's conversation poems turn against their origins in Shakespearean soliloquy. Because the fictive speaker does not form part of a dramatic scenario, this persona is haunted by an absence that inheres in its pretense. "Kubla Khan" brings an end to the naïve conversational mode, which it interrupts through the final acknowledgment: the dream is over. Whereas the conversation poems affirm the solitary voice, "Kubla Khan" shows its inadequacy, as it succumbs to a combination of external and internal pressures. The monologist, compelled to follow the peculiar constraints of written conversation, tends to lose touch with mimetic conventions. Pointing the way beyond Hamlet and toward poetic monologues by Shelley and Browning, "Kubla Khan" uncovers the affinity between monologue and madness. As developed by nineteenth-century authors, the conventions of poetic monologue both create and disrupt the illusion of a speaking subject. Monologue as a rhetorical swerve joins with monologue as a fiction of solitude. Mad monologues gradually displace the eolian monologue of meditation and move toward a new literary type that finds further expression in first-person narratives.

CAMILLE PAGLIA

"Christabel"

"Christabel" has an odd history. It has two parts, one written in 1797 and the other in 1800. Coleridge withheld it from publication, but it circulated privately in manuscript, and Byron declared it the source of all metrical tales of Sir Walter Scott. Its release in 1816 was at the urging of Byron himself, who greatly admired it. Coleridge never regarded "Christabel" as finished and claimed plans for three more parts. His mind returned fretfully to the poem for years, and his inability to complete it was an abiding disappointment. A century of scholars have advanced theories to account for this, none of them convincing. The corpus of commentary on "Christabel" is very small. Critics remain unsure what tone to take with it. Probably no poem in literary history has been so abused by moralistic Christian readings. Its blatant Lesbian pornography has been studiously ignored or blandly argued away. "Christabel" demonstrates the narrowness of assumptions of modern humanistic scholarship, whose liberalism is full of self-censorship.

The Christian interpretation of "Christabel" found ample justification in Coleridge's remark to his friend Gillman that the theme of the completed poem would be "that the virtuous of this world save the wicked." Little here can support what Coleridge declared to be his moral program. Piety is blasted by a daemonic night wind. Heaven is conquered by hell. Virtue does not and cannot redeem in the poem. The greatness of "Christabel" arises from its lurid pagan pictorialism. It is an epiphany of evil. Mother nature has returned to retake what she lost. "Christabel" is a daemonic screenplay, a script for an apocalyptic comeback. Behold the star: the Lesbian vampire Geraldine is the chthonian reawakened from its earthy grave. That this daemonic vision is the true heart of the poem is demonstrated by Shelley's reaction at first hearing. When one day in Geneva at the Villa Diodati Byron recited passages memorized from "Christabel," Shelley shrieked and rushed from the room. He was found trembling and bathed in sweat. At the description of Geraldine, he saw eyes in the nipples of Mary Godwin. This is reported by Polidori, who was present, and confirmed in a letter of Byron. Shelley's terrible vision of the archetypal phallic woman (aside from its hint of complications of attitude toward the hapless Mary!) show us that the amoral essence of the poem was instantaneously transmitted from one great poet to another. Coleridge's imagination is invested not in "the virtuous of this world" but in daemonic personae of hermaphrodite force. "Christabel" is a psychologically archaizing poem. Far from demonstrating the success of Christian aspiration, it abolishes Christianity and returns the psyche to a primitive world of ethical opacity and sexually malignant spirit-presences. Coleridge the Christian was the first misreader of Coleridge the poet.

At the opening of the poem, the lady Christabel ventures from her father's castle at midnight to pray for her betrothed knight. As at the opening of "The Ancient Mariner," there is an impulse toward conventional marriage which will be defeated. Christabel is an innocent who believes love and virtue go together. Her mission of heterosexual piety is to be grotesquely defiled by the poem. Sex will turn and sting the Christian will. Christabel's maiden voyage into archaic night is foolish and possibly provocative. She summons the very evil she hopes to quiet. Neither Christianity nor Wordsworthian nature can defend her. A bleak, decadent sterility has turned the green leaves gray. Persephone in the meadow is about to be raped, but her assailant is the earth-mother and her dark prison her own home.

Even as Christabel kneels in prayer, the daemonic drama begins. "It" has moaned, the brute sexless, sex-full thing, the stirring form of pagan nature waking from its long sleep. The poet's voice interjects: "Hush, beating heart of Christabel!/Jesu, Maria, shield her well!" We recall another appeal to heaven in "The Ancient Mariner," an appeal answered by a leprous vampire. The Coleridgean moral inversion operates again. Christian prayer produces pagan epiphany. Heaven is either deaf or sadistic. The materialization of the vampires in "Christabel" and "The Ancient Mariner" perversely awaits the invocation of a divine name. It is as if daemonic power is intensified by Christian assertion. A lust for profanation hangs in the air like a shadow-mist. This mist suddenly takes brilliant shape. In a burst of luminous, numinous cinema the vampire Geraldine appears in all her white beauty. "Mary mother, save me now!" says Christabel, pressed by that harsh Coleridgean irony. The Madonna has become the serpent in the garden. In her embrace Christabel will fall. Her touch will be the mark of Cain exiling Christabel from her own race. Christabel's trust and good will are a blank spot of tender passivity in nature, as in Blake's "Infant Joy." The benign is devoured by its context, hungry black flames of daemonic energy.

Geraldine gives birth to herself by the "infinite I AM" of Coleridgean imagination. She is poetry leaping full-armed from the unconscious, a hermaphrodite Muse. The voices of art in Coleridge prophesy not peace but war. Art is conflict, turbulence, negation. And art mirrors nature, from which Wordsworth has been finally driven. The vampire Muse makes poetry in "Christabel" by seduction and corruption. Poisoned words will lead to poisoned sex. She lies in order to lay. "Stretch forth thy hand, and have no fear!" Geraldine says to Christabel. A long falsehood follows, and the invitation is repeated, this time successfully Geraldine seems to evoke the unconscious complicity of her prey. Harold Bloom rightly speaks of Christabel as a "half-willing victim." The ritualistic temptations of Christabel are garnished by spurious sex-romance. Geraldine assumes the most frailly feminine of personae. Five warriors have carried her off from her father's house and abandoned her. "Me, even me, a maid forlorn." The irony of Geraldine's tale of rape is that she is herself a rapist. What Christabel hears is what is to be done to her. Psychologically, the tale translates to: men are brutes! Perhaps this is how Geraldine severs Christabel's mental connection with her betrothed knight and induces her to give her hand. The daemonic mother lures the bride backward, away from menarche and into the womb of regression. In Coleridge's plan for the unwritten conclusion, Geraldine was to impersonate Christabel's fiancé, by transsexual ruse. In part 1 we see that Geraldine has already replaced him. Once Geraldine has won her first victory, she has won everything. She has made her first penetration of Christabel's psyche and now manipulates her thoughts. It is Christabel who introduces the idea of "stealth" and who proposes they share the same bed. From this covertness come erotic intensity, trespass, and shame.

Geraldine's strategies are modeled on Spenser. Her woeful tale echoes the one told by duplicitous Duessa to the Redcrosse Knight in the first book of the *Faerie Queene*. In the forest Geraldine recalls Belphoebe and in the castle Malecasta. The sexual style of "Christabel," the combination of cool medieval beauty with voluptuous embowered evil, is uniquely Spenserian. Coleridge has sensed the decadent perversity in the *Faerie Queene* which so many scholars have missed. The rape theme of "Christabel" has come from the rape-infested *Faerie Queene*. But virginity has lost its Christian militancy. No armor defends Coleridge's heroine against sexual predators. Christabel's simple femininity is her undoing. Daemonic rapacity surges into her and obliterates her maidenhood. She is no match for hermaphrodite aggression. There is no longer a working

Christian scheme to divert lust into sublimation. The Spenserian bower in which Christabel is lost is her own.

Invitation to the rape: from Christabel's hospitable gesture to her actual seduction there are 140 lines. A long distance must be traversed. The Mariner's epic voyage is internalized. But "the moat" is crossed at the moment of Christabel's assent. This is her Rubicon, from which there is no turning back. The 140 lines are a ritual of dreamlike slowness, a sarabande which is both funeral and wedding procession. The poet traces step by step Geraldine's invasion of gate, court, hall, chamber. In Coleridge the castle of male society and history is entered and disordered by the chthonian. But the castle is also the body of Christabel herself which is systematically possessed by Geraldine. The "little door" unlocked by Christabel's key is her own chastity, her virgin autonomy. At the gate Geraldine sinks down and Christabel must carry her through it. Bloom says, "Geraldine cannot cross the threshold, which probably is charmed against her." In old Scandinavia, an ax was buried beneath the threshold to guard a house against lightning—and to prevent a witch from entering. Similarly, ancient cities were protected by the entombment of their founders' bones in the lintel of the gate. W. F. Jackson Knight has demonstrated that virgin goddesses were patrons of cities because the integrity of walls was imagined as a virgin's unbroken hymen. Hence the Trojan horse brought down Troy: as it passed the gate, it broke the magic spell protecting the city. Taboos governing the sanctity of walls were so extreme that a Roman soldier who leapt the wall of a camp instead of leaving by the gate was executed, for he had broken the defenses. This appears to be why Romulus kills Remus for jumping his wall. Thus in "Christabel" Geraldine's passage through the gate from which armies have marched is a Trojan subterfuge. Hidden in the arms of Christabel, she simultaneously overthrows male power and penetrates the virgin's body. She is the cunning sacker of cities dangling from the lamb's wool.

The breached gate of "Christabel" is the doorway which could not be crossed in "The Ancient Mariner." The Wedding Guest has finally become the Bridegroom. Christabel lifting Geraldine over the threshold is the groom with her bride. She has begun her daemonic marriage to Geraldine, from which there can be no divorce. Geraldine is a "weary weight," the terrible burden of our physical life. Christabel staggers under the tree of nature upon which Blake saw us crucified. The doorway is Coleridge's sexual crux, his via crucis. The slow passage of Geraldine and Christabel through the castle has an abstract formality, a religious solemnity. Seduction, leading astray, is here an induction, an initiation into daemonic mysteries. Much of the poem's eroticism is generated by this methodical movement, which inflames by anticipation and suspense. The darkness, seclusion, and silence create a sensuous impression of Christabel's tantalizing sexual vulnerability. For Geraldine as the poetic "I AM," progress is profanation. "Christabel" as poem moves forward on metric feet of spreading evil.

The procession moves through the castle as if through a church, nave to chancel to altar, which is the bed of seduction. No guard or hierarchical authority rises to block the queen's sweep of the board. The presiding male, Sir Leoline, is ill and asleep. The watchdog moans but does not wake. Only in the bedchamber does Geraldine meet resistance, from the ghost of Christabel's mother, a guardian spirit who springs out like the sacristan of the sanctuary. The mother died at the hour of Christabel's birth, vowing she would hear the castle bell strike twelve on her daughter's wedding-day. The poem begins with the tolling of midnight: this is indeed Christabel's wedding day, and she is about to consummate her perverse nuptials. In this poem good strangles itself. Birth leads to death: pregnancy is a terminal disease. The wine made by Christabel's mother from wildflowers—presumably Wordsworth's daffodils!—serves only to energize the vampire in her territorial war. Geraldine grapples with the ghost and repels her: "Off, wandering mother! . . . This hour is mine. . . . 'Tis given to me." Given by whom? God and fate take the side of evil. Archaic night makes her inexorable return. After her mother's defeat, Christabel is completely at Geraldine's mercy. The triumph of the daemonic is signified by Christabel kneeling at her side. Geraldine has subdued the cosmos of the poem, and she is now its deity. Christabel obeys without question Geraldine's command to unrobe herself: "So let it be!" In other words, "I do." They are married. She lies down in bed to await her master. The ceremonial character of "Christabel" is accentuated by the hieratic deliberativeness of the preparations for bed, a ritual sexual mime. This is one of the points the Christian Coleridge tried to fudge. Twenty years after writing the poem, Coleridge inserted seven lines (255–62) in which Geraldine "seeks delay" before lying down with Christabel and taking her in her arms. The reader must never be misled by the attempts of Coleridge the anxious reviser to cover the work of Coleridge the visionary. Vampire and conscience are mutually exclusive. The poem in its fine original inspiration presents a Geraldine who never hesitates, who cannot hesitate, who is implacable.

There is a mystery when Geraldine undresses. "Behold! her bosom and half her side—/A sight to dream of, not to tell!/O shield her! shield sweet Christabel!" What revelation comes with the unveiling of the daemon? G. Wilson Knight speaks of "some sort of sexual desecration, some expressly physical horror." In part 2 of the poem Christabel has a chilling flashback: "Again she saw that bosom old,/Again she felt that bosom cold." From the first, scholars recognized this as a detail from the *Faerie Queene*: when the beautiful Duessa is stripped, she has "dried dugs, like bladders lacking wind." When Christabel awakens the next morning, she sees Geraldine's "heaving breasts." One concludes that Geraldine is a classical vampire of great age, her breast withered only when she hungers. After she has sated herself, whether by drinking blood or somehow draining the life-energy of her victim, her breasts are restored to sensual fullness. In part 2 Christabel remembers "the touch and pain," so something surgical has definitely occurred! Whatever is repellent about Geraldine's bosom, it is the identifying mark of a witch. The witch's body is a perversion or parody of the maternal. It is therefore fitting that Geraldine's sole opponent is Christabel's benevolent mother, and it is a severe truth about the poem that this power is crushed and expelled. The witch, with her animallike teats reminiscent of the Ephesian Artemis, is virtually a third sex. She is the ugliness of procreative nature. She is the chthonian mother who eats her own children.

A third sex: how exactly does Geraldine sexually violate Christabel? Coleridge says of the two as they lie together:

> A star hath set, a star hath risen,
> O Geraldine! since arms of thine
> Have been the lovely lady's prison.
> O Geraldine! one hour was thine—
> Thou'st had thy will!

The star which was set is Jesus'. The star which has risen is the ancient sign of the daemon, the sexual scorpion. The prison is the embrace of mother nature, from which Jesus cannot redeem us. In "Christabel," female sexual receptivity is mysteriously transformed into the power to rape, perhaps more evil because the specifics of the act remain vague, diffuse. A female rape has few parallels in life and none in art. In the absence of phallic penetration, how is Christabel sexually possessed? If there is draining of blood, it must occur with a mentalized orgasmic excitement like the cloudy feverishness of J. Sheridan Le Fanu's *Carmilla*, a Victorian tale of a Lesbian vampire obviously inspired by "Christabel."

Christabel rising from her bed in the morning says, "Sure I have sinn'd!" She remembers nothing, but her sense of lost innocence is acute, for the hermaphrodite witch has entered her, body and mind. Geraldine sleeps satisfied like a man, the triumphant seducer, while the violated girl weeps in shame. She is humanity after the fall. Her eyes are open. She knows we are naked, defenseless against nature. Wordsworthian illusions about Mother Nature are over. Cannibalism and incest are the lovemaking of man's family romance. Christabel has been impregnated by the Muse and bears the burden of fear and suffering. "The vision of fear, the touch and pain": her sexual crucifixion is like a spectacle of sadomasochistic bondage. Her pain may be from the vampire's bite or from a sexually mutant penetration. In medieval covens the Devil performed ritual public intercourse with a forked penis, entering his devotees from two directions at once. Initiation into ancient nature cults always involved some abuse of the body, from flagellation to castration. In the pagan epiphany of "Christabel," the daemonic returns in an orgy of Dionysian pleasure-pain. Vampire and poem are a raptor-rapture of sexual monstrosity.

Most of Geraldine's daemonic aggression resides in her eye. The vampire has a phallic eye, probing, penetrating, riveting. In the hallway the hearth fire flames, "And Christabel saw the lady's eye,/And nothing else saw she thereby." She is obsessed, subjugated. At her moment of maximum power in the bedchamber, Geraldine rises to her full "lofty" height, an erection fueled by her dominance of the mother-spirit, the submission and genuflection of Christabel, and the wine which she will change into Christabel's blood. This is the full moon of the vampire eye: "Her fair large eyes 'gan glitter bright." In a note to "The Ancient Mariner" Bloom says, "Like Geraldine in 'Christabel,' the Mariner is a hypnotist or mesmerist." Christabel's seduction is by sexual hypnotism. Freud says, "The blind obedience evidenced by the hypnotized subject to the hypnotist causes me to think that the nature of hypnosis is to be found in the unconscious fixation of the libido on the person of the hypnotizer." Thus it can be said that Christabel spiritually participates beforehand in her own daemonic defloration.

As she lies down with Christabel, Geraldine says, "In the touch of this bosom there worketh a spell,/Which is lord of thy utterance, Christabel!" The next morning Christabel cannot tell her pain or appeal for help. Evil eye and magic spell: daemonic sorcery deprives its victims of speech, hurling them backward in history to the animal realm. Thus the alluring Circe's most sadistic torture is in stopping the mouths of Odysseus' men. Minds acute in their swine bodies, they can only grunt. The heroine of "Christabel" is plunged into muteness. Her "vision of fear" has obliterated language. Vision, silence, castration. We are approaching the sexual center of Coleridge's mystery poems.

Fascination is not only the principal theme but the poetic genesis of "Christabel." The first part of the poem ends with Christabel still in Geraldine's embrace. I will argue that part 1 encompasses the totality of Coleridge's vision and that the second part written three years later, as well as the rough plan he projected for three more parts, was born of fear at what he had already created. Coleridge's inability to finish "Christabel" came from the fact that, try as he might, he was powerless to turn his daemonic saga into a parable of Christian redemption. Bostetter rightly says, " 'Christabel' is a nightmare vision of the triumph of evil." Even part 2 ends with Christabel's father abandoning her and allying himself with the false Geraldine. Coleridge's conscious mind wills the victory of virtue. But his unconscious replies: evil is older and will endure. The closing of part 1 says of Christabel, "But this she knows, in joys and woes,/That saints will aid if men will call:/For the blue sky bends over all!" These lines have been read with naïve simplicity by Christian interpreters, missing their terrible irony. We have seen that calling heavenly powers in Coleridge brings disaster. Good, far from being a defense against evil, is a titillation to lust and provokes the vampire's assault. Paganism stakes its claim in the virgin heart of Christian virtue.

The transition from part 1 to part 2 of "Christabel" is jarring. We pass from the sinister dreaminess of the tale of seduction to forced and dry low comedy. The poem turns flat and schematic. Unimportant people pop up and down ringing bells and telling beads. We meet Christabel's father Sir Leoline, whom the poet would better have left snoring. The bustling busyness is in a distinctly minor mode. Part 1's mythic intensity has suffered sudden declension. Scholars have noticed this contrast but neither explored nor explained it. Humphry House, for example, says that "the two parts differ so much from each other, that they seem scarcely to belong to the same poem." I must amend my review: there are two fine passages in part 2. The first depicts Geraldine and Christabel waking together in the bedchamber (362–86); the second records the bard Bracy's ominous vision of the "bright green snake" coiled about the dove's body (549–56). But both these passages reinvoke the sexual intercourse of part 1. In other words, the best poetry of part 2 has been produced by daemonic infection from part 1, a contagion of vice.

Why is the first part of "Christabel" so much stronger? Bloom says, "The poem's vividness and energy belong to Geraldine; Christabel comes to life only in torment or when under the vampire's spell." The poetic greatness of "Christabel," its essence of imagination, is the seductive vampirism of Geraldine. The inspiration of the poem is a vision of a female persona of overwhelming hermaphroditic force. Everything in "Christabel" is subordinated to Geraldine. Character, time, place are manipulated by Coleridge to form an admiring circle about her, from which she radiates her cold hieratic glamour like a sun king. "Christabel" is structured by an archaic technique of ornamental display, a ritual exhibitionism. Gods descend when man is in crisis, but the daemon ascends from her bed of ghostly loam. Conventional heterosexuality has failed. Maternalism is weak and masculinity in decay. The father's armour is a musty relic. Art can see not but act: the bard warns but is not believed. Father spurns daughter in Lear-like disloyalty. The world of "Christabel" has run down and is ripe for apocalypse. Into this vacuum steps the Lesbian vampire, dazzlingly beautiful, relentlessly masculine. "Christabel," like Shakespeare's *As You Like*

It, is an alchemical experiment in which the main event is the crystallization of a *rebis* or hermaphroditic personality. The poem is an alembic of superheated psyche. Libido is released and bonded in new permutations, metamorphoses of daemonic energy. Vampires make vampires: Christabel, "hissing" (459), has been genetically altered, irradiated by the daemonic. Fascination, capture, possession, transfiguration. Geraldine is demiurge and architectus, the double-sexed great goddess of primeval nature.

"Christabel" is Coleridge dreaming aloud. Kathleen Coburn suggests that Coleridge could not finish the poem "because it was too closely a representation of his own experience." She connects Geraldine's advances to Christabel with the poet's nightmares, "in which one gathers he was frequently pursued by unpleasing female figures;" "Geraldine is a malignity out of Coleridge's own dreams." His notebooks describe the most striking of these dreams:

> a most frightful Dream of a Woman whose features were blended with darkness catching hold of my right eye & attempting to pull it out—I caught hold of her arm fast—a horrid feel. Wordsworth cried aloud to me hearing my scream—
>
> I was followed up & down by a frightful pale woman who, I thought, wanted to kiss me, & had the property of giving me a shameful Disease by breathing in the face & again I dreamt that a figure of a woman of a gigantic Height, dim & indefinite & smokelike appeared—& that I was forced to run up toward it—& then it changed to a stool—& then appeared again in another place—& again I went up in a great fright—& it changed to some other common thing—yet I felt no surprize.

Coleridge records many dreams of sexual assault, some by males. In one case there is a man "leaping on me, & grasping my Scrotum." These nightmares are united by a theme of rape and castration. Bostetter sees the analogy between "Christabel" and Coleridge's nightmares: "Geraldine is an incarnation of sadism, much like the women of Coleridge's dreams." Norman Fruman feels the dream image of the "woman of gigantic Height" resembles the "tall" and "lofty" Geraldine. If Geraldine is the imposing female figure who pursues Coleridge in his dreams, then we must logically infer some element of self-identification in Christabel. Coburn says that Christabel is "significantly one side of his own nature." Bostetter says, "The relationship between Christabel and Geraldine is the relationship between Coleridge and the dream woman." But these perceptions, which should have been so consequential for interpretation of the mystery poems, are left undeveloped, tottering on the edge of the sexually problematic but not daring to plunge into it.

"Christabel" contains one of the greatest transsexual self-transformations in literature. We have spoken of the drama of the male heroine in "The Ancient Mariner," a complex of self-identification which leads to episodic sentimentality. In "Christabel" the residual maleness of the male heroine is gone, and gender has shifted completely to the female. Christabel is Coleridge, a poet condemned to fascination by daemonic nature. This poem begins a peculiar nineteenth-century tradition in which a sexually ambivalent poet paints a scene of intense Lesbian eroticism in order to identify himself, by a daring warp of imaginative gender, with the passive partner. Balzac's Byronic (and therefore Coleridgean) *Girl with the Golden Eyes* starts the French version of this theme, which then returns to England. "Christabel" is mirrored by Baudelaire's "Delphine and Hippolyte," from which come Swinburne's "Anactoria" and Verlaine's and Pierre Louys' Sapphic idylls. "Christabel" is a mime-ritual of surrender to pagan corruption. Its heroine is entranced, morally drugged, powerless to flee from an irresistible power. The vampire Geraldine, an enlargement of the sea witch of "The Ancient Mariner," is the dominatrix of Coleridge's psychic and poetic life. She is cruel daemonic nature, whose second coming lays Wordsworth to rest.

Clues within the poem corroborate an identification of Coleridge with Christabel. The bard recounts a dream in which he sees Sir Leoline's pet dove, named for Christabel, lost in the forest, "a bright green snake/Coiled around its wings and neck": "And with the dove it heaves and stirs,/Swelling its neck as she swelled hers!" He wakes as the clock strikes twelve. It is the hour of Christabel's wedding day, and her marriage is being consummated. Dove and snake, locked in daemonic embrace, heave, stir, and swell in sexual spasms of pain and ecstasy. Coleridge was drawn to this heraldic hybrid image. In the ode "Dejection" (1802) he declares: "Hence, viper thoughts, that coil around my mind,/Reality's dark dream!" In defending his opium addiction he said that he "sought it only as the means of escaping from pains that coiled round my mental powers as a serpent around the body and wings of an eagle!" Thus we see that this metaphor, in which he is a bird in the grip of a snake, persistently abode with the poet and that he projected into it some crucial private experience. Man's body is the mortal coil, and imagination is the serpent-stung bird that would fly but cannot. Man lies in the chains of sex and nature.

Next is the curse laid by Geraldine upon Christabel's power of speech, which prevents her from informing her father of the rape. This detail probably comes from the classical story of Philomela, a rape victim whose tongue is cut out to ensure her silence. Coleridge in fact mentions Philomela by name in "The Nightingale" the following year (1798). Christabel struggles to speak but can utter only a single sentence. She is "O'ermastered by the mighty spell." Her hermaphrodite spouse is "lord of her utterance." Christabel is like Melville's Billy Budd, an innocent ensnared by a homosexual conspirator and undone by a speech impediment. Christabel laboring to speak is a self-portrait, half prophetic, half from life, of Coleridge the poet, whose achievement was to remain flawed and incomplete. By modern standards, Coleridge left an enormous body of work of vast scope. But he died under the burden of great expectations, his own and others' His masterpiece evaded him. Poetry came to him only in fragments. Hence his apologia, needless to us, for "Kubla Khan," with its spurious knock on the door. Toward the end of life Coleridge wrote in his notebooks, "From my earliest recollection I have had a consciousness of Power without Strength—a perception, an experience, of more than ordinary power with an inward sense of weaknesse." Hazlitt remarkably said of Coleridge's appearance, "His nose, the rudder of the face, the index of the will, was small, feeble, nothing—like what he has done." Coleridge believed he had "a *feeble*, unmanly face" The exceeding *weakness*, strengthlessness, in my face, was ever painful to me." Carlyle said upon first meeting Coleridge: "His cardinal sin is that he wants *will*. He has no resolution."

Christabel mute is Coleridge irresolute. Her truncated speech is like Lewis Carroll's stammer, which appeared in the challenging company of adults, never children. Carroll portrays himself in *Alice* as the earthbound and dowagerlike Dodo, whose name, it has been observed, is how the stammering Charles Dodgson would have rendered his own last name. Christabel's inability to speak is Coleridge stammering. It represents within the poem the poet's inability to complete the poem itself. Thus the spell laid upon Christabel is also laid upon Coleridge. It is his struggle with language, his fear of betrayal by and helpless alienation from language. The inability to speak is a dark spot in the poem, a melanoma which may spread and stop all poetry. The danger is that Coleridge will become a Philomela with her tongue torn out. Kiss but don't tell. This dark spot is a place of dangerous vision where words have not coalesced. It is a magic circle of frail tissue where there should be bone, like the soft spot on a baby's head. I think of that first great script of Rod Serling's *Twilight Zone*, "Little Girl Lost," where a hole in a bedroom wall sucks a child into another dimension. So in the boudoir-dominated "Christabel" the failure of speech is a zone of desolation which may draw Coleridge's poetry into non-being. The vampire Muse of "Christabel" is a Sphinx, literally a "strangler" (from the Greek *sphiggo*). She is the riddle of nature which the poet cannot solve. She brings vision but steals speech. Geraldine is the mother of lies. The serpent in the garden is a suave forked tongue, eating and entering the sanctified body of innocence.

Thus Coleridge as Christabel is a tongueless male heroine who is no longer identifiably male. He is the "coy maid half yielding to her lover" of "The Eolian Harp" and the "woman wailing for her demon-lover" of "Kubla Khan." Christabel in the vampire's arms is an Aeolian lyre, her body sadistically played upon by daemonic nature. But her music is silence. The story of nature cannot be told, for she will always betray the heart that loves her. The compulsive storytelling of the Ancient Mariner is an early, less effective version of Christabel's muteness. The Mariner tries to solve by excess of words the burden of mystery which silences Christabel. "Christabel" (in its original part 1) is the profounder poem. It is not marred by those eruptions of sentimentality of "The Ancient Mariner." Its language is grave, dignified, and seamless. Why? The Wedding Guest cannot get through the doorway of "The Ancient Mariner" because he is still male. The marriage may go on, but he will not see it. In "Christabel" the doorway is breached and the marriage occurs because the poet has jettisoned his gender. He disappears into his heroine and marries his Muse, who will speak for him. Geraldine is a ventriloquist. She writes the poem, and Christabel suffers it. Coleridge at his sexually most self-abased is at his poetically most potent. Art transfigures by self-mutilation.

Extremes meet in "Christabel." Vice and virtue, male and female, nature and society. All is dominated by the daemon. . . . The Christian element in this poem has been completely misread by scholars. Christabel is the Christian Coleridge, the hopeful moralist perpetually defeated by the daemonic. The she that is he will never emerge from her enslavement. In "Christabel" Christianity is abolished by a return of the chthonian. The "love and charity" at end of part 1 are the epitaph of the Christian Coleridge. Virtue is constantly violated in the text. Indeed, virtue is invoked only to increase the perversity of transgression. The rape is more passionate, more evil because of the borderlines set up for it to overcome. Resistance intensifies eroticism. Christabel, the beautiful Christ, meets her ruin in the barbaric ugliness of Mother Nature, the old, cold bosom in which every man is born and buried.

"Christabel" is a sexual apocalypse in which Coleridge no longer sees the hermaphrodite god through a glass darkly but face to face. The unholy sex act is so much the imaginative center of "Christabel" that the language of the poem degenerates whenever it gets too far away from it. Coleridge's fascination by Geraldine has made her the autocratic tyrannos of the poem, to the detriment of everything and everyone else in part 2. The figure is invested with so much psychic power that other characters lose fictive energy and become part of the unfinished background. Sir Leoline, for example, is merely a sketch, part of the decor.

Coleridge's Geraldine is one of the greatest androgynes of literature and art. She has a refined feminine beauty but a masculinity of spirit. She is spiritual menace and sexual fatality. She is like the narcissistic witch-queen of *Snow White*, the wicked stepmother of fairy tales who is a projection of the repressed negativity of the real mother. Christabel protests her father's fusion with Geraldine like a child who will not accept a widower's new wife. The Lesbianism of "Christabel" may be paralleled by the family romance of *Snow White*, in which Bloom has seen traces of mother-daughter incest. The witch-queen is a persona lying utterly outside the moral universe of Christianity, a pre-Christian form of the malevolent nature mother. In "Christabel" pagan imagism triumphs over the Judaeo-Christian word. The eyes of the vampire penetrate space and time. The voyeurism of "Christabel," like that of the *Faerie Queene*, reflects the unacknowledged voyeurism of all Western art. The vampire, as we see from the replay from Geraldine's point of view in the conclusion of part 1, has been watching all along, and most evilly, she makes the defeated mother watch the rape of her own daughter. The thousand hungry eyes of daemonic nature wait in the forest of the night.

"Christabel" shows the conflict, hostility, and ambivalence in love and poetry. It rebukes the liberal idealizers of emotion. The poem creates a hierarch of authoritarian glamour, beyond good and evil. Coleridge's lifelong desire to "finish" the poem was ill-conceived, for like Woolf's Lily Briscoe, he has had his vision. His additions to the poem, like the nervous marginalia of "The Ancient Mariner," are a form of self-thwarting, another stammering. They are a blatant deflection of the authentic inspiration of the poem, in which the vampire behind her feminine mask has a massive supernatural self-assurance. Geraldine is the daemonic spirit of archaic night, and in Coleridge's original and truer conception, her power has no beginning and no end.

Chronology

1772 Samuel Taylor Coleridge born in the vicarage at Ottery, St. Mary, Devonshire, on October 21.

1775 Begins formal schooling at Dame Key's Reading School.

1778 Attends Henry VIII Free Grammar School.

1781 His father, John Coleridge, dies.

1782 Admitted to Christ's Hospital School in July.

1791 Enters Jesus College, Cambridge, in July.

1793 Enlists in the King's Regiment, 15th Light Dragoons, under the pseudonym Silas Tomkyn Comberback.

1794 Obtains a discharge from the King's Regiment and returns to Cambridge. Meets Southey at Oxford. *The Fall of Robespierre* published (with Southey) under Coleridge's name. Meets Godwin. Leaves Cambridge in December, without a degree, in order to pursue the scheme of Pantisocracy.

1795 Moves to Bristol in January and meets William Wordsworth. Marries Sara Fricker of Bristol; they settle at Clevedon, Somerset. Lectures in Bristol through November on politics and history.

1796 Hartley Coleridge born. Publishes *Poems on Various Subjects* and edits the March–May issues of *The Watchman*. Moves with family to Nether Stowey.

1797 The Wordsworths move to Alfoxden to be near Coleridge. Composes "The Rime of the Ancient Mariner" and publishes *Poems* by himself, Charles Lamb, and Charles Lloyd.

1798 A second son, Berkeley, born, who later dies. Josiah and Thomas Wedgwood settle a lifetime annuity of £150 on Coleridge. Writes part 1 of "Christabel," "Frost at Midnight," "France: An Ode," "Fears in Solitude," and (?) "Kubla Khan." In September, the first edition of *Lyrical Ballads* is published anonymously with Wordsworth, while they are traveling through Germany with Dorothy Wordsworth and John Chester.

1799 Enters the University of Göttingen, alone, in February. Returns to England in July and contributes to the *Morning Post*. Meets Sara Hutchinson.

1800 Settles with family at Greta Hall, Keswick, where Derwent is born. Finishes translation of Schiller's *Wallenstein* in late spring. Second edition of *Lyrical Ballads* published with a preface by Wordsworth.

1802 The Southeys move to Greta Hall. Sara Coleridge born. Writes "Dejection: An Ode." Third edition of *Lyrical Ballads*.

1803 Abandons a tour of Scotland with William and Dorothy Wordsworth.

1804 In May leaves for Rome and Malta, having decided to separate from his wife, and with hopes that the climate will be good for his health, which has been weakened by rheumatism and opium addiction.

1806 Returns to England by way of Italy. Separates from his wife.

1807 De Quincey meets Coleridge in Somerset.

1808 January–June gives his first series of lectures, on "Principles of Poetry," at the Royal Institution in London. Later is guest, along with De Quincey, at the Wordsworth home at Grasmere.

1809 Begins *The Friend*. Contributions to *The Courier* to 1817.

1810 *The Friend* ended. Leaves the Lake District for London and breaks with Wordsworth.

1811 Lectures on the English poets in London. Josiah Wedgwood withdraws his half of the legacy.

1812 Lectures in London and Bristol. Makes up with Wordsworth.

1813	Early play *Osario*, revised as *Remorse*, performed at Drury Lane Theatre in London.
1814	Stays with his friend John Morgan in London and Calne, Wiltshire.
1815	Begins dictating *Biographia Literaria* in Calne. Health declining.
1816	Stays at Highgate, London, as patient of Dr. James Gillman. In June publishes a volume of poetry containing "Christabel," "Kubla Khan," and "The Pains of Sleep." Also brings out *The Statesman's Manual: or The Bible the Best Guide to Political Skill and Foresight.*
1817	Publishes *Biographia Literaria, Sibylline Leaves*, and his two *Lay Sermons*.
1818	Lectures on English poetry and history of philosophy. Publishes a selection from *The Friend* and *On Method*, a preliminary treatise to the *Encyclopaedia Metropolitana*.
1819	Ends lectures on history of philosophy.
1825	May–June publishes *Aids to Reflection in the Formation of a Manly Character*.
1828	*Poetical Works* published. Tours Germany with Wordsworth.
1830	*On the Constitution of Church and State* published.
1834	Dies on July 25 at Gillman residence, Highgate.
1836	Four volumes of Coleridge's *Literary Remains* edited by Henry Nelson Coleridge.
1840	*Confessions of an Enquiring Spirit* published.

Contributors

HAROLD BLOOM, Sterling Professor of the Humanities at Yale University, is the author of *The Anxiety of Influence*, *Poetry and Repression*, and many other volumes of literary criticism. His forthcoming study, *Freud: Transference and Authority*, attempts a full-scale reading of all of Freud's major writings. A MacArthur Prize Fellow, he is the general editor of five series of literary criticism published by Chelsea House.

KENNETH BURKE is the most eminent of living American literary theorists and critics. His crucial books are *A Grammar of Motives* and *The Rhetoric of Religion*.

OWEN BARFIELD was a lawyer by profession; after retiring he lectured as a Visiting Professor in Literature and Philosophy at Brandeis University and other schools. His books include *Saving the Appearances* and *Poetic Diction*.

M. H. ABRAMS is Class of 1916 Professor of English Literature at Cornell University. His studies of Romanticism, which include such works as *The Mirror and The Lamp* and *Natural Supernaturalism*, have been highly influential.

ANGUS FLETCHER is Distinguished Professor of English and Comparative Literature at Herbert H. Lehman College and the Graduate Center of the City University of New-York. His books include *Allegory*, *The Prophetic Moment*, and *The Transcendental Masque*.

E. S. SHAFFER is a lecturer in Comparative Literature at the University of East Anglia.

KATHLEEN COBURN is Professor Emeritus in Victoria College at the University of Toronto and Honorary Fellow of St. Hugh's College, Oxford. She has edited the *Notebooks of Samuel Taylor Coleridge* and a volume of Coleridge's philosophical lectures of 1818–19, and is general editor of the Bollingen edition of the *Collected Works*.

THOMAS McFARLAND is Professor of English Literature at Princeton University. He is the author of *Romanticism and the Forms of Ruin* and *Coleridge and the Pantheist Tradition*.

JEROME CHRISTENSEN is Professor of English at Johns Hopkins University. Besides his study of Coleridge, he has written extensively on Romantic poetry.

LESLIE BRISMAN is Professor of English at Yale University. His books include a study of Milton.

TIMOTHY CORRIGAN is Professor of English at Temple University. Besides his book on Coleridge, he is the author of works on contemporary German cinema.

ARDEN REED is Assistant Professor of English at Pomona College.

SUSAN J. WOLFSON is an Assistant Professor of English at Rutgers University.

KEN FRIEDEN is the author of *Genius and Monologue* and *The Dream of Interpretation*. He is an Assistant Professor in the Department of Modern Languages and Classics at Emory University.

CAMILLE PAGLIA teaches at the Philadelphia College of Art. She is the author of *Sexual Personae*.

Bibliography

Abrams, M. H. *The Correspondent Breeze: Essays on English Romanticism*. New York: Norton, 1984.

———. *The Mirror and the Lamp: Romantic Theory and the Critical Tradition*. Oxford: Oxford University Press, 1953.

Barfield, Owen. *What Coleridge Thought*. Middletown, Conn.: Wesleyan University Press, 1971.

Beer, John, ed. *Coleridge's Variety*. Pittsburgh: University of Pittsburgh Press, 1975.

Bloom, Harold. *Figures of Capable Imagination*. New York: The Seabury Press, 1976.

———. *The Visionary Company: A Reading of English Romantic Poetry*. Revised edition. Ithaca: Cornell University Press, 1971.

Boulger, James D. *Coleridge as Religious Thinker*. New Haven: Yale University Press, 1961.

———, ed. *Twentieth Century Interpretations of "The Rime of the Ancient Mariner."* Englewood Cliffs, N. J.: Prentice-Hall, 1969.

Brisman, Leslie. *Romantic Origins*. Ithaca: Cornell University Press, 1978.

Burke, Kenneth. *Language as Symbolic Action: Essays on Life, Literature, and Method*. Berkeley: University of California Press, 1966.

Christensen, Jerome. *Coleridge's Blessed Machine of Language*. Ithaca: Cornell University Press, 1981.

———. "Philosophy/Literature: The Associationist Precedent for Coleridge's Late Poems." In *Literature and Philosophy: New Perspectives on Nineteenth and Twentieth Century Texts*, edited by William E. Cain. Bucknell, Pa: Bucknell University Press, 1983.

———. "Politerotics: Coleridge's Rhetoric of War in *The Friend*." *Clio* 8 (1979): 339–64.

Coburn, Kathleen, ed. Coleridge. Twentieth Century Views. Englewood Cliffs, N. J.: Prentice-Hall, 1967.

———. *Experience into Thought: Perspectives in the Coleridge Notebooks*. Toronto: University of Toronto Press, 1979.

Crawford, Walter B., ed. *Reading Coleridge: Approaches and Applications*. Ithaca: Cornell University Press, 1979.

Delson, Abe. "The Function of Geraldine in *Christabel*: A Critical Perspective and Interpretation." *English Studies* 61 (1980): 130–41.

De Man, Paul. "The Rhetoric of Temporality." In *Interpretation: Theory and Practice*, edited by Charles Singleton. Baltimore: The Johns Hopkins University Press, 1969.

Ferguson, Frances. "Coleridge and the Deluded Reader: 'The Rime of the Ancient Mariner.'" *Georgia Review* 31 (1977): 191–207, 617–35.

Fry, Paul. *The Poet's Calling in the English Ode*. New Haven: Yale University Press, 1980.

———. "Coleridge on Language and Delusion." *Genre* 11 (1978).

Hartman, Geoffrey, ed. *New Perspectives on Coleridge and Wordsworth: Selected Papers from the English Institute*. New York: Columbia University Press, 1972.

Havens, Michael K. "Coleridge on the Evolution of Language." *Studies in Romanticism* 29 (1981): 163–83.

House, Humphry. *Coleridge*. The Clark Lectures 1951–52. London: Rupert Hart-Davis, 1953.

Isaacs, J. "Coleridge's Critical Terminology." *Essays and Studies by Members of the English Association* 21 (1936): 86–104.

Knight, G. W. "Coleridge's Divine Commedy." In *English Romantic Poets: Modern Essays in Criticism*, edited by M. H. Abrams. Oxford: Oxford University Press, 1960.

Levere, Trevor H. "Coleridge, Chemistry, and the Philosophy of Nature." *Studies in Romanticism* 16 (1977): 349–79.

McFarland, Thomas. *Coleridge and the Pantheist Tradition*. Oxford: The Clarendon Press, 1969.

———. *Originality and Imagination*. Baltimore: The Johns Hopkins University Press, 1985.

———. *Romanticism and the Forms of Ruin: Wordsworth, Coleridge, and Modalities of Fragmentation*. Princeton: Princeton University Press, 1981.

Modiano, Raimonda. "Words and 'Languageless' Meanings: Limits of Expression in *The Rime of the Ancient Mariner*." *Modern Language Quarterly* 38 (1977): 40–77.

Parker, Reeve. *Coleridge's Meditative Art*. Ithaca: Cornell University Press, 1975.

Rand, Richard. "Geraldine." *Glyph* 3 (1978).

Randel, Fred. V. "Coleridge and the Contentiousness of Romantic Nightingales." *Studies in Romanticism* 21 (1982): 33–55.

Reed, Arden. *Romantic Weather: The Climates of Coleridge and Baudelaire.* Hanover, N. H.: Brown University Press and University Press of New England, 1983.

Shaffer, E. S. *"Kubla Khan" and the Fall of Jerusalem: The Mythological School in Biblical Criticism and Secular Literature 1770–1880.* Cambridge: Cambridge University Press, 1975.

Simpson, David. *Irony and Authority in Romantic Poetry.* Totowa, N. J.: Rowman & Littlefield, 1979.

Weiskel, Thomas. *The Romantic Sublime: Studies in the Structure and Psychology of Transcendence.* Baltimore: The Johns Hopkins University Press, 1976.

Acknowledgments

Introduction by Harold Bloom from *Samuel Taylor Coleridge: Selected Poetry*, edited by Harold Bloom, © 1972 by Harold Bloom. Reprinted by permission.

"Wisdom and Dejection: Four Poems" (originally entitled "Samuel Taylor Coleridge") by Harold Bloom from *The Visionary Company: A Reading of English Romantic Poetry* by Harold Bloom, © 1961 by Harold Bloom. Reprinted by permission of Cornell University Press and the author.

" 'Kubla Khan': Proto-Surrealist Poem" by Kenneth Burke from *Language as Symbolic Action: Essays on Life, Literature, and Method* by Kenneth Burke, © 1966 by The Regents of the University of California. Reprinted by permission of University of California Press.

"Ideas, Method, Laws" by Owen Barfield from *What Coleridge Thought* by Owen Barfield, © 1975 by Wesleyan University Press. Reprinted by permission of the publisher.

"Coleridge's 'A Light in Sound'" (originally entitled "Coleridge's 'A Light in Sound' Science, Metascience, and Poetic Imagination") by M. H. Abrams from *The Correspondent Breeze: Essays on English Romanticism*, © 1984 by M. H. Abrams and Jack Stillinger. Reprinted by permission of Norton. The footnotes in the original essay have been omitted.

" 'Positive Negation' " (originally entitled "Personification and Negation" and "The Dramatic Personification") by Angus Fletcher from *New Perspectives on Coleridge and Wordsworth: Selected Papers from the English Institute*, edited by Geoffrey Hartman, © 1972 by Columbia University Press. Reprinted by permission.

"The Oriental Idyll" by E. S. Shaffer from *"Kubla Khan" and The Fall of Jerusalem:*

The Mythological School in Biblical Criticism and Secular Literature 1770–1880 by E. S. Shaffer, © 1975 by Cambridge University Press. Reprinted by permission of Cambridge University Press.

"Experience into Thought" (originally entitled "Lecture One") by Kathleen Coburn from *Experience into Thought: Perspectives in the Coleridge Notebooks* by Kathleen Coburn, © 1979 by University of Toronto Press. Reprinted by permission of the publisher.

"The Origin and Significance of Coleridge's Theory of Secondary Imagination" by Thomas McFarland from *Originality and Imagination* by Thomas McFarland, © 1985 by The Johns Hopkins University Press. Reprinted by permission.

"The Marginal Method of the *Biographia Literaria*" by Jerome Christensen from *Coleridge's Blessed Machine of Language* by Jerome Christensen, © 1981 by Cornell University Press. Reprinted by permission of the publisher.

"Coleridge and the Supernatural" by Leslie Brisman from *Studies in Romanticism* 21 (1982), © 1982 by the Trustees of Boston University. Reprinted by permission.

"The *Biographia Literaria* and the Language of Science" by Timothy Corrigan from *Coleridge, Language, and Criticism* by Timothy Corrigan, © 1982 by the University of Georgia Press. Reprinted by permission of the publisher.

"'Frost at Midnight'" (originally entitled "The Wedding Garment and the Shroud") by Arden Reed from *Romantic Weather: The Climates of Coleridge and Baudelaire* by Arden Reed, © 1983 by Brown University. Reprinted by permission of University Press of New England.

"The Language of Interpretation" (originally entitled "The Language of Interpretation in Romantic Poetry: 'A Strange Working of the Mind'") by Susan J. Wolfson from *Romanticism and Language*, edited by Arden Reed, © 1984 by Cornell University. Reprinted by permission of Cornell University Press.

"Conversational Pretense in 'Kubla Khan'" (originally entitled "Coleridge's Conversational Pretense in 'Kubla Khan'") by Ken Frieden from *Genius and Monologue* by Ken Frieden, © 1985 by Cornell University. Reprinted by permission of Cornell University Press.

"'Christabel'" by Camille Paglia © 1986 by Camille Paglia. Published for the first time by Chelsea House. Printed by permission.

Index